Pocket
NEW YORK CITY

TOP SIGHTS · LOCAL LIFE · MADE EASY

D1040924

Brandon Presser

In This Book

QuickStart Guide

Your keys to understanding the city – we help you decide what to do and how to do it

Need to Know
Tips for a smooth trip

Neighborhoods
What's where

Explore New York City

The best things to see and do, neighborhood by neighborhood

Top Sights
Make the most of your visit

Local Life
The insider's city

The Best of New York City

The city's highlights in handy lists to help you plan

Best Walks
See the city on foot

New York City's Best...
The best experiences

Survival Guide

Tips and tricks for a seamless, hassle-free city experience

Getting Around
Travel like a local

Essential Information
Including where to stay

Our selection of the city's best places to eat, drink and experience:

◎ **Sights**

✖ **Eating**

⊖ **Drinking**

✪ **Entertainment**

🔒 **Shopping**

These symbols give you the vital information for each listing:

☏	Telephone Numbers	👪	Family-Friendly
⊙	Opening Hours	🐾	Pet-Friendly
P	Parking	🚍	Bus
⊘	Nonsmoking	🚢	Ferry
@	Internet Access	M	Metro
⊚	Wi-Fi Access	S	Subway
✔	Vegetarian Selection	🚊	Tram
📖	English-Language Menu	🚆	Train

Find each listing quickly on maps for each neighborhood:

Bar Hemingway

16 ⊖ Map p233, B2

Legend has it that Hemi
self, wielding a machine
...rate this timber-pan
...ered bar during
... showpiece is a
...en by Papa a
... town. Dress
...s.com; Hôtel Rit
..., ⊙6.30pm-2a

6 ◎ Plac

Lonely Planet's New York City

Lonely Planet Pocket Guides are designed to get you straight to the heart of the city.

Inside you'll find all the must-see sights, plus tips to make your visit to each one really memorable. We've split the city into easy-to-navigate neighborhoods and provided clear maps so you'll find your way around with ease. Our expert authors have searched out the best of the city: walks, food, nightlife and shopping, to name a few. Because you want to explore, our 'Local Life' pages will take you to some of the most exciting areas to experience the real New York City.

And of course you'll find all the practical tips you need for a smooth trip: itineraries for short visits, how to get around, and how much to tip the guy who serves you a drink at the end of a long day's exploration.

It's your guarantee of a really great experience.

Our Promise

You can trust our travel information because Lonely Planet authors visit the places we write about, each and every edition. We never accept freebies for positive coverage, so you can rely on us to tell it like it is.

QuickStart Guide 7

Explore New York City 21

Worth a Trip:

The Best of New York City **199**

New York City's Best Walks

New York City's Best...

Survival Guide **229**

QuickStart Guide

Welcome to New York City

No other place does big-city charm quite like Gotham. Take a bite of the Big Apple's diverse dining scene, swig cocktails all night, enjoy mind-blowing performances in venues ranging from Broadway theaters to back-alley comedy joints, and shop 'til you drop among the veritable UN of international brands and unique boutiques. New York is truly one helluva town.

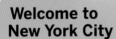

Empire State Building (p128)
RICHARD I'ANSON/LONELY PLANET IMAGES ©

New York City
Top Sights

Central Park (p174)

One of the world's most renowned green spaces checks in with 843 acres of rolling meadows, boulder-studded outcroppings, elm-lined walkways and manicured European-style gardens. There's also a lake and a reservoir.

JEAN-PIERRE LESCOURRET/LONELY PLANET IMAGES ©

Empire State Building (p128)

This towering ode to Gotham is the New York skyline's queen bee. Don't miss the view from the top – a sea of twinkling lights awaits at sunset.

New York Harbor (p24)

Stellar skyline views, free ferry service, a lookout atop Lady Liberty and a reverential tribute to America's immigrants at Ellis Island – what more could you ask for?

Metropolitan Museum of Art (p154)

Known as 'The Met,' this museum of encyclopedic proportions has over two million objects in its permanent collections, many of which are displayed in the 17 acres' worth of galleries.

Museum of Modern Art (p130)

This superstar of the art scene contains a veritable who's who of modern masters. It's a thrilling crash course in all that is beautiful and addictive about the world of art and design. Right: Museum of Modern Art exterior (architects: Yoshio Taniguchi and Kohn Pedersen Fox)

Guggenheim Museum (p158)

This stunning museum has an enviable collection of 20th-century art and welcomes exhibits from all over the world. Right: *The Shapes of Space*, Solomon R. Guggenheim Museum, New York, April 14–September 5, 2007. ©The Solomon R. Guggenheim Foundation, New York. Used with permission.

The High Line (p84)

Refurbished rail tracks have been transformed into grassy catwalks in the sky. It's the paradigm of urban renewal gone right, enjoying its status as one of the city's most beloved public spaces.

ALAN COPSON/CORBIS ©

Times Square (p126)

Like it or loathe it, Times Square offers the quintessential New York conglomeration of bright lights and oversized billboards that soar above the relentless crowds and thick streamers of concrete.

IZZET KERIBAR/LONELY PLANET IMAGES ©

World Trade Center Site (p28)

A soaring new tower, a memorial museum and a pair of reflecting pools are as much a symbol of hope and renewal as they are a tribute to those who perished on 9/11.

JON HICKS/CORBIS ©

New York City
Local Life

Insider tips to help you find the real city

NYC has tons of big-ticket attractions, but it's the tucked-away rooftops, unexpected art installations and secreted speakeasy pubs that truly give the city its unique flair. The real New York will gladly welcome you in if you're daring enough to explore.

Chelsea Galleries (p86)

▶ Emerging artists
▶ Tapas snacks

Western Chelsea was once an unbecoming district with dozens upon dozens of industrial warehouses. These days, however, with factory smoke long gone, the area's empty spaces have been filled with myriad galleries – over 300, in fact – all touting the latest and greatest in the art world.

Harlem (p192)

▶ African American history
▶ Trendy eats

New York's gridiron doesn't end at 100th St – there's lots more of the city to explore, starting with Harlem, a bastion of African American culture.

There are good eats and jazz beats on offer here, not to mention a riveting history captured in the brick and stone of its churches, landmarks and theaters.

South Brooklyn (p194)

▶ Unfurling green space
▶ Vintage shopping

It would be a pity not to snoop around Brooklyn during any New York foray. Though the borough is decidedly on the tourist radar, most folks seem to opt out of crossing waterways. For those who do, there's rolling spaces of green, world-class cuisine and a famous flea market.

Williamsburg (p196)

▶ Designer drinks
▶ Funky boutiques

One stop over the bridge in the borough of Brooklyn, Williamsburg is the undeniable poster child of the hipster movement. Its cache of vintage warehouses, themed cocktail lounges, live music hangouts and highbrow eateries is definitely worth checking out – especially on weekends.

Wall mural in Harlem

Bedford Ave, Williamsburg

Other great places to experience the city like a local:

Lincoln Center (p187)

Lower East Side Galleries (p68)

Koreatown (p140)

St Marks Addresses (p77)

Eating at Chelsea Market (p96)

New York Road Runners Club (p162)

Garment District (p150)

Merchant's House Ghosts (p50)

Curry Hill (p117)

New York City
Day Planner

Day One

With only one day in the city, it's all about quintessential New York moments. Zip down to Lower Manhattan to hop aboard a ferry right in New York Harbor, which will take you to the **Statue of Liberty** (p25) and **Ellis Island** (p25) to learn about the city's (and nation's) immigrant past.

Make a beeline for the Upper West Side and pack a picnic at **Zabar's** (p182) to enjoy on the verdant hillocks of **Central Park** (p174) – weather permitting, of course. Take in the park's many architectural and landscaped wonders before pausing at the **Loeb Boathouse** (p183) for snacks and a boat or bicycle rental. Then, saunter over to the **Museum of Modern Art** (p130) for the very best in contemporary classics.

Bathe in the impossibly bright lights of **Times Square** (p126) after sunset before treating your eyes and ears to an unforgettable Broadway show, such as **Book of Mormon** (p145). Dinner and drinks are on order afterwards – splurge at **Le Bernardin** (p137) – then sling your tipples back at **Don't Tell Mama** (p147). Warning: you will break into song.

Day Two

Start your second day on the Upper East Side's Museum Mile, attacking the colossal **Metropolitan Museum of Art** (p154) first and – if time permits – tacking on the **Guggenheim Museum** (p158). Strut your stuff along Madison Avenue in search of ritzy wares and check out the **Frick Collection** (p161) if you're still in a museum mood.

Head downtown to the refurbished **Chelsea Market** (p90) where you can choose from a colorful assortment of lunchtime nibbles. Grab a gelato to go and climb up to **The High Line** (p84) for a stroll amid green stretching over the gridiron. Spend the latter half of the afternoon wandering among the Chelsea Galleries, which sit in lovingly restored factory warehouses. Walk over to the **Empire State Building** (p128) and take in the twinkling metropolitan lights as the sun sets over the city.

After dark, head back to the West Village for some vino at **Vin Sur Vingt** (p98) and sample Asian-fusion fare at **RedFarm** (p93). Then hit up **Village Vanguard** (p103) or **Blue Note** (p103) for some jazz tunes, or try the **Upright Citizens Brigade Theatre** (p101) if you're looking for laughs.

Short on time?
We've arranged New York City's must-sees into these day-by-day itineraries to make sure you see the very best of the city in the time you have available.

Day Three

As the local youngsters are crawling back to their shoebox apartments after a raucous night out, make your way to the **Lower East Side Tenement Museum** (p67) to learn about life in the area long before gentrification. Pair your visit with the **New Museum of Contemporary Art** (p66) if you're in search of mind-bending art at the other end of the spectrum.

Head up to the East Village for lunch at one of the area's many street-side cafes, then explore the city's punk rock roots along **St Marks Place** (p66), before swinging through **Union Square** (p113) to catch the flurry of pedestrians and the popular **Union Square Greenmarket** (p122). Snap your camera at the photogenic **Flatiron Building** (p113) further along, then pause for an early-evening cocktail with the after-work crowd at **Raines Law Room** (p118).

Bust out the plastic for an extended retail therapy session in SoHo, where you'll find a healthy mix of international brand names – like **Prada** (p61) – and unique boutiques, such as **Kiosk** (p57). Then go easy on the wallet in Chinatown, home to dozens of noodle and dumplings houses, such as **Joe's Shanghai** (p54).

Day Four

Pay your respects to those who perished in the 9/11 tragedy at the **World Trade Center site** (p28), while glimpsing the city's most anticipated homage to resurrection and progress: the 'Freedom Tower'. Afterwards, get the blood pumping with a walk along the famed **Brooklyn Bridge** (p33), an inspired neo-Gothic gesture bathed in iron.

On the other side of the bridge, you'll find Brooklyn – one of New York's other boroughs, though it largely feels like its own city. Enjoy the views of Manhattan's skyline then hop over to Fort Greene to browse artisanal wonders at the **Brooklyn Flea** (p195). Pause for smoke meat at **Mile End** (p195), then check out the **Brooklyn Academy of Music** (p195) to see what's on.

If you're diggin' Brooklyn's (hipster, ahem) vibe, stick around for the evening and check out Williamsburg, New York's of-the-moment Bohemia. Do dinner at **Dressler** (p197), then the neighborhood's night scene is yours for the taking – try **Commodore** (p197) for '70s-style snifters or dial the time machine back even further with a drink at **Maison Premiere** (p197).

Need to Know

For more information, see Survival Guide (p229)

Currency
US dollar (US$)

Language
English

Visas
The US Visa Waiver program allows nationals of 27 countries to enter the US without a visa.

Money
ATMs widely available and credit cards accepted at most hotels, stores and restaurants. Farmers markets, food trucks and some smaller eateries are cash-only.

Cell Phones
Most US cell phones, apart from the iPhone, operate on CDMA, not the European standard GSM. Check compatibility with your phone service provider.

Time
Eastern Standard Time (GMT/UTC minus five hours)

Plugs & Adaptors
The US electric current is 110V to 115V, 60Hz AC. Outlets are made for flat two-prong plugs (which often have a third, rounded prong for grounding).

Tipping
At restaurants and in taxis, leave between 15% and 20% of the total bill. Hotel housekeepers get $1 to $5 per day.

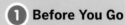 **Before You Go**

Your Daily Budget

Budget less than $100
► Hostel dorm bed $25–$80
► Self-catering supermarkets and cheap eats at cafes and food trucks $5–$25
► Exploring the city on foot

Midrange $100–$300
► Double room $150–$300
► Two-course dinner with a cocktail $30–$75; brunch on the town
► Discount Broadway TKTS tickets $70

Top End over $300
► Luxury sleeps or boutique digs $350+
► Tasting menus at high-end restaurants $190
► Metropolitan Opera orchestra seats $95

Useful Websites

Lonely Planet (www.lonelyplanet.com/usa/new-york-city) Destination information, hotel bookings, traveler forum and more.

NYC: the Official Guide (www.nycgo.com) New York City's official tourism portal.

New York Magazine (www.nymag.com) Comprehensive bar, restaurant, entertainment and shopping listings.

Advance Planning

Two months before Book your hotel reservations – prices increase closer to your arrival date – and snag Broadway tickets.

Three weeks before Score a table at your favorite high-end restaurant.

One week before Surf the interwebs for the newest and coolest in the city and join email news blasts.

② Arriving in New York City

With its three bustling airports, two train stations and a monolithic bus terminal, New York City rolls out the welcome mat for the more than 50 million visitors who come to take a bite out of the Big Apple each year.

✈ From John F Kennedy International Airport (JFK)

Destination	Best Transport
Brooklyn	Subway A line
Lower Manhattan	Subway A line
Midtown	Subway E line
Greenwich Village	Subway A line
Upper West Side	Subway A line

✈ From LaGuardia Airport (LGA)

Destination	Best Transport
Harlem	Bus M60
Upper East Side	Bus M60 & Subway 4/5/6 line
Midtown	Taxi
Union Square	Taxi
Greenwich Village	Taxi

✈ From Newark International Airport (EWR)

Take the AirTrain to Manhattan's Midtown – there's only one transfer. Shared shuttles and buses are also available. From Midtown, you can hop on a subway to reach your final destination.

③ Getting Around

Once you've arrived in NYC, getting around is fairly easy. The 660-mile subway system is cheap and (reasonably) efficient. The sidewalks of New York, however, are the real stars in the transportation scheme – this city is made for walking.

S Subway

The subway system is inexpensive, somewhat efficient and open around the clock, though it can be confusing to the uninitiated. Check out www.mta.info for public transportation information, including a handy travel planner and regular notifications of delays and alternate travel routes during frequent maintenance. Subway travel is particularly useful when traveling large distances uptown or downtown, or venturing over to Brooklyn.

🚌 Bus

Buses are convenient during off hours and are a good choice when trying to travel 'crosstown' – there are buses that ply the east–west/west–east route on most two-way streets in Manhattan. Buses are also handy for travel along First and Tenth Aves. Avoid Second Ave buses due to the heavy construction.

🚗 Taxi

Taxi travel is the most convenient means of transportation, especially outside of rush hour. Taxis are handy if your trajectory is a zigzag through Manhattan as subway and bus lines follow the city's linear avenues and major streets. It can very difficult to grab a taxi in inclement weather.

⛴ Ferry

There are hop-on-hop-off services and free rides to Staten Island. Check out **New York Waterway** (☎800-533-3779; www.nywaterway.com) and **New York Water Taxi** (☎212-742-1969; www.nywatertaxi.com; hop-on-hop-off service 1 day $26).

New York City
Neighborhoods

Upper West Side & Central Park (p172)
Home to Lincoln Center and Central Park – the city's antidote to the endless stretches of concrete.

👁 **Top Sights**
Central Park

Greenwich Village, Chelsea & the Meatpacking District (p82)
Quaint streets and well-preserved brick townhouses lead to neighborhood cafes mixed with trendy nightlife options.

👁 **Top Sights**
The High Line

SoHo & Chinatown (p46)
Hidden temples and steaming dumpling houses dot Chinatown. Next door are SoHo's streamlined streets and retail storefronts.

Lower Manhattan & the Financial District (p22)
Home to Wall Street, the 9/11 Memorial and the Statue of Liberty. Tribeca hums with restaurants and lounges.

👁 **Top Sights**
New York Harbor
World Trade Center Site

Times Square 👁

Empire State Building 👁

The High Line 👁

World Trade Center Site 👁

New York Harbor 👁

Upper East Side (p152)

High-end boutiques and sophisticated mansions culminate in an architectural flourish called Museum Mile.

◉ Top Sights

Metropolitan Museum of Art

Guggenheim Museum

Midtown (p124)

This is the NYC found on postcards: Times Sq, Broadway theaters, canyons of skyscrapers and bustling crowds.

◉ Top Sights

Times Square

Empire State Building

Museum of Modern Art

Union Square, Flatiron District & Gramercy (p110)

The tie that binds the colorful menagerie of surrounding areas. It's short on sights but big on buzz-worthy restaurants.

East Village & Lower East Side (p62)

Old meets new on every block of this downtown duo – two of the city's hottest 'hoods for nightlife and cheap eats.

Central Park

Guggenheim Museum

Metropolitan Museum of Art

Museum of Modern Art

Explore
New York City

Taxis at Times Sq (p126)
KARSTEN BIDSTRUP/LONELY PLANET IMAGES ©

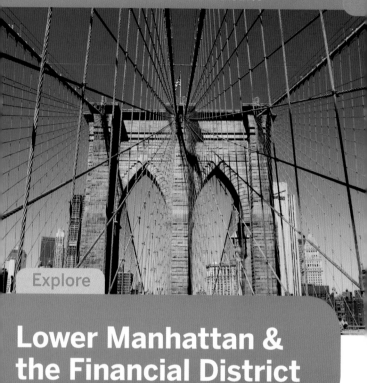

Explore

Lower Manhattan & the Financial District

Home to icons like Wall Street, the 9/11 Memorial and the Statue of Liberty, the southern end of Manhattan is the city's true historical heart. And these days it pulses with businesslike energy during the day before settling into quieter nights. Tribeca, however, continues to hum well after dark with its cache of restaurants and lounges.

The Sights in a Day

☼ Beat the crowds and catch the New York Harbor ferry when it opens to tour the **Statue of Liberty** (p25) and **Ellis Island** (p25). Those with smaller wallets can hop on the **Staten Island Ferry** (p32) for a free ride in the harbor, which offers post-card-worthy photo ops of the southern portion of Manhattan.

☼ Head back to Manhattan for lunch at Anthony Bourdain's **Les Halles** (p37). After you've packed an artery, head over to the **Brooklyn Bridge** (p33) for a wander along the cantilevered Gothic wonder. As evening nears, pay your respects to the fallen at the **World Trade Center site** (p28), then lighten the mood with some retail therapy during a round of whirlwind shopping at **Century 21** (p43).

☾ Do dinner and a show in Tribeca, stopping first at brasserie-style **Locanda Verde** (p35), then hitting up the **Flea Theater** (p41), one of the best respected off-off-Broadway institutions in town. End the night at **Brandy Library** (p39), where you can choose from a veritable encyclopedia of spirits.

◉ Top Sights

New York Harbor (p24)

World Trade Center Site (p28)

♥ Best of New York City

Fine Dining

Locanda Verde (p35)

Les Halles (p37)

Drinking

Brandy Library (p39)

Weather Up (p40)

Keg No 229 (p40)

Entertainment

Flea Theater (p41)

92YTribeca (p41)

Getting There

S Subway Fulton St is the area's main interchange station, serv-icing the A/C, J/M/Z, 2/3 and 4/5 lines. The 1 train terminates at South Ferry, from where the Staten Island Ferry departs.

☗ Boat The Staten Island Ferry leaves at the southern end of Whitehall St. Services to Liberty and Ellis Islands depart from Battery Park.

Top Sights
New York Harbor

Since its unveiling in 1886, Lady Liberty has welcomed millions of immigrants sailing into New York Harbor in the hope of a better life. It now welcomes millions of tourists, many of whom head up to her crown for one of New York City's finest skyline and water views. Close by lies Ellis Island, the American gateway for over 12 million new arrivals between 1892 and 1954. These days it's home to one of the city's most moving museums, paying tribute to these immigrants and their indelible courage.

👁 Map p18, B8

www.statuecruises.com

ferry adult/child $13/5

🕙 9am-5pm, ferries every 20min 8:30am-6pm Jun-Aug

Ⓢ 1 to South Ferry, 4/5 to Bowling Green

Statue of Liberty

Don't Miss

Statue of Liberty

Following the **statue's** (☎877-523-9849; www.nps.gov/stli; Liberty Island; admission free; ⏱9:30am-5pm) 125th anniversary celebrations on October 28, 2011, the crown, museum and pedestal were closed for a major renovation and are due to reopen in late 2012. Once the renovations are complete, folks who reserve in advance will once again be able to climb the (steep) 354 steps to Lady Liberty's crown, where the city and harbor are even more impressive. Crown access is, however, extremely limited, and the only way in is to reserve your spot in advance – you can do it up to a full year in advance. Each customer may only reserve a maximum of four crown tickets.

Ellis Island Immigration Museum

Ellis Island's three-level **Immigration Museum** is a poignant tribute to the immigrant experience. It is estimated that 40% of Americans today have at least one ancestor who was processed at Ellis Island, confirming the major role this tiny harbor island has played in the making of modern America. To get the most out of your visit, opt for the 50-minute self-guided audio tour ($8, available from the museum lobby). The tour features narratives from a number of sources, including historians, architects and the immigrants themselves, and brings to life the museum's hefty collection of personal objects, official documents, photographs and film footage. It's an evocative experience to relive personal memories – both good and bad – in the very halls and corridors in which they occurred.

The collection itself is divided into a number of permanent and temporary exhibitions. If you're very short on time, skip the *Journeys: the Peopling of America 1550–1890* exhibit on the 1st

☑ Top Tips

▶ The ferry ride from Battery Park in Lower Manhattan is only 15 minutes, but a trip to both the Statue of Liberty and Ellis Island is an all-day affair, and you need to set out by 1pm to be allowed to visit both sites.

▶ A reservation to visit the grounds and pedestal (the latter closed until late 2012) is recommended, as it gives you a specific time and guaranteed entry. You can also buy a Flex Ticket, which lets you enter any time within a three-day period.

✗ Take a Break

Skip the cafeteria fare at Lady Liberty and pack a picnic lunch. On Sundays, stop by the New Amsterdam Market (p36) for take-away eats before riding the ferry over. Or, take to the harbor early and return to Lower Manhattan for lunch at the much loved Locanda Verde (p35) – make sure to reserve a table!

floor and focus on the exhibitions on the 2nd floor. It's here you'll find two of the most fascinating exhibitions. The first, *Through America's Gate*, examines the step-by-step process faced by the newly arrived, including the chalk-marking of those suspected of illness, a wince-inducing eye examination and 29 questions in the beautiful, vaulted Registry Room. The second must-see exhibition, *Peak Immigration Years*, explores the motives behind the immigrants' journeys and the challenges they faced once they were free to begin their new American lives. For a history of the rise, fall and resurrection of the building itself, make time for the *Restoring a Landmark* exhibition on the 3rd floor; its tableaux of trashed desks, chairs and other abandoned possessions are strangely haunting. Best of all, the audio tour

offers optional, in-depth coverage for those wanting to delve deeper into the collections and the island's history. If you don't feel like opting for the audio tour, you can always pick up one of the phones in each display area and listen to the recorded memories of real Ellis Island immigrants, taped in the 1980s. Another option is the free, 45-minute guided tour with a park ranger (also available in American Sign Language).

American Immigrant Wall of Honor & Fort Gibson Ruins

Accessible from the 1st-floor *Journeys: the Peopling of America* exhibit is the outdoor American Immigrant Wall of Honor, inscribed with the names of over 700,000 immigrants. Believed to be the world's longest wall of names, it's a fund-raising project, allowing

---

Understand
Building Lady Liberty

One of America's most powerful symbols of kinship and freedom, 'Liberty Enlightening the World' was a joint effort between America and France to commemorate the centennial of the Declaration of Independence. It was created by commissioned sculptor Frédéric-Auguste Bartholdi. The artist spent most of 20 years turning his dream – to create the hollow monument and mount it in the New York Harbor – into reality. Bartholdi's work on the statue was delayed by structural challenges – a problem resolved by the metal framework mastery of railway engineer Gustave Eiffel (of, yes, the famous tower). The work of art was finally completed in France in 1884. It was shipped to NYC as 350 pieces packed into 214 crates, reassembled over a span of four months and placed on a US-made granite pedestal. Its spectacular October 1886 dedication included New York's first ticker-tape parade and a flotilla of almost 300 vessels. The monument made it onto the UN's list of World Heritage Sites in 1984.

any American to have an immigrant relative's name recorded for the cost of a donation. Construction of the wall in the 1990s uncovered the remains of the island's original structure, Fort Gibson – you can see the ruins at the southwestern corner of the memorial. Built in 1808, the fortification was part of a harbor defense system against the British that also included Castle Clinton in Battery Park and Castle Williams on Governors Island. During this time, Ellis Island measured a modest 3.3 acres of sand and slush. Between 1892 and 1934, the island expanded dramatically thanks to landfill brought in from the ballast of ships and construction of the city's subway system.

Ellis Island Immigration Museum

Main Building Architecture

With their Main Building, architects Edward Lippincott Tilton and William A Boring created a suitably impressive and imposing 'prologue' to America. The designing duo won the contract after the original wooden building burnt down in 1897. Having attended the Ecole des Beaux Arts in Paris, it's not surprising that they opted for a beaux arts aesthetic for the project. The building evokes a grand train station, with majestic triple-arched entrances, decorative Flemish bond brickwork, and granite quoins (cornerstones) and belvederes. Inside, it's the 2nd-floor, 338ft-long Registry Room (also known as the Great Hall) that takes the breath away. It was under its beautiful vaulted ceiling that

the newly arrived lined up to have their documents checked, and that the polygamists, paupers, criminals and anarchists were turned back. The original plaster ceiling was severely damaged by an explosion of munition barges at nearby Black Tom Wharf. It was a blessing in disguise and the rebuilt version is adorned with striking, herringbone-patterned tiles by Rafael Guastavino. The Catalan-born engineer is also behind the beautiful tiled ceiling at the **Grand Central Oyster Bar & Restaurant** (www.oysterbarny.com; Grand Central Terminal, 42nd St at Park Ave; mains $23.95-33.95; ⊘closed Sun) at Grand Central Terminal.

TOM GRILL/CORBIS ©

Top Sights
World Trade Center Site

Plagued by design controversies, budget blowouts and construction delays, the first part of the World Trade Center (WTC) redevelopment – the National September 11 Memorial, known more simply as the 9/11 Memorial – opened to the public on September 12, 2011. The wait was worth it. Titled *Reflecting Absence,* its two massive reflecting pools are as much a symbol of hope and renewal as they are a tribute to the thousands who lost their lives to terrorism.

Map p30, B5

www.911memorial.org

cnr Greenwich & Albany Sts

9/11 Memorial free

S A/C/E to Chambers St, R to Rector St, 2/3 to Park Pl

9/11 Memorial (designer: Michael Arad)

Don't Miss

One World Trade Center

At the northwest corner of the WTC site is architect David M Childs' *One World Trade Center* (1 WTC). Upon completion in late 2012, the tapered skyscraper will be America's tallest, with 105 stories and a total height of 1776ft. An observation deck 1362ft above the ground is also planned.

Reflecting Pools

Surrounded by a plaza planted with 400 swamp white oak trees, the 9/11 Memorial's reflecting pools occupy the very footprints of the ill-fated twin towers. From their rim, a steady cascade of water pours 30ft down toward a central void. Bronze panels frame the pools, inscribed with the names of those who died in the terrorist attacks of September 11, 2001, and in the World Trade Center car bombing on February 26, 1993.

Memorial Museum

When it opens, the National September 11 Memorial Museum will document the terrorist attacks of September 11, 2001 and February 26, 1993 in state-of-the-art subterranean galleries.

WTC Tribute Visitor Center

Until the museum's opening, visitors can reflect at the temporary WTC Tribute Visitor Center, which features a gallery of moving images and artifacts, and join 75-minute tours of the WTC site's perimeter. Admission to the center also includes access to the neighboring 9/11 Memorial.

☑ Top Tips

▸ Until surrounding construction projects at the World Trade Center are complete, you will need to reserve a visitor pass for a specific date and time. Visitor passes are free and available through the memorial's online reservation system.

▸ While checking out the WTC Tribute Visitor Center, don't miss the temporary **9/11 Memorial Preview Site** (Map p30, B4; www.911memorial. org; 20 Vesey St; admission free; ⏰9am-7pm Mon-Fri, 8am-7pm Sat & Sun), which has models, renderings, artifacts and films related to the site and redevelopment.

✗ Take a Break

Escape the swarm of restaurants serving the lunching Wall St crowd and head to Tribeca for a variety of in-demand eats, like Locanda Verde (p35) or Kutsher's Tribeca (p36).

For reviews see
⊙ Top Sights	p24
⊙ Sights	p32
✗ Eating	p35
⊕ Drinking	p39
✿ Entertainment	p41
⚅ Shopping	p42

Sights

Staten Island Ferry OUTDOORS

1 Map p30, D8

Staten Islanders know these hulking, dirty-orange ferryboats as commuter vehicles, while Manhattanites like to think of them as their secret, romantic vessels for a spring-day escape. Yet many a tourist is clued into the charms of the Staten Island Ferry, whose 5.2-mile journey between Lower Manhattan and the Staten Island neighborhood of St George is one of NYC's finest free adventures. (www.siferry.com; Whitehall Terminal at Whitehall & South Sts; fare free; ⏰24hr; Ⓢ1 to South Ferry)

Fraunces Tavern Museum MUSEUM

2 Map p30, C7

Combining five early-18th-century structures, this unique museum/restaurant combo is an homage to the nation-shaping events of 1783, when the British relinquished control of New York at the end of the Revolutionary War and General George Washington gave a farewell speech to the officers of the Continental Army in the 2nd-floor dining room on December 4. (www.frauncestavernmuseum.org; 54 Pearl St btwn Broad St & Coenties Slip; adult/child $7/free; ⏰noon-5pm; Ⓢ J/M/Z to Broad St, 4/5 to Bowling Green)

National Museum of the American Indian MUSEUM

3 Map p30, C7

An affiliate of the Smithsonian Institution, this elegant museum of Native American culture is set in Cass Gilbert's spectacular 1907 Custom House, one of NYC's finest beaux arts buildings. Beyond a vast elliptical rotunda, sleek galleries play host to changing exhibitions documenting Native American culture, life and beliefs. The museum's permanent collection includes stunning decorative arts, textiles and ceremonial objects. (www.nmai.si.edu; 1 Bowling Green; admission free; ⏰10am-5pm Fri-Wed, to 8pm Thu; Ⓢ4/5 to Bowling Green)

Federal Hall MUSEUM

4 Map p30, C6

A Greek Revival masterpiece, Federal Hall houses a museum dedicated to postcolonial New York. Exhibition themes include George Washington's inauguration, Alexander Hamilton's relationship with the city and the struggles of John Peter Zenger, who was jailed, tried and acquitted of libel here for exposing government corruption in his newspaper. There's also a visitor information hall which covers downtown cultural happenings. (www.nps.gov/feha; 26 Wall St, entrance on Pine St; admission free; ⏰9am-5pm Mon-Fri; Ⓢ J/M/Z to Broad St, 2/3, 4/5 to Wall St)

Understand
Brooklyn Bridge

A New York icon, the **Brooklyn Bridge** (Map p30, E4) was the world's first steel suspension bridge. When it opened in 1883, the 1596ft span between its support towers was the longest in history. Its construction was fraught with disaster, but the bridge became a magnificent example of urban design, inspiring poets, writers and painters. Today, it continues to dazzle – many regard it as the most beautiful bridge in the world.

Building the Bridge
Prussian-born engineer John Roebling designed the bridge, which spans the East River from Manhattan to Brooklyn. He died of tetanus poisoning before construction of the bridge even began. His son, Washington Roebling, supervised construction, which lasted 14 years and managed to survive budget overruns and the deaths of 20 workers. The younger Roebling himself suffered from the bends while helping to excavate the riverbed for the bridge's western tower and remained bedridden for much of the project; his wife Emily oversaw construction in his stead.

There was one final tragedy to come in June 1883, when the bridge opened to pedestrian traffic. Someone in the crowd shouted, perhaps as a joke, that the bridge was collapsing into the river, setting off a mad rush in which 12 people were trampled to death.

The Bridge Today
The bridge entered its second century as strong and beautiful as ever following an extensive renovation in the early 1980s. The pedestrian walkway just east of City Hall affords a wonderful view of Lower Manhattan; observation points under the support towers offer brass 'panorama' histories of the waterfront. Just stay on the side of the walkway marked for folks on foot – one half is designated for cyclists, who use it en masse for both commuting and pleasure rides. Frustrated pedalers have been known to get nasty with tourists who wander into the bike lane. Barring any such run-ins, you should reach Brooklyn in 20 minutes. Bear left to Empire-Fulton Ferry State Park or Cadman Plaza West, which runs alongside Middagh St in the heart of Brooklyn Heights, taking you to Brooklyn's downtown area. Don't miss the ornate Brooklyn Borough Hall and the Brooklyn Heights Promenade.

New York Stock Exchange

NOTABLE BUILDING

5 Map p30, C6

Home to the world's best-known stock exchange, Wall Street is an iconic symbol of US capitalism. About one billion shares, valued at around $73 billion, change hands daily behind the portentous Romanesque facade, a sight no longer accessible to the public due to security concerns. Feel free to gawk outside the building, protected by barricades and the hawk-eyed New York Police Department (NYPD). (The online shop has souvenirs like a hooded NYSE sweatshirt, as if you'd actually been inside.) (NYSE; www.nyse.com; 11 Wall St; ⏰closed to the public; **S** J/M/Z to Broad St, 2/3, 4/5 to Wall St)

Trinity Church

CHURCH

6 Map p30, B6

New York City's tallest building upon completion in 1846, Trinity Church features a 280ft-high bell tower, an arresting stained glass window over the altar and a small museum of historical church artifacts. Famous residents of its serene cemetery include Founding Father Alexander Hamilton, while its excellent music series includes Concerts at One (1pm Thursdays) and magnificent choir concerts, such as an annual December rendition of Handel's Messiah. (www.trinitywallstreet. org; Broadway at Wall St; ⏰7am-6pm Mon-Fri, 8am-4pm Sat, 7am-4pm Sun; **S** R to Rector St, 2/3, 4/5 to Wall St)

St Paul's Chapel

CHURCH

7 Map p30, C4

Despite George Washington worshiping here after his inauguration in 1789, this classic revival brownstone chapel found new fame in the aftermath of September 11. With the World Trade Center destruction occurring just a block away, the mighty structure became a spiritual support and volunteer center, movingly documented in its exhibition *Unwavering Spirit: Hope & Healing at Ground Zero.* (www. trinitywallstreet.org; Broadway at Fulton St; ⏰10am-6pm Mon-Fri, to 4pm Sat, 7am-4pm Sun; **S** A/C, J/Z, 2/3, 4/5 to Fulton St)

Bowling Green

PARK

8 Map p30, C7

New York's oldest – and possibly tiniest – public park is purportedly the spot where Dutch settler Peter Minuit paid Native Americans the equivalent of $24 to purchase Manhattan Island. At its northern edge stands Arturo Di Modica's 7000lb bronze *Charging Bull,* placed here permanently after it mysteriously appeared in front of the New York Stock Exchange in 1989, two years after a market crash. (cnr Broadway & State St; 📶; **S** 4/5 to Bowling Green)

Hudson River Park

PARK

9 Map p30, A2

Stretching from Battery Park to Hell's Kitchen, the 5-mile, 550-acre Hudson River Park runs along the lower western side of Manhattan. Diversions include a bike/run/skate path snaking along its entire length, community gardens, playgrounds and renovated piers reinvented as riverfront esplanades, miniature golf courses, and alfresco summertime movie theaters and concert venues. Visit the website for a detailed map. (www.hudsonriverpark.org; Manhattan's west side from Battery Park to 59th St; S 1 to Franklin St, 1 to Canal St)

New York City Police Museum

MUSEUM

10 Map p30, D7

Get the brief on 'New York's Finest,' with cool old police vehicles, as well as the mug shots and weapons of notorious New York criminals like Willie Sutton and Al Capone. There's a collection of NYPD uniforms throughout the decades, insight into anti-terrorism tactics, and a 'Hall of Heroes' memorial to officers killed in the line of duty since 1845. The museum itself is housed in a neo-Renaissance palazzo on a landfilled inlet. (www.nycpolicemuseum.org; 100 Old Slip; adult/child $8/5; ◷10am-5pm Mon-Sat, noon-5pm Sun; S 1 to South Ferry, 2/3 to Wall St)

Museum of American Finance

MUSEUM

11 Map p30, C6

Money makes this museum go round, with exhibits focusing on historic moments in American financial history. Permanent collections include rare, 18th-century documents, stock and bond certificates from the Gilded Age, the oldest known photograph of Wall

St, and a stock ticker from around 1875. The museum also runs themed walking tours of the area, advertised on the museum website. (www.moaf.org; 48 Wall St btwn Pearl & William Sts; adult/child $8/free; ◷10am-4pm Tue-Sat; S 2/3, 4/5 to Wall St)

Museum of Jewish Heritage

MUSEUM

12 Map p30, B7

This waterfront memorial museum explores all aspects of modern Jewish identity, with often poignant personal artifacts, photographs and documentary films. Its outdoor Garden of Stones – created by artist Andy Goldsworthy (and his first permanent exhibition in NYC) – is dedicated to those who lost loved ones in the Holocaust. It holds 18 boulders that form a narrow pathway for contemplating the fragility of life. (www.mjhnyc.org; 36 Battery Pl; adult/child $12/free, 4-8pm Wed free; ◷10am-5:45pm Sun-Tue & Thu, to 8pm Wed, to 5pm Fri; S 4/5 to Bowling Green)

Eating

Locanda Verde

ITALIAN $$$

13 Map p30, A2

Step through the red velvet curtains and into a sexy, buzzing scene of loosened Brown Brothers' shirts, black dresses and slick barmen behind a long, crowded bar. Part of the Greenwich Hotel, this sprawling, brasserie-style hot spot is the domain of celebrity chef Andrew Carmellini, whose contemporary Italian grub is seasonal, savvy and insanely flavorful. (☎212-925-3797; www.locandaverdenyc.com; 377 Greenwich St at Noore St; pasta $17-19, mains $15-31 ; [S]A/C/E to Canal St, 1 to Franklin St)

Kutsher's Tribeca JEWISH $$$

14 🍴 Map p30, A2

Thank Yahweh for new-kid-on-the-block Kutsher's, where Jewish comfort food gets a refreshing makeover. Forget the starch and stodge, here you'll be grazing on crispy artichokes with lemon, garlic and Parmesan; borscht salad with marinated goat cheese; or latkes with local apple compote. (☎212-431-0606; www.kutsherstribeca.com; 186 Franklin St btwn Greenwich & Hudson Sts; mains $19-29; 🕓dinner ; [S]A/C/E to Canal St, 1 to Franklin St)

New Amsterdam Market MARKET $

15 🍴 Map p30, E5

Sophisticated locavore or basic glutton, do not miss this Sunday food market outside the old Fulton Fish Market. Usually held from late April to mid-December, its 40-odd stalls showcase some of the region's top food and drink producers. Pick up everything from organic Finnish Ruis bread to handmade sausages and pasta. The porchetta sandwiches ($6) have converted vegetarians. (www.newamsterdammarket.org; South St btwn Peck Slip & Beekman St; 🕓11am-4pm Sun late Apr–mid-Dec; [S]A/C, J/Z, 1/2, 4/5 to Fulton St)

Understand

Long Before New York

Long before the days of European conquest, the swath that would eventually become NYC belonged to Native Americans known as the Lenape – 'original people' – who resided in a series of seasonal campsites. They lived up and down the eastern seaboard, along the signature shoreline, and on hills and in valleys sculpted by glaciers after the Ice Age left New York with glacial debris now called Hamilton Heights and Bay Ridge. Glaciers scoured off soft rock, leaving behind Manhattan's stark rock foundations of gneiss and schist. Around 11,000 years before the first Europeans sailed through the Narrows, the Lenape people foraged, hunted and fished the regional bounty here. Spear points, arrowheads, bone heaps and shell mounds testify to their presence. Some of their pathways still lie beneath streets such as Broadway. In the Lenape language of Munsee, the term Manhattan may have translated as 'hilly island.' Others trace the meaning to a more colorful phrase: 'place of general inebriation.'

Locanda Verde (p35)

Les Halles FRENCH $$

16 Map p30, C5

Vegetarians need not apply at this packed and serious brasserie, owned by celebrity chef Anthony Bourdain. Among the elegant light-fixture balls, dark wood paneling and stiff white tablecloths you'll find a buttoned-up, meat-lovin' crowd who've come for rich and decadent favorites like cote de boeuf and steak au poivre. (☎212-285-8585; www.leshalles.net; 15 John St btwn Broadway & Nassau St; mains $14.50-28.50; ⏰11:30am-midnight; 🛜; 🚇A/C, J/M/Z, 2/3, 4/5 to Fulton St)

Thalassa GREEK $$$

17 Map p30, A2

Owned by a family of passionate food importers, this upmarket, mosaic-laced spot injects some much needed attitude into Greek nosh (there's even a cheese cave in the basement). Ditch sad souvlakis for refreshing dishes like baby arugula with graviera cheese, beets, walnuts and honey oregano dressing, or super-succulent calamari stuffed with Dodonis fetta, tomato and pine nuts. (☎212-941-7661; www.thalassanyc.com; 179 Franklin St btwn Hudson & Greenwich Sts; lunch prix fixe $24, dinner mains $28-46 ; ⏰lunch & dinner; 🚇1 to Franklin St)

Tiny's & the Bar Upstairs

AMERICAN $$

18 Map p30, B3

Snug and adorable (book ahead!), Tiny's comes with a crackling fire in the back room and an intimate bar upstairs – try the signature hot buttered wassail (chamomile, apple cider, allspice, cinnamon and whipped cream). Heading the kitchen is chef John Martinez (formerly of Michelin-starred Jean Georges), whose seasonal, well-balanced dishes are served on vintage porcelain. You can expect to find soulful options like meatballs and garlic toast, beet and crispy goat cheese salad, or a beautifully cooked pan-roasted hake here. (☎212-374-1135; 135 W Broadway btwn Duane & Thomas Sts; mains $18-29; ⏱11:30am-11pm Mon-Thu, to 1am Fri, 10:30am-1am Sat; Ⓢ A/C, 1/2/3 to Chambers St)

Barbarini

ITALIAN $$

19 Map p30, E5

Is it a deli? A cafe? A restaurant? Barbarini is all three, sleekly packaged in a combination of concrete floors, charcoal hues and brickwork. Stock the larder with artisanal pasta, salami, cheeses and mini pistachio cannoli.... but not before nabbing a table in the light-filled backroom for better-than-mamma's offerings like buckwheat pasta with wild boar. If you're in a hurry, opt for the buonissimi panini. (www.barbarinimercato.com; 225 Front St btwn Peck Slip & Beekman St; pasta $15, mains $16-20; ⏱10am-10:30pm Mon-Sat, 11am-9:30pm Sun; Ⓢ A/C, J/Z, 2/3, 4/5 to Fulton St)

Moomah

CAFE $

20 Map p30, A1

Bond with your little munchkins at this trendy cafe/creative space hybrid in Tribeca, where you can buy art projects off the shelf and undertake them on-site. Whether you're making jewelry or a superhero costume, you'll be sensibly fueled by wholesome edibles, including a variety of soups, wraps and salads. There are dairy- and gluten-free options for sensitive bellies and Counter Culture Coffee for caffeine snobs. (www.moomah.com; 161 Hudson St btwn Laight & Hubert Sts; meals $7-13; ⏱7:30am-6pm Mon-Thu, to 7pm Fri, 8am-7pm Sun, art space 9am-5pm Mon-Thu, to 6pm Fri & Sat ; 🛜♿; Ⓢ A/C/E, 1/2 to Canal St)

Nelson Blue

PUB $$

21 Map p30, E4

Good for a drink as well as a lamb curry pie, Nelson Blue is the only Kiwi pub in town. The wine list is heavy on New Zealand drops, which are perfect matches for standout dishes such as zucchini and corn fritters, and green-lipped mussels in a curry and coconut broth. In true antipodean style, the vibe is friendly, laid-back and attitude-free. (☎212-346-9090; www.nelsonblue.com; 233-235 Front St at Peck Slip; mains $15-26; Ⓢ 2/3, 4/5, A/C, J/Z to Fulton St)

Drinking

Kaffe 1668 CAFE

22 Map p30, B3

One for the coffee cognoscenti, with clover machines, coffee urns and dual synessos pumping out superlative single-origin magic. Seating includes a large communal table, speckled with a mix of office workers, designer Tribeca parents and laptop-hugging creatives. The vibe is chilled, the cafe latte seriously smooth and the triple ristretto a hair-raising thrill. (www. kaffe1668.com; 275 Greenwich St btwn Warren & Murray Sts; ⏱6:30am-10pm Mon-Fri, 7:30am-10pm Sat & Sun; 🛜; Ⓢ A/C, 1/2/3 to Chambers St)

Macao COCKTAIL BAR

23 Map p30, B1

Skip the lines for Macao restaurant and duck into the dark, red-walled opium-den-turned-lounge downstairs. A fusion of Portuguese and Asian grub and liquor, Macao remains a top spot for late-night drinking and snacking, especially if you've a soft spot for creative, sizzle-on-the-tongue cocktails. (☎212-431-8750; www.macaonyc.com; 311 Church St btwn Lispenard & Walker Sts; Ⓢ A/C/E, N/R/Q, 4/6 to Canal St)

Brandy Library BAR

24 Map p30, B1

When sipping means serious business, settle into this uber-luxe library, with soothing reading lamps and club chairs facing backlit, floor-to-ceiling, bottle-filled shelves. Go for top-shelf cognac, malt scotch or 90-year-old brandies (prices range from $9 to $340). Libation-friendly nibbles includes the sublime house specialty Gougeres (Gruyere cheese puffs). Call ahead about tastings and other events. (www.brandylibrary.com; 25 N Moore St at Varick St; ⏱5pm-1am Sun-Wed, 4pm-2am Thu, 4pm-4am Fri & Sat; Ⓢ 1 to Franklin St)

Smith & Mills COCKTAIL BAR

25 Map p30, A2

This petite drinking hole marks all the cool boxes: unmarked exterior, kooky industrial interior (think early-20th-century factory) and smooth libations – the 'Carriage House' is a nod to the bar's previous incarnation. Space is limited so head in early if you fancy kicking back on a plush banquette. A seasonal menu spans light snacks to more substantial options. (www.smith andmills.com; 71 N Moore St btwn Hudson & Greenwich Sts; Ⓢ 1 to Franklin St)

Ward III COCKTAIL BAR

26 Map p30, B3

Ward III channels old-school jauntiness with its elegant cocktails, vintage vibe (tin ceilings, dark wood and old Singer sewing tables behind the bar) and gentlemanly house rules (number two: 'Don't be creepy'). Reminisce over a Moroccan martini or line the stomach with top-notch bar grub, available every day 'til close at 4am. (www.ward3tribeca.com;

ANDRIA PATINO/CORBIS ©

Staten Island Ferry (p32)

111 Reade St btwn Church St & W Broadway;
 A/C/E, 1/2/3 to Chambers St)

Weather Up
COCKTAIL BAR

27 🍸 Map p30, B3

Softly lit subway tiles, eye candy bar staff and smooth, seductive libations underlie Weather Up's magic. Sweet talk the staff over a None But the Brave (cognac, homemade ginger syrup, fresh lime, Pimeto Dram Allspice and soda). Failing that, comfort yourself with some seriously fine bar grub, including spectacular green chili-spiked oysters. (www.weatherupnyc.com; 159 Duane St btwn Hudson St & W Broadway; S 1/2/3 to Chambers St)

Keg No 229
BEER HALL

If you know that a Flying Dog Raging Bitch is a craft beer – not a nickname for your ex – this curated beer bar near Barbarini (see 19 ✗ Map p30; E5) is for you. From Mother's Milk Stout to Whale's Tail Pale Ale, its booty of drafts, bottles and cans are a who's who of boutique American brews. On hand to soak it all up is a solid selection of comfort grub, including fried pickles and mini cheeseburgers. Sibling bar Bin 220 across the street offers a similar set-up for vino-philes. (www.kegno229.com; 229 Front St btwn Beekman St & Peck Slip; S A/C, J/Z, 1/2, 4/5 to Fulton St)

Blue Bar at India House
COCKTAIL BAR

28 🍸 Map p30, D6

Head up the stairs to the lobby, turn left and slip into this blue-walled, wooden-floored beauty. A private members' bar during the day, it's a handsome, grown-up hideaway for all after 4pm. There's no shortage of Wall St old-timers, known by name and drink by the barmen. Reminisce about the crash of '87 over a smooth whiskey or a remastered 19th-century cocktail. (www.indiahouseclub.org; 1 Hanover Sq at Stone St; ⊙4-11pm Mon-Fri; **S** R to Whitehall St, 1 to South Ferry)

Another Room
BAR

29 🍸 Map p30, B1

Charcoal walls, candlelight and velvet banquettes: Another Room is a perfect spot to slip into darkness with a luscious glass of red. It's all beer and wine – no mixed drinks – with chalkboard scrawl announcing the daily catch, from boutique Italian drops to seasonal domestic brews. Expect a 30- and 40-something Tribeca crowd, clinking glasses over indie-folk tunes. (www.anotherroomtribeca.com; 249 W Broadway btwn Beach & White Sts; **S**1/2 to Franklin St)

La Colombe
CAFE

30 🍸 Map p30, B1

Coffee and a few baked treats are all you'll get at this roaster but, man, are they good. The espresso is dark and intense, brewed by hipster baristas and swilled by an endless stream of eye-candy creatives and clued-in Continentals. Don't leave without a bottle of 'Pure Black Coffee,' steeped in oxygen-free stainless steel wine tanks for 16 hours. (www.lacolombe.com; 319 Church St at Lispenard St; ⊙7:30am-6:30pm Mon-Fri, 8:30am-6:30pm Sat & Sun; **S**A/C/E, N/Q/R, 4/6 to Canal St.)

Entertainment

Flea Theater
THEATER

31 ⭐ Map p30, B2

The Flea is one of New York's top off-off-Broadway companies, performing innovative, timely new works in its two intimate performance spaces. Luminaries, including Sigourney Weaver and John Lithgow, have tread the boards here, and the year-round program also includes cutting-edge music and dance performances. (www.theflea.org; 41 White St btwn Church St & Broadway; **S**1 to Franklin St, A/C/E, N/Q/R, J/M/Z, 6 to Canal St)

92YTribeca
CINEMA

32 ⭐ Map p30, A1

Festival-circuit indies, underground classics, camp tear-jerkers – the film screenings at this Tribeca cultural center are as eclectic as they are brilliant. One night you're wincing at *The House by the Cemetery*, then next

✅ Top Tip
Downtown TKTS

If you're after cut-price tickets to Broadway shows, ditch the main TKTS Booth in Times Sq and head for the TKTS branch at **South Street Seaport** (Map p30, D5; www.tdf.org/tkts; cnr Front & John Sts; ⏰11am-6pm Mon-Sat, to 4pm Sun; 🚇A/C to Broadway-Nassau; 2/3, 4/5, J/Z to Fulton St). Queues usually move a little faster and you can also purchase tickets for next-day matinees (something you can't do at the Times Sq outlet). Smartphone users can download the free TKTS app, which offers real-time listings of what's on sale.

you're psychoanalyzing Woody Allen in *Broadway Danny Rose*. Regular themed events include 'sing-a-long' screenings (go on, you're dying to sing 'Wind Beneath My Wings' in public, admit it!). (📞212-601-1000; www.92y.org; 200 Hudson St at Vestry St; 🚇A/C/E, N/Q/R, J/M/Z, 6 to Canal St)

Tribeca Cinemas   CINEMA

33 ⭐ Map p30, B1

This is the physical home of the Tribeca Film Festival, founded in 2003 by Robert De Niro and Jane Rosenthal. Throughout the year, the space hosts a range of screenings and educational panels, including festivals dedicated to video art, experimental films or kids' movies. Check the website for upcoming events and screening schedules. (www.tribecacinemas.com; 54 Varick St at Laight St; 🚇A/C/E, N/Q/R, J/M/Z, 6 to Canal St)

Shopping

Philip Williams Posters   VINTAGE

34 🔒 Map p30, B3

You'll find over half a million posters in this cavernous treasure trove, from oversized French advertisements for perfume and cognac to Soviet film posters and retro-fab promos for TWA (we even found an Italian-language film poster for Billy Wilder's *Some Like It Hot*). Prices range from $15 to a few thousand bucks and most of the stock is original. (www.postermuseum.com; 122 Chambers St btwn Church St & W Broadway; ⏰11am-7pm Tue-Sat; 🚇A/C, 1/2/3 to Chambers St)

Steven Alan   FASHION

35 🔒 Map p30, B2

Head to this unisex boutique for cognoscenti labels like Sweden's Our Legacy, Canada's Dace and New York's very own Steven Alan. The look is chic, silhouetted and fun, with whimsical frocks, vintage-inspired shirts, woolen ties and detailed denim in the mix. Accessories include hard-to-find colognes, bags, jewelry and a lust-inducing selection of shoes from the likes of Saville Row. (www.stevenalan.com; 103 Franklin St btwn Church St & W Broadway; 🚇A/C/E to Canal St, 1 to Franklin St)

Century 21

Century 21   FASHION

36 🔒 Map p30, B5

If you're a fashionista with more style
than cents, this cut-price department
store is your promised land. Raid the
racks for designer duds at up to 70%
off. Not everything is a knockout or
a bargain, but persistence pays off. It
gets crowded and competitive, so if
you see something you like, get hold
of it fast. (www.c21stores.com; 22 Cortlandt
St btwn Church St & Broadway; ⏰7:45am-
9pm Mon-Wed, to 9:30pm Thu & Fri, 10am-
9pm Sat, 11am-8pm Sun; **S**A/C, J/Z, 2/3, 4/5
to Fulton St)

Pasanella & Son   WINE

37 🔒 Map p30, E5

Oenophiles will adore this savvy
wine peddler, its 400-plus drops both
inspired and affordable. Long sheets
of butcher's paper run down the wall,
offering handwritten wine suggestions
based on your menu. There's an impressive choice of American whiskeys,
free wine tastings of the week's new
arrivals on Sundays, and themed wine
and cheese tastings throughout the
year (check the website). (www.pasanel
laandson.com; 115 South St btwn Peck Slip &
Beekman St; ⏰10am-9pm Mon-Sat, noon-
7pm Sun; **S**A/C, J/Z, 2/3, 4/5 to Fulton St)

JEM Fabric Warehouse

HANDICRAFTS

38 Map p30, C2

Looking for triple-layered satin topped with tulle and metallic spray paint? Chances are you'll find it here. Aside from stocking rare retro fabrics, JEM functions as a creative hub, with short- and longer-term workshops in anything from fabric dyeing to fashion illustration. There's even a drop-in sewing workshop on Thursdays between 5:30pm and 7pm. Check the website for upcoming events. (www.houseofjem. blogspot.com; 355 Broadway btwn Franklin & Leonard Sts; S N/R, 4/6 to Canal St)

Understand
Buying Manhattan

In 1624, the Dutch West India Company sent 110 settlers to begin a trading post in present-day New York City. They settled in Lower Manhattan and called their colony New Amsterdam, touching off bloody battles with the unshakable Lenape tribe. It all came to a head in 1626, when the colony's first governor, Peter Minuit, became the city's first – but certainly not the last – unscrupulous real estate agent by purchasing Manhattan's 14,000 acres from the Lenape for 60 guilders ($24) and some glass beads.

Urban Archaeology

HOMEWARES

39 Map p30, B2

A pioneer in recycled design, owner Gil Shapiro continues his tradition of remixing, reconstructing and reclaiming old parts from abandoned buildings and construction sites. What he salvages and restores (or repurposes) is now sought after in the hippest Manhattan apartments: even Robert De Niro headed here when furnishing his Greenwich Hotel. Check out the Tribeca showroom/studio for Shapiro's latest creations. (www.urbanarchaeology. com; 143 Franklin St btwn Hudson & Varick Sts; ⏱8am-6pm Mon-Fri; S 1 to Franklin St)

J&R Music & Computer World

MUSIC

40 Map p30, C4

Located on what was once known as Newspaper Row – the center of NYC's newspaper publishing biz from the 1840s to the 1920s – this trio of electronics stores sells everything related to computers, phones, stereos, iPods, iPads, recording equipment and other electronic gadgetry. It's also packed with CDs, DVDs and video games. (www.jr.com; 15-23 Park Row; S A/C, J/Z, M, 2/3, 4/5 to Fulton St-Broadway-Nassau St)

Citystore

BOOKS

41 Map p30, C3

This small, little-known city-run shop stocks all manner of New York memorabilia, including Brooklyn Bridge posters, NYPD baseball caps, actual streets signs ('No Parking,' 'Don't Feed the Pigeons'), and authentic taxi medallions, manhole coasters, silk ties and baby clothes bearing the official 'City of New York' seal. There's also a great collection of city-themed books. (www.nyc.gov/citystore; Municipal Bldg, North Plaza, 1 Centre St; ⏰10am-6pm Mon-Fri; Ⓢ J/M/Z to Chambers St, 4/5/6 to Brooklyn Bridge-City Hall)

New York Yankees Clubhouse
SPORTS

42 🔒 Map p30, D5

It's on Schermerhorn Row, a block of old warehouses bordered by Fulton, Front and South Sts, that you'll find this commercial shrine to America's mightiest baseball dynasty. Salute the ballpark legends with logo-pimped jerseys, tees, caps...even dog bowls. Hardcore fans will appreciate the booty of signed bats, balls and posters. You can even purchase fee-free game

New York Yankees merchandise

tickets. (8 Fulton St btwn Front & Water Sts; ⏰10am-9pm Mon-Sat, 11am-8pm Sun; Ⓢ A/C, J/Z, 2/3, 4/5 to Fulton St)

Explore

SoHo & Chinatown

Like a colorful quilt of subneighborhoods sewn together in mismatched patches, the areas orbiting SoHo feel like urban crumbs mopped up from other countries and sprinkled throughout lower Manhattan. While So-Ho's sidewalks unfurl in a regal manner, there's an anything-goes spirit that wafts up like stall smoke in Chinatown, where frenzied crowds and hawkers mingle under the winking lights of aging billboards.

The Sights in a Day

☀ The morning is all about meditation before a fanciful and furious day of shop-til-you-drop fun. Kneel before the giant gilded Buddha at the **Mahayana Temple** (p51), then stroll over to Little Italy for a calming wander through **St Patrick's Old Cathedral** (p51). And who said pizza wasn't good for breakfast?

☼ Nothing beats lunch at **Dutch** (p53) or brunch at **Balthazar** (p53), followed by a round of serious shopping. Warm up your swiping arm as you wield your plastic at the big-name boutiques along Broadway before hitting up hidden wonders like **Kiosk** (p57), **Purl Soho** (p58) and **Built By Wendy** (p59). Step into the past with a visit to the **Merchant's House Museum** (p50) – the best-preserved Federalist mansion in all of New York.

☾ Return to Chinatown in the evening as the twinkling billboards and dangling lanterns replace the sun in the sky. Go for soup dumplings at **Joe's Shanghai** (p54) and dessert at the **Original Chinatown Ice Cream Factory** (p56), then end the evening with chic, Russified drinks at **Pravda** (p56).

♥ Best of New York City

Drinking
Pravda (p56)

Shopping
Housing Works Book Store (p57)

Kiosk (p57)

McNally Jackson (p57)

Purl Soho (p58)

Museums
Merchant's House Museum (p50)

New York City Fire Museum (p52)

Museum of Comic & Cartoon Art (p52)

Fine Dining
Dutch (p53)

Getting There

S **Subway** The subway lines dump off along various points of Canal St (J/M/Z, N/Q/R/W and 6). Once you arrive, it's best to explore on foot. Other useful stops are Brooklyn Bridge–City Hall (4/5/6) and Chambers St (J/Z) for southern access (with a bit of walking).

🚕 **Taxi** Avoid taking cabs – especially in Chinatown – as the traffic is full-on.

EAST VILLAGE

NOHO

NOLITA

SOHO

GREENWICH VILLAGE

Washington Sq Park

New York University

Sara D Roosevelt Park

Fourth Ave

200 m
0.1 miles

For reviews see

Sights	p50
Eating	p53
Drinking	p56
Shopping	p57

Forsyth St
Chrystie St
Stanton St
Rivington St
Delancey St
Second Ave
Lower East Side-2nd Ave
Elizabeth St
Mott St
Mulberry St
Jersey St
Spring St
Prince St
Crosby St
Bowery
E Houston St
Bleecker St
Bond St
Great Jones St
Lafayette St
Broadway-Lafayette St
Broadway
Mercer St
W Houston St
W 4th St
W 3rd St
Bleecker St
LaGuardia Pl
W Broadway
Thompson St
Sullivan St
Prince St
Spring St
E 4th St
E 3rd St
E 2nd St
E 1st St

34
1
15
39
17
6
22
29
19
27
10
38
21
13
28
41
11
26
12
7

Grand St

Bowery

Bowery

24

Kenmare St

Broome St

Grand St

Elizabeth St

Hester St

LITTLE
ITALY

35

Center Market Pl

Cleveland Pl

Old Police
Headquarters

Centre St

Mulberry St

2

8

16

Baxter St

4

Canal St

5

Manhattan
Bridge
Entrance

Confucius
Plaza

14

25

Doyers St

Pell St

18

20

Bayard St

Canal St

Mott St

40

3

CHINATOWN

NYC &
Company

Columbus
Park

9

Hogan Pl

Centre St

Chatham
Sq

Division St

Bowery

E

D

Howard St

33

Lafayette St

Cortlandt Alley

Canal St

C

36

32

37

30

31

Broome St

Mercer St

Greene St

Broadway

Lispenard St

Walker St

White St

Franklin St

Leonard St

Canal St

Church St

Church St

B

Wooster St

Grand St

Watts St

23

Canal St

Sixth Ave (Ave of the Americas)

St Johns La

Hudson
Sq

Beach St

Varick St

W Broadway

Franklin St

TRIBECA

A

5

6

7

8

Sights

Merchant's House Museum
MUSEUM

1 Map p48, D1

Walking through the doors of this perfectly preserved mansion is like stepping into a time machine that has transported you 150 years into the past. Everything in the house – from the polished floors to the crown molding – is as it was during the bygone era. The facade is also intact. The gorgeous red-brick house was once the home of merchant magnate Seabury Tredwell and his family. It remains to this day the most authentic Federal-style house (of which there are about 300) in New York City. (☎212-777-1089; www.merchantshouse.org; 29 E 4th St btwn Lafayette St & Bowery; adult/senior & student $10/5; 🕐11am-6pm Tue-Wed & Fri-Sun, to 9pm Thu; [S]6 to Bleecker St)

> Local Life
> ### Merchant's House Ghosts
> Perhaps just as well known as its antiques are the Merchant's House Museum's (p50) clan of ghosts and ghouls. It is popularly believed that many of the former residents haunt the old mansion, making cameo appearances late in evenings and sometimes at public events. In fact, at a Valentine's Day concert several years back many attendees spotted the shadow of a woman sitting in the parlor chairs. It was commonly believed to be the ghost of Gertrude Tredwell, the last inhabitant of the brownstone. Each year during the last couple of weeks of October, the museum offers special ghost tours after dark.

Mulberry Street
STREET

2 Map p48, D6

New York's tribute to the Boot-land is mostly concentrated on Mulberry St between Broome and Canal Sts. Here you'll find scores of restaurants with their signature checkerboard tablecloths spooning out bowlfuls of homemade pasta and spinning hot tin trays of Neapolitan slices. There's a pick-a-table-and-enjoy kinda vibe, so put down the guidebook and enjoy the dolce vita. ([S]6 to Spring St)

Canal Street
STREET

3 Map p48, D7

Walking down Canal St is like a game of Frogger played on the streets of Shanghai. This is Chinatown's main artery, where you'll dodge oncoming human traffic as you scurry into back alleys to scout treasures from the Far East. You'll pass mysterious herb shops displaying a witch's cauldron's worth of roots and potions; restaurants with whole, roasted ducks and pigs hanging by their skinny necks in the windows; and street vendors selling every iteration of knock-off, from Gucci sunglasses to faux Prada bags. ([S]M/Z, N/Q/R/W, 6 to Canal St)

Museum of Chinese in America

MUSEUM

4 Map p48, C6

Housed in a 12,350-sq-ft space designed by architect Maya Lin (who created the famed Vietnam Memorial in Washington DC), the Museum of Chinese in America is a multifaceted space with exhibit galleries, a bookstore and a visitors lounge. It serves as a national center of information about Chinese American life. Take some time to browse through interactive multimedia exhibits, maps, timelines, photos, letters, films and artifacts. (☎212-619-4785; www.mocanyc. org; 211-215 Centre St near Grand St; admission $7; ⏰11am-5pm Mon & Fri, to 9pm Thu, 10am-5pm Sat & Sun; 🅂N/Q/R/W, J/M/Z, 6 to Canal St)

Mahayana Temple

TEMPLE

5 Map p48, E7

The Mahayana Buddhist Temple holds one golden, 16ft-high Buddha statue, which sits on a lotus and is edged with offerings of fresh oranges, apples and flowers. This is the largest Buddhist temple in Chinatown, and the facade, right near the frenzied vehicle entrance to the Manhattan Bridge, features two giant golden lions for protection. The interior is simple, with a wooden floor, red chairs and red paper lanterns. (133 Canal St at Manhattan Bridge Plaza; ⏰8am-6pm; 🅂B/D to Grand St, J/M/Z, 6 to Canal St)

Merchant's House Museum

St Patrick's Old Cathedral

CHURCH

6 Map p48, D3

St Patrick's Cathedral is now famously located on Fifth Ave in Midtown, but its first congregation was housed here, on the northern edge of Little Italy, in this 1809–15 Gothic Revival church designed by Joseph-François Mangin. In its heyday, the church was the seat of religious life for the archdiocese of New York, and an important community center for new, mainly Irish, immigrants. Its ancient cemetery out the back is a beautiful respite in the midst of city chaos. (www.oldsaintpatricks. com; 263 Mulberry St; ⏰rectory 8am-5pm Mon-Fri; 🅂R/W to Prince St)

LEE SNIDER/CORBIS ©

New York City Fire Museum

MUSEUM

7 Map p48, A4

Situated in an old firehouse dating from 1904, this museum houses a collection of horse-drawn firefighting carriages and modern-day red firetrucks. Exhibits show the development of the NYC firefighting system, which began with the 'bucket brigades.' The New York Fire Department (FDNY) lost half of its members in the collapse of the World Trade Center, and memorials and exhibits have become a permanent part of the collection. (☎212-219-1222; www.nycfiremuseum.org; 278 Spring St btwn Varick & Hudson Sts; suggested donation adult/child $5/1; 🕒10am-5pm Tue-Sat, to 4pm Sun; 👪; [S]C/E to Spring St)

Italian American Museum

MUSEUM

8 Map p48, D6

This small museum sits where one of the most important buildings in Little Italy once stood: the Banca Stabile. It was once the unofficial headquarters of the community, helping immigrants with their monetary needs and providing a lifeline back to the homeland. Today, the former bank makes up much of the main exhibition space, which tells the New York Italian community's unique story of struggle. (www.italianamericanmuseum.org; 155 Mulberry St; admission free; 🕒11am-6pm Wed, Thu, Sat & Sun, to 8pm Fri; [S]J/Z, N/Q, 4/6 to Canal St, B/D to Grand St)

Columbus Park

PARK

9 Map p48, D8

This is where outdoor mah-jongg and domino games take place at bridge tables while tai chi practitioners move through lyrical, slow-motion poses under shady trees. Judo-sparring folks and relaxing families are also common sights in this active communal space originally created in the 1890s and popular with local residents. (Mulberry & Bayard Sts; [S]J/M/Z, 6 to Canal St)

Museum of Comic & Cartoon Art

MUSEUM

10 Map p48, C3

Cartoon aficionados can't get enough of this museum and its wealth of graphic novels, comic lore and long-lost posters. Special exhibits include both well-known cartoonists and up-and-coming artists, with frequent opening parties and various festivals. Check the website for online exhibits and upcoming lecture series. (☎212-254-3511; www.moccany.org; 594 Broadway; admission $5; 🕒noon-5pm Fri-Mon, by appointment Tue-Thu; 👪; [S]R/W to Prince St)

New York Earth Room

GALLERY

11 Map p48, B3

Since 1980 the oddity of the New York Earth Room, the work of artist Walter De Maria, has been wooing the curious with something not easily found in the city: dirt (250 cu yd, or 280,000lb, of it, to be exact). Walking into the small space is a heady experience, as the scent will make you feel like you've entered a wet forest; the sight of such beautiful, pure earth in the midst of this crazy city is surprisingly moving. (www.earthroom.org; 141 Wooster St; admission free; 🕐noon-6pm Wed-Sun, closed 3-3:30pm; [S]N/R/W to Prince St)

Eating

Dutch

AMERICAN **$$**

12 🍴 Map p48, A3

The foodie folks from Locanda Verde have done it again at the Dutch, which has simple pleasures on a cobalt-blue chalkboard and a shortlist of supper regulars inspired by the new American table. Oysters on ice and freshly baked homemade pies are the notable bookends of the dining experience – in the middle is unfussy cuisine, fresh from the farm and served in casseroles with the perfect amount of ceremony. (☎212-677-6200; www.thedutchnyc.com; 131 Sullivan St btwn Prince & Houston Sts; mains $16-48; 🕐11:30am-3pm Mon-Fri, 5:30pm-midnight Mon-Thu & Sun, 5:30pm-1am Fri & Sat, 10am-3pm Sat & Sun; [S]A/C/E to Spring St, N/R to Prince St, 1/2 to Houston St)

Balthazar

FRENCH **$$$**

13 🍴 Map p48, C4

Retaining its long-held status as a superstar among the city's glut of French bistros, this bustling spot still pulls in the discriminating mobs. That's thanks to three winning details: the location, which makes it a convenient shopping-spree rest area; the uplifting ambiance, shaped by mounted mirrors, booth seating, high ceilings and wide windows; and, of course, the something-for-everyone menu featuring everything from an outstanding raw bar to the immensely popular *steak*

Understand

Chinatown's Residents

The history of Chinese immigrants in New York City is long and tumultuous. The first Chinese people to arrive in America came to work on the Central Pacific Railroad under difficult conditions. Others were lured to the west coast in search of gold. When prospects dried up, many moved east to NYC to work in factory assembly lines and in the laundry houses of New Jersey.

A rising racist sentiment gave way to the Chinese Exclusion Act (1882–1943), which made naturalization an impossibility and largely squashed the opportunity for mainland Chinese to find work in the US. When the ban was lifted, the Chinese were given a limited immigration quota that eventually expanded and grew. Today it's estimated that over 150,000 citizens fill the bursting, tenement-like structures orbiting Mott St.

Café Gitane

frites. (☎212-965-1414; www.balthazarny.
com; 80 Spring St btwn Broadway & Crosby
St; mains $11-34; ☺breakfast, lunch & dinner
daily, brunch Sat & Sun; **S**6 to Spring St)

Joe's Shanghai   CHINESE $

14 Map p48, E8

Gather a gaggle of friends and descend upon Joe's en masse to spin the
plastic lazy Susans and savor some of
the best dumplings in town. A Flushing transplant, this Chinatown staple
also tempts the budget-friendly palate
with crispy beef, sticky pork buns and
finger-licking shrimp platters. (☎212-
233-8888; www.joeshanghairestaurants.com;
9 Pell St btwn Bowery & Doyers St; mains
$5-16; ☺11am-11pm Mon-Sun; **S**J/Z, N/Q,
4/6 to Canal St, B/D to Grand St)

Café Gitane   MOROCCAN $

15 Map p48, D3

Clear the Gauloise smoke from your
eyes and blink twice if you think
you're in Paris – Gitane has that
louche kind of vibe. Label-conscious
shoppers love this authentic bistro,
which serves dark, aromatic coffee.
Its menu includes dishes such as yel-
lowfin tuna seviche, spicy meatballs
in tomato turmeric sauce with a
boiled egg, Greek salad on focac-
cia and heart-of-palm salad. There's
also a winelist filled with plenty of
lusty wines. (☎212-334-9552; www.
cafegitanenyc.com; 242 Mott St; mains $12-18;
☺9am-midnight Sun-Thu, to 12:30am Fri &
Sat; **S**N/R/W to Prince St)

Mulberry Project

MODERN AMERICAN **$$**

16 🍴 Map p48, D6

An unmarked set of stairs – like those of a secret Prohibition-Era speakeasy – leads down to the doorway of the Mulberry Project, a veritable cocktail laboratory and the playground of the international owners and their coterie of server-friends. Lip-smacking beverages – the product of wisdom and whimsy in equal measure – are best enjoyed with the tasty assortment of small plates. Come in summer when the courtyard out back fills with wafting DJed beats, curious graffiti art and a casual scatter of tables. (☎646-448-4536; www.mulberryproject.com; 149 Mulberry St btwn Hester & Grand Sts; mains $14-25; 🕒6pm-2am Mon-Wed, to 4am Thu-Sat; [S] J/Z, N/Q, 4/6 to Canal St, B/D to Grand St)

Balaboosta

MODERN AMERICAN **$$$**

17 🍴 Map p48, D4

As the Yiddish name suggests, 'The Perfect Housewife' truly does feel like a cram-packed evening at your bubbie's...if your bubbie were an amazing cook with an uncanny flair for whipping up delightfully inventive appetizers (crispy cauliflower!) and scrumptious mains (flavor-intensive lamb chops!). Seating is tight, but neighbors become fast friends when united by the collective chorus of 'yums.' (☎212-966-7366; www.balaboostanyc.com; 214 Mulberry St btwn Spring & Prince Sts; mains $20-29, small plates $5-10; 🕒5:30-11pm Mon-Thu, noon-3pm Tue-Fri, 5:30-10pm Fri & Sat, 11am-4pm Sat & Sun, 5:30-10pm Sun; [S] J to Bowery, N/R to Prince St, 4/6 to Spring St)

Nice Green Bo

CHINESE **$**

18 🍴 Map p48, E8

Not a shred of effort – not even a new sign (you'll see!) – has been made to spruce up Nice Green Bo, and that's the way we like it. It's all about the food here: gorgeous soup dumplings served in steaming drums, heaping portions of noodles and savory pancakes. (New Green Bow; ☎212-625-2359; 66 Bayard St btwn Elizabeth & Mott Sts; mains $4-10; 🕒11am-11pm; [S] J/Z, N/Q, 4/6 to Canal St, B/D to Grand St)

Rubirosa

PIZZERIA **$$**

19 🍴 Map p48, D4

Rubirosa's infallible family recipe for the perfect, whisper-thin pie crust lures a steady stream of patrons from every corner of the city. Shovel slices from the bar stools or grab a table

Local Life

Family-Style Dining

Chinatown has the best dining deals around and locals love to head downtown to satisfy their hankering for hole-in-the-wall fare. Experience the area's bustling dining dens with a handful friends by eating 'family style' (order a ton of dishes and sample spoonfuls of each). You'll be sure the waiter left a zero off the bill.

amid cozy surrounds and make room for savory appetizers and antipasti. (212-965-0500; www.rubirosanyc.com; 235 Mulberry St btwn Spring & Prince Sts; mains $12-25; 11:30am-11pm Mon-Wed & Sun, to midnight Thu-Sat; S N/R to Prince St, B/D/F, M to Broadway-Lafayette St, 4/6 to Spring St)

Original Chinatown Ice Cream Factory
ICE CREAM $

20 Map p48, E8

Totally overshadowing the nearby Häagen-Dazs is this busy ice-cream shop, where you can savor scoops of green tea, ginger, passion fruit and lychee sorbet among dozens of flavors. The Factory also sells ridiculously cute, trademark yellow T-shirts with an ice-cream-slurping happy dragon on them. (212-608-4170; www.chinatown icecreamfactory.com; 65 Bayard St; scoop $4; 11am-10pm; S J/M, N/Q/R/W, 6 to Canal St)

Dean & DeLuca
DELI $$

21 Map p48, C4

New York City loves its luxury grocers and Dean & DeLuca is one of the biggest names around town. This reputation is well earned, as it boasts a seemingly infinite assortment of edibles from around the globe. Curious palates should make a beeline for the bakery. (212-226-6800; www. deananddeluca.com; 560 Broadway at Prince St; 7am-8pm Mon-Fri, 8am-8pm Sat-Sun; S R/W to Prince St)

Drinking

Pravda
COCKTAIL BAR

22 Map p48, C3

This subterranean bar and brasserie lays on the Soviet-era nostalgia with heavy brushstrokes, from the Cyrillic lettering on the walls to the extensive vodka menu, which includes caviar martini (vodka with dill, cucumber and a spoonful of you-know-what). Red leather banquettes and inviting armchairs provide a fine spot to enjoy blinis with a side of eavesdropping on neighboring apparatchiks from the fashion or banking industry. (212-226-4944; 281 Lafayette St btwn Prince & Houston Sts; S B/D/F/V to Broadway-Lafayette St)

Jimmy
BAR

23 Map p48, A6

Lofted atop the James New York hotel in SoHo, Jimmy is a sky-high hangout with sweeping views of the city below. During the summer months, it's teeming with tipsy patrons who spill out onto the open deck; in cooler weather, drinks are slung indoors from the centrally anchored bar guarded by floor-to-ceiling windows. (212-201-9118; www.jimmysoho.com; James Hotel, 15 Thompson St; S A/C/E, 1/2 to Canal St, A/C/E to Spring St)

Randolph
COCKTAIL BAR

24 Map p48, E5

Brewing coffee by day and swirling cocktails after dark (you can't go wrong with a 'Brambie'), Randolph has a low-key Europe-meets-NYC vibe with a shiny tin ceiling, knickknacks stacked on wobbly shelves and an extended happy hour that slashes prices around the clock. (www.randolphnyc.com; 349 Broome St btwn Bowery & Elizabeth St; Ⓢ J to Bowery)

Apotheke Bar
BAR

25 🔒 Map p48, E8

It takes a little effort to track down this former opium-den-turned-apothecary-bar located on Doyers St. Look for a Golden Flower sign – that's the clue you've arrived. The sleek red interior and the marble bar adorned with mortars, pestles and cylinders gives Apotheke Bar a cool vibe, enhanced when the owner passes around his homemade absinthe. (☎212-406-0400; www.apothekenyc.com; 9 Doyers St; ⏱6pm-2am Mon-Sat, 8pm-2am Sun; Ⓢ J/M/Z to Canal St)

MiLady's
BAR

26 🔒 Map p48, A3

The last of the dive bars in SoHo where you can still score a brewski for under $5, MiLady's has all the ambiance of the old neighborhood before high-end shops and sleek eats took over. The salads here are surprisingly fresh and you can't go wrong with the chicken wings and mac 'n' cheese – just avoid everything else. (☎212-226-9340; 160 Prince St btwn W Broadway & Thompson St; Ⓢ A/C/E to Spring St, N/R to Prince St, 1/2 to Houston St)

Shopping

Housing Works Book Store
BOOKS

27 🔒 Map p48, C3

Relaxed, earthy and featuring a great selection of fabulous books you can buy for a good cause (proceeds go to the city's HIV-positive and AIDS homeless communities), this spacious cafe is a great place to while away a few quiet afternoon hours. (☎212-334-3324; www.housingworks.org/usedbookcafe; 126 Crosby St; ⏱10am-9pm Mon-Fri, noon-9pm Sat; Ⓢ B/D/F/V to Broadway-Lafayette St)

Kiosk
HANDICRAFTS

28 🔒 Map p48, B4

'Things from places' – the motto is as simple as that. Kiosk's owners scour the planet for the most interesting and unusual found items, which they bring back to SoHo and proudly vend with museum-worthy acumen. Shopping adventures have brought back designer booty from the likes of Japan, Iceland, Sweden and Hong Kong. (☎212-226-8601; www.kioskkiosk.com; 2nd fl, 95 Spring St btwn Mercer St & Broadway; ⏱noon-7pm Mon-Sat; Ⓢ N/R to Prince St, B/D/F to Broadway-Lafayette St)

McNally Jackson
BOOKS

29 🔒 Map p48, C4

This inviting indie bookshop stocks an excellent selection of magazines and books covering contemporary fiction, food writing, art, history, and architecture and design. The cozy cafe is a fine spot to settle in with some reading material or to catch one of the frequent readings and book signings held here. (212-274-1160; www.mcnallyjackson.com; 52 Prince St btwn Lafayette & Mulberry Sts; 10am-10pm Mon-Sat, to 9pm Sun; S R/W to Prince St)

Jack Spade
CLOTHING, ACCESSORIES

30 Map p48, B5

Men's wear in rustic plaids along with a spectacular array of woven and leather satchels make this a must for the urban gentleman. Perfectly folded sweaters sit alongside a carefully curated selection of found objects, dog-eared paperbacks and vintage knickknacks undoubtedly found at the bottom of a cereal box in the '70s. (56 Greene St btwn Broome & Spring St; S N/R to Prince St, N/R to Canal St, 4/6 to Spring St)

Purl Soho
HANDICRAFTS

31 Map p48, B5

The brainchild of the former Martha Stewart Living editor, Purl is a colorful library of fabric and yarn that feels like an in-person Etsy boutique, with

☑ Top Tip
Shopping Blogs
Serious shopaholics should consult the city's in-the-know retail blogs before hitting the streets of SoHo – there's always some sort of 'sample sale' or marked-down giveaway going on.

inspiration for DIY crafts galore and a scatter of finished products that make unique stocking stuffers. (www.purlsoho.com/purl; 459 Broome St btwn Greene & Mercer Sts; S N/R to Canal St, N/R to Prince St, 4/6 to Spring St)

Pearl River Mart
HOMEWARES

32 Map p48, C5

An Asian emporium that stocks all sorts of knickknacks, Pearl River Mart's swanky storefront showcases bright kimonos, bejeweled slippers, Japanese teapots, paper lanterns, jars of mysterious spices, herbs, teas (and a Zen-like tea room) and more. (212-431-4770; www.pearlriver.com; 477 Broadway; 10am-7pm; S J/M/Z, N/Q/R/W, 6 to Canal St)

Opening Ceremony
FASHION

33 Map p48, C6

Just off the beaten SoHo path, Opening Ceremony is a favorite among fashion insiders for its unique collection of indie labels. Owners Carol Lim and Humberto Leon showcase a changing roster of labels from across the globe – though the look is always avant-garde, the prices are decidedly uptown. (212-219-2688; 35 Howard St btwn Broadway & Lafayette St; 11am-8pm Mon-Sat, noon-7pm Sun; S N/Q/R/W, 6 to Canal St)

Screaming Mimi's
VINTAGE

34 Map p48, C1

A warm and colorful storefront that just begs to be entered. You'll find accessories and jewelry up front, and an excellent selection of clothing – organized, ingeniously, by decade, from the '50s to the '90s. It's all in great condition, from the prim, beaded wool cardigans to the suede minidresses and white leather go-go boots. (☎212-677-6464; 382 Lafayette St; ⏰noon-8pm Mon-Sat, 1-7pm Sun; Ⓢ6 to Bleecker St)

Built by Wendy
CLOTHING

35 🔒 Map p48, D5

Hidden out of reach from the SoHo masses, Built by Wendy is a cozy boutique where sweaters, dresses, and men's and women's denim sport a classic, flattering cut with interesting details. You can also pick up owner-designer Wendy Mullin's clever sewing book *Sew U* or one of her ultrasuede guitar straps. There's a second branch in Williamsburg, Brooklyn. (☎212-925-6538; 7 Centre Market Pl; ⏰noon-7pm Mon-Sat, to 6pm Sun; Ⓢ6 to Spring St)

Scoop
FASHION

36 🔒 Map p48, C5

Scoop is a great one-stop destination for unearthing top contemporary fashion by Theory, Stella McCartney, Marc Jacobs, James Perse and many others. While there's nothing particularly edgy about the selections, there's a lot on offer (over 100 designers covering men's, women's and children's clothing) and you can often score deals at season-end sales. Scoop

MICHAEL COHEN/GETTY IMAGES ©

Scoop

has several stores in the city. (☎212-925-3539; 473 Broadway btwn Broome & Grand Sts; ⏰11am-8pm Mon-Sat, to 7pm Sun; Ⓢ N/Q/R/W to Canal St)

Joe's Jeans
CLOTHING

37 🔒 Map p48, B5

The newest link in the elite Joe's Jeans chain firmly plants the name brand's flag in the heart of shop-happy SoHo. Clean lines and sparsely stalked racks of carefully curated denim give Joe's an effortlessly trendy vibe. (☎917-243-5043; www.joesjeans.com; 77 Mercer St btwn Spring & Broome Sts; ⏰11am-7pm Mon-Sat, noon-6pm Sun; Ⓢ N/R to Prince St; N/R to Canal St; 4/6 to Spring St)

Understand

New York City in Print & on Screen

New York City – more than any other place in the world – is the setting of countless works of literature, television and film. From critical commentary on class and race to the lighter foibles of falling in love, NYC's stories are not just entertainment, they are carefully placed tiles in a diverse mosaic of tales. Here are some of our favorite movies and books that take place in – and are inspired by – this wild and wonderful city.

Books

The Amazing Adventures of Kavalier & Clay (Michael Chabon, 2000) Beloved Pulitzer-winning novel that touches upon Brooklyn, escapism and the nuclear family.

A Tree Grows in Brooklyn (Betty Smith, 1943) An Irish-American family living in the Williamsburg tenements at the start of the 20th century.

Down These Mean Streets (Piri Thomas, 1967) Memoirs of tough times growing up in Spanish Harlem.

Invisible Man (Ralph Ellison, 1952) Poignant prose exploring the situation of African Americans in the early 20th century.

The Age of Innocence (Edith Wharton, 1920) Tales and trials of NYC's social elite in the late 1800s.

Film

Annie Hall (1977) Oscar-winning romantic comedy by the king of New York neuroses, Woody Allen.

Manhattan (1979) Allen's at it again with tales of twisted love set among NYC's concrete landscape.

Taxi Driver (1976) Martin Scorsese's tale of a troubled taxi driver and Vietnam vet.

West Side Story (1961) A modern-day Romeo and Juliet set on the gang-ridden streets of New York.

Prada
FASHION, ACCESSORIES

38 Map p48, C3

Don't come just for the shoes: check out the space. Dutch architect Rem Koolhaas has transformed the old Guggenheim into a fantasy land full of elegant hardwood floors and small dressing spaces. Don't be afraid to try something on – the translucent changing-room doors do fog up when you step inside. (212-334-8888; 575 Broadway; 11am-7pm Mon-Sat, noon-6pm Sun; N/R/W to Prince St)

Resurrection
VINTAGE

39 Map p48, D4

A boudoir to the eye, Resurrection is a sleek and pricey red-walled boutique that gives new life to cutting-edge designs from past decades. Striking, mint-condition pieces cover the eras of mod, glam-rock and new-wave design, and well-known designers like Marc Jacobs have visited the shop for inspiration. Top picks include Gucci handbags, Halston dresses and Courrèges jackets. (212-625-1374; www.resurrectionvintage.com; 217 Mott St; 11am-7pm Mon-Sat, noon-7pm Sun; 6 to Spring St)

Kam Man
HOMEWARES

40 Map p48, D7

Head past hanging ducks to the basement of this classic Canal St food store for cheap Chinese and Japanese

Local Life
Bunya Citispa

After a tiring day of strutting your stuff down the concrete catwalks of downtown in search of the perfect new outfit, rest those spend-y bones at **Bunya Citispa** (Map p48, 3A; 212-388-1288; www.bunyacitispa. com; 474 W Broadway btwn Prince & W Houston Sts; 10am-9pm Mon-Sat, to 7pm Sun; N/R/W to Prince St; C/E to Spring St) day spa, which mixes SoHo's savviness with Chinatown's traditions.

tea sets, plus kitchen products such as chopsticks, stir-frying utensils and rice cookers. (212-571-0330; 200 Canal St btwn Mulberry & Motts Sts; 9am-9pm; J/M/Z, N/Q/R/W, 6 to Canal St)

American Apparel
CLOTHING

41 Map p48, B4

Pick up American classics made with a conscience: no sweatshop labor goes into the making of these clothes. Everything is done with above-board in-house production. Sweats, hoodies, underwear and other apparel available in a range of colors. (212-226-4880; www.americanapparel.net; 121 Spring St at Greene St; 10am-8pm Mon-Thu, to 9pm Fri & Sat, 11am-8pm Sun; R/W to Prince Street)

Explore

East Village & Lower East Side

If you've been dreaming of those quintessential New York City moments – graffiti on crimson brick, skyscrapers rising overhead, punks and grannies walking side by side, and cute cafes with rickety tables spilling out onto the sidewalks – then the East Village and the Lower East Side is your Holy Grail.

The Sights in a Day

Have a wander around the Lower East Side as its youngsters are walk-of-shame-ing home from a raucous night out on town. Stop at the **Lower East Side Tenement Museum** (p67) to learn about the area's immigrant past. Then warp time with a trip into the future at the **New Museum of Contemporary Art** (p66) to check out the latest iterations of mind-bending modern art.

Pause for a bite at one of the quaint cafes in the East Village, such as **Cafe Orlin** (p69), then slurp down a cappuccino at **Abraço** (p70). If you're still feeling peckish, wander down **St Marks Place** (p66) with a dessert from **ChiKaLicious** (p72), stopping for punk rock wares (and wears) at **Trash & Vaudeville** (p78). Burn off the calories with a Frisbee toss in **Tompkins Square Park** (p67) during warmer weather.

Capitalize on the area's cheap-eats vibe for dinner with a slurp-worthy bowl of noodles at **Ippudo NY** (p70) or **Minca** (p73), then enjoy an evening of revelry. Start at old-school **McSorley's Old Ale House** (p73) then spice things up at **Cienfuegos** (p75) or **Eastern Bloc** (p74), depending on what you're into.

♥ Best of New York City

Local Eats

Katz's Delicatessen (p71)

ChiKaLicious (p72)

Cafe Orlin (p69)

Drinking

Terroir (p73)

McSorley's Old Ale House (p73)

Abraço (p70)

LGBT

Eastern Bloc (p74)

Shopping

Trash & Vaudeville (p78)

Museums

Lower East Side Tenement Museum (p67)

Getting There

S Subway Trains don't reach most East Village locations, but it's a quick walk from the 6 at Astor Pl or the L at First Ave. The F line will let you off in the thick of the Lower East Side.

🚌 Bus If you're traveling from the west side, take the M14 as it will take you further into the East Village.

E   F   G   H

: 14th St

E 13th St

0 _____ 500 m
0 _____ 0.25 miles

For reviews see
- ◉ Sights   p66
- ✗ Eating   p69
- 🍷 Drinking   p73
- ⭐ Entertainment   p76
- 🔒 Shopping   p78

E 10th St

ompkins
Sq
Park

Ave B

Ave C

Szold Pl

Ave D

E 9th St

E 8th St

ALPHABET CITY

Franklin D Roosevelt Dr

East
River
Park

East River

E 5th St

✗
24

E 4th St

E 3rd St

9 ◉   **E Houston St**

Sheriff St

Hamilton
Fish Park

Stanton
St

Baruch Dr

✗
19

Attorney St

Stanton St

Pitt St

Columbia St

Ridge St

Williamsburg Bridge

Rivington St

Attorney St

Clinton St

Delancey St

Delancey St

86

Suffolk St

Bernard Downing
Playground

Abraham E
Kazan St

Lewis St

Broome St

Ridge St

Pitt St

Willett St

**LOWER
EAST SIDE**

Jackson St

Grand St

E Broadway

Henry St

Madison St

Corlears
Hook Park

Sights

St Marks Place

STREET

1 🎯 Map p64, C2

One of the most magical things about New York is that every street tells a story, from the action unfurling before your eyes to the dense history hidden behind colorful facades. St Marks Pl is one of the best strips of pavement in the city for story telling, as almost every building on these hallowed blocks is rife with tales from a time when the East Village embodied a far more lawless spirit. When things get too crowded, hop a block over in either direction for some local retail and restaurant finds. (St Marks Pl, Ave A to Third Ave; ⓢ N/R/W to 8th St-NYU, 6 to Astor Pl)

New Museum of Contemporary Art

GALLERY

2 🎯 Map p64, C4

Any modern-day museum worth its salt has to have a structure that makes as much of a statement as the artwork inside. The New Museum of Contemporary Art's Lower East Side avatar accomplishes just that and more with its inspired design by noted Japanese architecture firm SANAA. The Lower East Side has seen its fair share of physical changes over the last decade as the sweeping hand of gentrification has cleaned up slummy nooks and replaced them with glittering residential blocks. The New Museum punctuates the neighborhood with something truly unique, and its cache of artistic work will dazzle and confuse just as

---

Understand

SANAA's Vision

While exhibits rotate through the New Museum of Contemporary Art (p66), regularly changing the character of the space within, the shell – an inspired architectural gesture – remains a constant. It acts as a unique structural element in the diverse cityscape, simultaneously fading into the background to allow the exhibits to shine.

The building's structure is the brainchild of the hot Japanese firm SANAA – a partnership between two great minds, Sejima Kazuyo and Nishizawa Ryue. In 2010, SANAA won the much-coveted Pritzker Prize for its contributions to the world of design (think the Oscars of architecture). Its trademark vanishing facades are known worldwide for abiding by a strict adherence to a form-follows-function design aesthetic, sometimes taking the land plot's footprint into the overall shape of the structure. The box-atop-box scheme provides a striking counterpoint to the clusters of crimson brick and iron fire escapes outside, while alluding to the geometric exhibition chasms within.

RAYMOND PATRICK/CORBIS ©

New Museum of Contemporary Art (designer SANAA)

much as its facade. (☎212-219-1222; www.newmuseum.org; 235 Bowery btwn Prince & Rivington Sts; adult/child $14/free, 7-9pm Thu free; ⏰11am-6pm Wed & Fri-Sun, to 9pm Thu; Ⓢ N/R to Prince St, F to 2nd Ave, J/Z to Bowery, 6 to Spring St)

Lower East Side Tenement Museum MUSEUM

3 Map p64, D5

No other museum humanizes NYC's colorful past quite like the Lower East Side Tenement Museum, which puts the neighborhood's heartbreaking but inspiring heritage on full display in several recreations of turn-of-the-20th-century tenements. These include the late-19th-century home and garment shop of the Levine fam-

ily from Poland, and two immigrant dwellings from the Great Depressions of 1873 and 1929. The museum has a variety of tours and talks beyond the museum's walls as well and it's worth stopping by in the evenings when – at least twice a week – the staff hosts 'Tenement Talks,' a lecture and discussion series on wide-reaching topics about the city and its people. (☎212-431-0233; www.tenement.org; 108 Orchard St btwn Broome & Delancey Sts; admission $22; ⏰10am-6pm; Ⓢ B/D to Grand St, J/M/Z to Essex St, F to Delancey St)

Tompkins Square Park PARK

4 Map p64, D2

The 10.5-acre Tompkins Sq Park honors Daniel Tompkins, who served

Local Life
LES Galleries

Though Chelsea may be the heavy hitter when it comes to the New York gallery scene, the Lower East Side has about a dozen quality showplaces. Check out **Participant Inc** (Map p64, D4; ☎212-254-4334; www.participantinc.org; 253 E Houston St btwn Norfolk & Suffolk Sts; [S]F to Lower East Side-2nd Ave), which showcases emerging talent and hosts varied performances. The **Sperone Westwater** (Map p64, C4; www.speronewestwater.com; 257 Bowery; [S]F to Lower East Side-2nd Ave) gallery represents heavy hitters like William Wegman and Richard Long, and its new home was designed by Norman Foster, who's already made a splash in NYC with his Hearst Building and Avery Fisher Hall designs.

as governor of New York from 1807 to 1817 (and as the nation's vice president after that, under James Monroe). It's like a friendly town square for locals, who gather for chess at concrete tables, picnics on the lawn on warm days and spontaneous guitar or drum jams on various grassy knolls. It's also the site of basketball courts, a fun-to-watch dog run (a fenced-in area where humans can unleash their canines) and frequent summer concerts. Kids will enjoy the always-lively playground. (www.nycgovparks.org; E 7th & 10th Sts btwn Aves A & B; admission free; 🕒6am-midnight; [S]6 to Astor Pl)

Eldridge Street Synagogue — JEWISH

5 👁 Map p64, D5

This landmarked house of worship, built in 1887, was once the center of Jewish life, before falling into squalor in the 1920s. Left to rot, it's only recently been reclaimed, and now shines with original splendor. Its on-site museum gives tours every half hour ($10; 10am to 5pm), with the last one departing at 4pm. (☎212-219-0888; www.eldridgestreet.org; 12 Eldridge St btwn Canal & Division Sts; donations suggested; 🕒10am-5pm Sun-Thu; [S]F to East Broadway)

St Mark's in the Bowery — CHURCH

6 👁 Map p64, C2

Though it's most popular with East Village locals for its cultural offerings – such as poetry readings hosted by the Poetry Project or cutting-edge dance performances from Danspace and the Ontological Hysteric Theater – this is also a historic site. This Episcopal church stands on the site of the farm, or *bouwerie*, owned by Dutch Governor Peter Stuyvesant, whose crypt lies under the grounds. (☎212-674-6377; www.stmarksbowery.org; 131 E 10th St at Second Ave; 🕒10am-6pm Mon-Fri; [S]L to 3rd Ave, 6 to Astor Pl)

Ukrainian Museum — MUSEUM

7 👁 Map p64, C2

Ukrainians have a long history and still a strong presence here, hence the existence of several (though rapidly disappearing) pierogi joints –

including the famous Veselka – and this interesting museum. Its collection of folk art includes richly woven textiles, ceramics, metalwork and traditional Ukrainian Easter eggs, as well as the research tools needed for visitors to trace their own Ukrainian roots. (☏212-228-0110; www.ukrainianmu seum.org; 222 E 6th St btwn Second & Third Aves; adult/senior & student/child under 12yr $8/6/free; ⏱11:30am-5pm Wed-Sun; Ⓢ F/V to Lower East Side-2nd Ave, L to 1st Ave)

Sara D Roosevelt Park PARK

8 ◎ Map p64, C4

Spiffed up just in time for the arrival of its new luxury-condo neighbors, this remade little park is a place that most New Yorkers will remember as more of a junkie's spot for scoring than an actual plot of green space. But it's joined the ranks of other rejuve-nated 'needle parks' – such as Bryant Park and Tompkins Sq Park – and is now a three-block respite from urban chaos. (Houston St at Chrystie St; Ⓢ F to Delancey-Essex Sts)

Le Petit Versailles GARDENS

9 ◎ Map p64, E3

After a stretch of arboreal abstinence in New York City, the community gar-dens of Alphabet City – created from abandoned lots – are breathtaking. Le Petit Versailles is a unique marriage of a verdant oasis and an electrifying art organization, offering a range of quirky performances and screenings to the public. Also worth a look is

the 6th & B Garden, which hosts free music events, workshops and yoga sessions. (www.alliedproductions.org; 346 E Houston St at Ave C)

Eating

Cafe Orlin MIDDLE EASTERN $

10 ✕ Map p64, C2

Toeing the line between Middle East-ern and homegrown American fare, Cafe Orlin is the star of the brunching and lunching scene along St Marks Pl. The perfect omelets, with fresh fixings folded deep within, lure a colorful assortment of characters from angsty hipster types guzzling red wine while toying with their iPads to hungover SNL cast members recovering from last night's show. (☏212-777-1447; www. cafeorlin.com; 41 St Marks Pl btwn First & Second Aves; mains $7-14; ⏱breakfast, lunch & dinner; Ⓢ L to 3rd Ave, N/R to 8th St-NYU, 4/6 to Astor Pl)

Cocoron NOODLES $

11 ✕ Map p64, D5

Oh Cocoron, if soba weren't so messy, we'd fill our pockets with your brilliant recipes. A short menu of delicious hot and cold noodle dishes (go for the cold) reads like a haiku dedicated to savory, vegetable-driven fare. Minimalist surrounds and clean wooden tables help offset the cramped quarters, though the tight seating means that you'll have a front-row seat to watch the pan-wielding

geniuses. (☎212-925-5220; www.cocoron-soba.com; 61 Delancey St btwn Eldridge & Allen Sts; dishes $9-13; ⏰noon-3pm Tue-Sun, 6-11pm Tue-Sat, to 10:30pm Sun; [S]F to Delancey St, B/D to Grand St, J to Bowery)

Freemans

AMERICAN $$$

12 🍴 Map p64, C4

Tucked down a back alley befitting the metropolitan likes of Paris or London, Freemans is staunchly reserved for hipster brunchophiles who let their chunky jewelry clang on the wooden tables as they lean over to sip overflowing martinis. Potted plants and taxidermic antlers lend an endearing hunting-cabin vibe – a charming escape from the bustle (when there isn't a crowd inside). (☎212-420-0012; www.freemansrestaurant.com; end of Freeman Alley; mains $24-30; ⏰5-11:30pm; [S]F to 2nd Ave)

Abraço

CAFE $

13 🍴 Map p64, C2

With hardly room to move – let alone sit – Abraço is an East Village refuge where good coffee and good taste combine to form one of the finest cafes in the entire city. Slurp your perfectly crafted espresso while inhaling a slice of delicious olive cake. If you're stopping by with a friend you'll each need to order a slice – fights are known to break out over the last bite. (www.abraconyc.com; 86 E 7th St btwn First & Second Aves; snacks $2-7; ⏰8am-6pm Tue-Sat, 9am-6pm Sun; [S]F to 2nd Ave, L to 1st Ave, 4/6 to Astor Pl)

Ippudo NY

NOODLES $$

14 🍴 Map p64, B2

In Tokyo, Ippudo is the veritable equivalent of the America's Olive Garden, with hundreds of franchised outposts tucked into every urban fold. In New York City, the good folks from Ippudo have kicked things up a notch – they've taken their mouth-watering ramen recipe (truly, it's delicious) and spiced it up with sleek surrounds (hello, shiny black surfaces and streamers of cherry red) and blasts of rock and roll on the overhead speakers. (☎212-388-0088; www.ippudo.com/ny; 65 Fourth Ave btwn 9th & 10th Sts; ramen $10-13; ⏰11am-3:30pm Mon-Sat, 5-11:30pm Mon-Thu, 5pm-12:30am Fri & Sat, 11am-10:30pm Sun; [S]N/R to 8th St-NYU, 4/5/6 to 14th St-Union Sq, 4/6 to Astor Pl)

Westville East

MODERN AMERICAN $$

15 🍴 Map p64, D1

Market-fresh veggies and mouthwatering mains are the names of the game at Westville, and it doesn't hurt that the cottage-chic surrounds are undeniably charming. The chicken reuben is the ultimate hangover cure-all, though most people opt to take four vegetable side dishes and turn them into a gorgeous meal (the brussels sprouts are heavenly). There are two other locations in the West Village and Chelsea, but this one's our favorite. (☎212-677-2033; www.westvillenyc.com; 173 Ave A; mains $12-20; ⏰11:30am-11pm Mon-Fri, 10am-11pm Sat & Sun; [S]L to 1st Ave, 4/6 to Astor Pl)

DBIMAGES / ALAMY ©

Pastrami sandwich at Katz's Delicatessen

Katz's Delicatessen DELI $

16 Map p64, D4

Though visitors to New York City won't find many remnants of the classic, old-world Jewish Lower East Side dining scene, there are a few stellar holdouts around. One of the most well-known is Katz's Delicatessen, where Meg Ryan faked her famous orgasm in the 1989 Hollywood flick *When Harry Met Sally*. If you love classic deli grub, such as pastrami and salami on rye, it just might have the same effect on you. (212-254-2246; www.katzsdelicatessen.com; 205 E Houston St at Ludlow St; pastrami on rye $15, knockwurst $6; breakfast, lunch & dinner; S F/V to Lower East Side-2nd Ave)

Luzzo's PIZZERIA $$

17 Map p64, C1

Fan-favorite Luzzo's occupies a thin sliver of real estate in the East Village, which gets stuffed to the gills each evening as discerning diners feast on thin-crust pies kissed with ripe tomatoes and cooked in an illusive coal-fired oven. (212-473-7447; 211-213 First Ave btwn 12th & 13th Sts; pizzas $14-17; noon-11pm Tue-Sun, 5-11pm Mon; S L to 1st Ave)

Vanessa's Dumpling House CHINESE $

18 Map p64, D5

If it weren't for Vanessa, the entire campus of NYU would starve. Tasty

Top Tip

Snagging Tables

A lot of the restaurants in this neck of the woods don't take reservations, so stop by the restaurant of your choosing in the early afternoon (2pm should do the trick) and place your name on the roster for the evening meal – chances are high that they'll take your name and you'll get seated right away when you return for dinner later on.

dumplings – served steamed, fried or in soup (our favorite) – are whipped together in iron skillets at lightning speed and tossed into hungry mouths at unbeatable prices. There's a second location at 14th St and Third Ave. (☏212-625-8008; 118 Eldridge St btwn Grand & Broome Sts; dumplings $1-5; ☷7:30am-10:30pm; Ⓢ B/D to Grand St, J to Bowery, F to Delancey St)

Clinton Street Baking Company
AMERICAN $

 19 Map p64, E3

Mom-and-pop shop extraordinaire, Clinton Street Baking Company gets the blue ribbon in so many categories – best pancakes (blueberry! Swoon!), best muffins, best po'boys (Southern-style sandwiches), best biscuits etc – that you're pretty much guaranteed a stellar meal no matter which time of day (or night) you stop by. Half-priced vino sweetens the already sweet pot on Mondays and Tuesdays, officially keeping the doors spinning every

night of the week. (☏646-602-6263; www.clintonstreetbaking.com; 4 Clinton St btwn Stanton & Houston Sts; mains from $8.50-17; ☷8am-4pm Mon-Fri, 6-11pm Mon-Sat, 9am-4pm Sat, 9am-6pm Sun; Ⓢ J/M/Z to Essex St, F to Delancey St, F to 2nd Ave)

Momofuku Noodle Bar
NOODLES $$$

 20 Map p64, C1

With just 30 stools and a no-reservations policy, you will always have to wait to cram into this tiny phenomenon. It's part of a crazily popular restaurant group that includes Momofuku Ko for pricey tasting menus and a prohibitive, we-dare-you-to-try reservations scheme; Momofuku Ssäm Bar for large and small meat-heavy dishes; and Momofuku Milk Bar with its to-die-for desserts and snacks. (☏212-777-7773; www.momofuku.com/noodle-bar/; 171 First Ave btwn 10th & 11th Sts; ☷lunch & dinner; Ⓢ L to 1st Ave, 6 to Astor Pl)

ChiKaLicious
DESSERT $

 21 Map p64, C2

An ice cream served atop an éclair instead of a cone? We're in! ChiKaLicious is an East Village favorite taking traditional sweet-tooth standards and transforming them into inspired calorie concoctions. Transcontinental desserts – like green-tea ice cream – are a big hit too. Due to popular demand, ChiKaLicious recently opened a 'dessert club' (more seating space) across the street. (☏212-995-9511; www.chikalicious.com; 203 E 10th St btwn First &

Second Aves; desserts $3-12; ⊙3pm-10:30pm Thu-Sun; **S**L to 1st Ave, 4/6 to Astor Pl)

Veselka

UKRAINIAN $

22 Map p64, C2

A bustling tribute to the area's Ukrainian past, Veselka dishes out borscht and stuffed cabbage amid the usual suspects of greasy comfort food. The cluttered spread of tables is available to loungers and carbo-loaders all night long, though it's a favorite any time of day. (☎212-228-9682; www.veselka. com; 144 Second Ave at 9th St; mains $6-14; ⊙24hr; **S**L to 3rd Ave, 6 to Astor Pl)

Caracas Arepa Bar

SOUTH AMERICAN $

23 Map p64, D2

Cram into this tiny joint and order a crispy, hot arepa (corn tortilla stuffed with veggies and meat) such as the Pepi Queen (chicken and avocado) or La Pelua (beef and cheddar). You can choose from 17 types of arepa (plus empanadas and daily specials like oxtail soup), served in baskets with a side of nata (sour cream) and fried plantains. (☎212-529-2314; www. caracasarepabar.com; 93 1/2 E 7th St btwn First Ave & Ave A; dishes $6-16; ⊙noon-11pm; ✈; **S**6 to Astor Pl)

Minca

NOODLES $

24 Map p64, E3

The epitome of an East Village hole-in-the-wall, Minca focuses all of its attention on the food: cauldron-esque bowls of steaming ramen served with a recommended side order of fried gyoza. When you're nearing the end, the waitress will bring you a mug of complimentary tea. Yum. (☎212-505-8001; www.newyorkramen.com; 536 E 5th St btwn Aves A & B; ramen $10-13; ⊙noon-11:30pm Mon-Sun; **S**F to 2nd Ave, J/M/Z to Essex St, F to Delancey St)

Drinking

Terroir

WINE BAR

25 Map p64, D1

Removing the pretension from the wine-bar experience, Terroir spins vino by the tome-ful on smooth communal tables made from large scraps of wood. A delightful assortment of bar bites (including superlative paninis) makes a strong case for tee-totalers with boozy friends. There are two other locations – one in Tribeca and a newer one shaking things up in Murray Hill. (☎646-602-1300; www. wineisterroir.com; 413 E 12th St btwn First Ave & Ave A; **S**L to 1st Ave, L to 3rd Ave, 4/6 to Astor Pl)

McSorley's Old Ale House

BAR

26 Map p64, B2

Around since 1854, McSorley's feels far removed from the East Village veneer of cool: you're more likely to drink with firemen, Wall St refugees and a few tourists. But (didn't you know?) that's become cool again. It's hard to beat the cobwebs, sawdust floors

ALLAN MONTAINE / ALAMY ©

McSorley's Old Ale House (p73)

and flip waiters who slap down two mugs of the house's ale for every one ordered. (☎212-474-9148; 15 E 7th St btwn Second & Third Aves; **S**6 to Astor Pl)

Death + Co
LOUNGE

27 Map p64, D2

'Death & Co' is scrawled in ornate cursive on the ground at Death's door, so to speak – the only hint that you're in the right place to try some of the most perfectly concocted cocktails in town. Relax amid dim lighting and thick wooden slatting, and let the bartenders – with their PhDs in mixology – work their magic as they shake, rattle and roll your blended poison of choice. (☎212-388-0882; www. deathandcompany.com; 433 E 6th St btwn First Ave & Ave A; ☺6pm-1am Mon-Thu & Sun, to 2am Fri & Sat; **S**F to 2nd Ave, L to 1st Ave, 4/6 Astor Pl)

Eastern Bloc
GAY

28 Map p64, D2

Though the theme may be 'Iron Curtain,' the drapery is most definitely velvet and taffeta at this East Village gay bar. Hang your jacket at the 'Goat Czech' and spring forth into the cramped and crowded sea of boys – some flirting with the topless barkeeps, others pretending not to stare at the retro '70s porno playing on the TVs. (☎222-777-2555; www.easternblocnyc. com; 505 E 6th St btwn Aves A & B; ☺7pm-4am; **S**F/V to Lower East Side-2nd Ave)

Milk & Honey   BAR

29 🚇 Map p64, D5

You can't beat the '40s-era low-key ambience of the most infamous bar on the Lower East Side – the cocktails are superb (and priced accordingly at $15 each) and the staff are even friendly – it's just that you have to know people to get in. No number listed, no sign outside but a graffitied door. (www.mlkhny.com; 134 Eldridge St btwn Delancey & Broome Sts; **S** B/D to Grand St)

Heathers   BAR

30 🚇 Map p64, D1

Heathers is a tiny and stylish unsigned drinking den with frosted windows, a painted tin ceiling and white-washed brick walls. A mish-mash of regulars linger over eye-catching artworks (courtesy of the artist owner and her friends), two-for-one drink specials and gluten-free beer options. The DJ tucked in the corner spins eclectic sounds: sometimes indie rock, other times bubble-gum pop. (🗹212-254-0979; 506 E 13th St btwn Aves A & B; **S** L to 1st Ave)

Ten Degrees Bar   WINE BAR

31 🚇 Map p64, D2

The decor doesn't suggest anything particularly special about this St Marks stalwart, but one glance at the drinks list and you'll quickly appreciate one of the best happy-hour deals around town: half-priced bottles of wine. And it's no gimmick; a fantastic selection from across the globe (grab the Malbec) comes heavily discounted when you show up early – go for the couches up front or grab a tiny table in the back nook. (🗹212-358-8600; www.10degreesbar.com; 121 St Marks Pl btwn First Ave & Ave A; ⏱noon-4am Mon-Sun; **S** F to 2nd Ave, L to 1st Ave, L to 3rd Ave)

Immigrant   WINE BAR

32 🚇 Map p64, C2

Wholly unpretentious, this East Village wine bar – housed in a former tenement (hence the name) – could easily become your *Cheers* if you decide to stick around town. The owners are on the floor doing the dirty work, mingling with faithful regulars while dishing out tangy olives and topping up glasses with imported snifters. (🗹212-677-2545; www.theimmigrantnyc.com; 341 E 9th St btwn First & Second Aves; ⏱5pm-1am Mon-Wed & Sun, to 2am Thu, to 3am Fri & Sat; **S** L to 1st Ave, L to 3rd Ave, 4/6 to Astor Pl)

Cienfuegos   BAR

33 🚇 Map p64, D2

If Fidel Castro had a stretched Cadillac, it's interior would look something like the inside of New York's foremost rum-punch joint. A sampler of tasty Cuban dishes makes the perfect midnight snack. If you like this place, then make a pit stop at the connected Amor y Amargo – Cienfuegos' bitters-centric brother. (🗹212-614-6818; www.cienfuegosny.com; 95 Ave A btwn 6th & 7th Sts ; **S** F to 2nd Ave, L to 1st Ave, 4/6 to Astor Pl)

Whiskey Ward BAR

34 Map p64, D4

Once upon a time, city officials divided Manhattan into wards, and the Lower East Side was the 'Whiskey Ward,' courtesy of its many drinking establishments. The modern owners of the Whiskey Ward apparently appreciate history as much as they adore single malts, rye whiskey, blended Scotch, Irish whiskey and bourbon. Patrons enjoy the single-mindedness of this brick-walled bar. (☑212-477-2998; www.thewhiskeyward.com; 121 Essex St btwn Delancey & Rivington Sts; ⊙5pm-4am; Ⓢ F, J/M/Z to Delancey-Essex Sts)

Jimmy's No 43 BAR

35 Map p64, C2

It doesn't look like much from outside – the generic awning and plastic weather shield do it no favors – but when you enter the basement beer hall, the story quickly changes. Barrels and stag antlers line the walls up to the ceiling as locals chug their drinks. Select from over 50 imported favorites to go with a round of delectable bar nibbles (betcha didn't think a hot plate could cook pork belly so darn well!). (☑212-982-3006; www.jimmysno43.com; 43 E 7th St btwn Third & Second Aves; ⊙noon-2am Mon-Thu & Sun, to 4am Fri & Sat; Ⓢ N/R to 8th St-NYU, F to 2nd Ave, 4/6 to Astor Pl)

Nurse Bettie COCKTAIL BAR

36 Map p64, E4

Something a bit new is going on with this pint-sized charmer: plenty of

roaming space between slick '00s-modern lounges and '50s-style ice-cream-shop stools and painted pin-ups on the brick walls. Cocktails get freaky: fruity vodka and brandies, plus bubble-gum martinis. You can bring food in, and many won-over locals do. (☑917-434-9072; www.nursebettieles.com; 106 Norfolk St btwn Delancey & Rivington Sts; ⊙6pm-2am Sun-Tue, to 4am Wed-Sat; Ⓢ F, J/M/Z to Delancey-Essex Sts)

Entertainment

Performance Space 122 THEATER

37 Map p64, D2

This former schoolhouse has been committed to fostering new artists and their far-out ideas since its inception in 1979. Its two stages have hosted such now-known performers as Meredith Monk, Eric Bogosian and the late Spalding Gray, and it's also home to dance shows, film screenings and various festivals for up-and-coming talents. (PS 122; ☑212-477-5288; www.ps122.org; 150 First Ave at 9th St; Ⓢ R/W to 8th St-NYU, 6 to Astor Pl)

Sweet COMEDY

38 Map p64, D3

There are tons of small comedy houses scattered around the city, but we're pretty sure you haven't heard of this one – a local gig hosted every Tuesday by Seth Herzog and his gang of friends (including his mother who loves to get up in front of the small crowd and discuss her weekly list of grievances). Seth brings in his industry friends – everyone from unknown up-and-comers to SNL mainstays – to test out their new material. Laughs aplenty. (Comedy at Ella's; ☎ 212-777-2230; sethzog@aol.com; 9 Ave A near Houston St; admission $5; ⏱ show starts 9pm Tue; **S** F to 2nd Ave, F to Delancey St, J/M/Z to Essex St)

Arlene's Grocery   LIVE MUSIC

39 ⭐ Map p64, D4

Formerly a bodega and butcher shop, Arlene's Grocery now serves up heaping portions of live talent with frequent shows. Drinks are cheap and the crowd is good-looking – make an impression on Monday night with Rock 'n' Roll Karaoke. It's free and you're backed by a live band. Probably your best shot at getting a groupie. (☎ 212-358-1633; www.arlenesgrocery.net; 95 Stanton St; cover charge for bands Tue-Sun $8-10; ⏱ 6pm-4am; **S** F, V to Lower East Side-Second Ave)

Anthology Film Archives   CINEMA

40 ⭐ Map p64, C3

This theater, opened in 1970 by film buff Jonas Mekas and a supportive crew, is dedicated to the idea of film as an art form. It screens indie works by new filmmakers and also revives classics and obscure oldies, which are usually shown in programs organized around a specific theme or director, from Luis Buñuel to Ken Brown's psychedelia. (☎ 212-505-5181; www.anthologyfilmarchives.org; 32 Second Ave at 2nd St; **S** F/V to Lower East Side-2nd Ave)

New York Theater Workshop   THEATER

41 ⭐ Map p64, C3

This innovative production house is a treasure to those seeking cutting-edge, contemporary plays with purpose. It was the originator of two big Broadway hits, Rent and Urinetown, and offers a constant supply of high-quality drama. (☎ 212-460-5475; www.nytw.org; 79 E 4th St btwn Second & Third Aves; **S** F/V to Lower East Side-2nd Ave)

Sing Sing Karaoke   KARAOKE

42 ⭐ Map p64, B2

A chuckle-worthy reference to the nearby state prison, Sing Sing Karaoke is exactly what it sounds like – swing by to belt your heart out. Go for a classic ballad or try for a top-40 hit – no matter what you choose,

Local Life

St Marks Addresses

St Marks Place (p66) is jam-packed with historical tidbits that would delight any trivia buff. A cast of colorful characters has left its mark at 4 St Marks Pl. Alexander Hamilton's son built the structure, James Fenimore Cooper lived here in the 1830s and Yoko Ono's Fluxus artists descended upon the building in the 1960s. And don't miss the buildings at 96 and 98 St Marks Pl, which are immortalized on the cover of Led Zepplein's *Physical Graffiti* album.

you're likely to be joined by a chorus of tipsy back-up singers. (☎212-387-7800; www.karaokesingsing.com; 9 St Marks Pl; Ⓢ N/R to 8th St-NYU, L to 3rd Ave, 4/6 to Astor Pl)

La MaMa ETC
THEATER

 43 ⭐ Map p64, C3

A long-standing home for onstage experimentation (the ETC stands for Experimental Theater Club), La MaMa is now a three-theater complex with a cafe, an art gallery and a separate studio building that features cutting-edge dramas, sketch comedy and readings of all kinds. (☎212-475-7710; www.lamama.org; 74A E 4th St; Annex Theater $20, 1st fl Theater $15, the Club $15; ⏱hours vary; Ⓢ F/V to Lower East Side-2nd Ave)

Bowery Poetry Club
LITERARY

44 ⭐ Map p64, B3

Just across from the old CBGB site on the East Village/NoHo border, this funky cafe and performance space has eccentric readings of all genres, from plays to fiction, plus frequent themed poetry slams and literary-focused parties that celebrate new books and their authors. (☎212-614-0505; www.bowerypoetry.com; 308 Bowery btwn Bleecker & Houston Sts; Ⓢ 6 to Bleecker St)

Amore Opera
OPERA

45 ⭐ Map p64, D3

This new company, formed by several members of the recently defunct Amato Opera, presents affordable ($35) works. Its inaugural season

offerings included La Bohème, The Merry Widow, The Mikado and Hansel and Gretel, performed at its East Village theater. (www.amoreopera.com; Connelly Theater, 220 E 4th St btwn Aves A & B; Ⓢ F/V to Lower East Side-2nd Ave)

Pianos
LIVE MUSIC

46 ⭐ Map p64, D4

Nobody's bothered to change the sign at the door, a leftover from the location's previous incarnation as a piano shop. Now it's a musical mix of genres and styles, leaning more toward pop, punk and new wave, but throwing in some hip-hop and indie bands for good measure. Sometimes you get a double feature – one act upstairs and another below. (☎212-505-3733; www.pianosnyc.com; 158 Ludlow St at Stanton St; cover charge $8-17; ⏱noon-4am; Ⓢ F/V to Lower East Side-2nd Ave)

Shopping

Trash & Vaudeville
CLOTHING

 47 🔒 Map p64, B2

The capital of punk-rocker-dom, Trash & Vaudeville is the veritable costume closet for singing celebs like Debbie Harry, who found their groove in the East Village when it played host to a much grittier scene. On any day of the week, you'll find everyone from drag queens to themed partygoers scouting out the most ridiculous shoes, shirts and hair dye. (4 St Marks Pl; Ⓢ 6 to Astor Pl)

WALIK GOSHORN/CORBIS ©

Patricia Field

Amé Amé

FASHION

48 🛍 Map p64, C2

Rain gear and candy? Teresa Soroka, the kindly owner of this shop, will explain what Amé Amé means if you're perplexed by this unusual juxtaposition. She'll also tell you that there's no such thing as bad weather – only bad fashion. This teeny hipster haven will set you straight when it comes to drizzle-friendly fashion. Don't forget to spot by on a rainy day, when the imported candy is discounted. Score! (☎646-867-2342; www.amerain.com; 318 E 9th St btwn First & Second Aves; 🕐1-7pm Tue-Sun; [S]L to 3rd Ave, L to 1st Ave, 4/6 to Astor Pl)

Patricia Field

FASHION

49 🛍 Map p64, B4

The move from its SoHo digs to the new Bowery location brings much-needed space (4000 sq ft to be exact) to this fun, whimsical design shop. The fashion-forward stylist for *Sex and the City*, Patricia Field isn't afraid of flash, with feather boas, pink jackets, disco dresses, graphic and color-block T-shirts, and leopard-print heels, plus colored frizzy wigs, silver spandex and some wacky gift ideas for good measure. (☎212-966-4066; 302 Bowery at 1st St; 🕐11am-8pm Mon-Thu, to 9pm Fri & Sat, to 7pm Sun; [S]F/V to Lower East Side-2nd Ave)

Kiehl's

BEAUTY

50 🔒 Map p64, B1

Making and selling skincare products since it opened in NYC as an apothecary in 1851, this Kiehl's flagship store has doubled its shop size and expanded into an international chain. The personal touch remains – as do the coveted, generous sample sizes. (☏212-677-3171, 800-543-4571; 109 Third Ave btwn 13th & 14th Sts; ⏰10am-8pm Mon-Sat, 11am-6pm Sun; Ⓢ L to 3rd Ave)

Edith Machinist

VINTAGE

51 🔒 Map p64, D4

To properly strut about the Lower East Side, you've got to dress the part. Edith Machinist can help you get that rumpled but stylish look in a hurry – a bit of vintage glam via knee-high soft suede boots, 1930s silk dresses and ballet-style flats, with military jackets and weather-beaten leather satchels for the gents. (☏212-979-9992; 104 Rivington St at Essex St; ⏰1-8pm; Ⓢ F, J/M/Z to Delancey-Essex Sts)

Essex Street Market

MARKET

52 🔒 Map p64, D4

This 60-year-old historic shopping destination is the local place for produce, seafood, butcher-cut meats, cheeses, Latino grocery items and even a barber. It's a fun place to explore, with snack stands and an attached restaurant when you really want to get down to business. (☏212-312-3603; www.essexstreetmarket.com; 120 Essex St btwn Delancey & Rivington Sts;

⏰8am-7pm Mon-Sat; Ⓢ F/V to Delancey St, J/M/Z to Delancey-Essex Sts)

TG170

CLOTHING

53 🔒 Map p64, D5

One of the first boutiques to blaze the trail into the Lower East Side way back in 1992, TG170 is still a major destination for downtown style-seekers. Inside the graffiti-covered storefront, you'll find both young and established designers pushing a fashion-forward look. Vivienne Westwood dresses, Lauren Moffatt jackets and vinyl Freitag bags look all the better beneath the wild ice-planet-style chandeliers. (☏212-995-8660; 77 Ludlow St; ⏰noon-8pm; Ⓢ F, J/M/Z to Delancey-Essex Sts)

Tokio 7

CONSIGNMENT STORE

54 🔒 Map p64, C2

This revered, hip consignment shop, down a few steps on a shady stretch of E 7th St, has good-condition designer labels for men and women at some fairly hefty prices. Best of all is the selection of men's suits – there's nearly always something tip-top in the $100 to $150 range that's worth trying on. (☏212-353-8443; 83 E 7th St near First Ave; ⏰noon-8:30pm Mon-Sat, to 8pm Sun; Ⓢ 6 to Astor Pl)

Sustainable NYC

CLOTHING

55 🔒 Map p64, D2

Across from Tompkins Sq Park, this eco-friendly shop offers all sorts of home and office gear for living green.

Organic T-shirts, shoes made out of recycled auto tires, compost bins, biodegradable beauty products, recycled stationery and books on going green are all on hand. The store itself sets a fine example: the interior is built from 300-year-old reclaimed lumber and fixtures are recycled (and for sale). (212-254-5400; 139 Ave A btwn St Marks Pl & 9th St; 8am-9pm Mon-Fri, 9am-9pm Sat & Sun; 6 to Astor Pl)

C'H'C'M
CLOTHING

56 Map p64, B3

The acronym-y shortening of Clinton Hill Classic Menswear shows not a pinch of pretension when displaying carefully selected threads for the fashion-forward man. The store's decor is unadulterated by design decoys, letting shoppers focus solely on the beautifully crafted wares. (212-673-8601; www.chcmshop.com; 2 Bond St btwn Broadway & Lafayette St; B/D/F, M to Broadway-Lafayette St, N/R to 8th St-NYU, 4/6 to Bleecker St)

John Varvatos
CLOTHING, SHOES

57 Map p64, B3

Set in the hallowed halls of former punk club CBGB, the John Varvatos Bowery store is either a grievous insult to rock history or a creative reconfiguration of the past – depending on which side of the gentrification aisle you happen to stand on. The store goes to great lengths to tie fashion to rock and roll, with records, '70s audio equipment and even electric guitars for sale alongside JV's wares. (212-358-0315; 315 Bowery btwn 1st & 2nd Sts; noon-9pm Mon-Sat, to 7pm Sun; F/V to Lower East Side-2nd Ave, 6 to Bleecker St)

Moo Shoes
SHOES

58 Map p64, D5

Socially and environmentally responsible fashion usually tends to entail certain sacrifices in the good-looks department. Bucking the trend is Moo Shoes, a vegan boutique where style is no small consideration in the design of inexpensive microfiber (faux leather) shoes, bags and motorcycle jackets. Look for smart-looking Novacas, Crystalyn Kae purses, Queenbee Creations messenger bags and sleek Matt & Nat wallets. (212-254-6512; www.mooshoes.com; 78 Orchard St btwn Broome & Grand Sts; 11:30am-7:30pm Mon-Sat, noon-6pm Sun; F, J/M/Z to Delancey-Essex Sts)

Explore

Greenwich Village, Chelsea & the Meatpacking District

There's a very good reason why this area is known as the Village: it kinda looks like one! Quaint, quiet lanes carve their way between brown-brick townhouses offering endless strolling fodder. The Meatpacking District – once filled with slaughterhouses and now brimming with sleek boutiques and roaring nightclubs – leads to Chelsea, stocked with galleries and gay-friendly haunts.

The Sights in a Day

☀️ Wander along **The High Line** (p84) – an inviting emerald strand zipping over the gridiron – to get yourself oriented in this charming corner of the city. Exit at 14th St and ogle designer threads in the Meatpacking District, then slip into the West Village for more unique buys. Don't miss the **Strand Book Store** (p106) just beyond.

☀️ An afternoon of art is in store for those who explore the Chelsea galleries, located in a swath of former warehouses. Fuel up at the wonderfully refurbished **Chelsea Market** (p90), or hit up one of the neighborhood eateries such as **Cookshop** (p94) or **Le Grainne** (p95).

🌙 Blues-y tunes often get tangled in the trees of **Washington Square Park** (p90) – swing by before a delicious dinner at one of the dozens of up-and-comers such as **RedFarm** (p93). For a taste of the Prohibition-chic craze that has take the city by storm, try **Little Branch** (p98) or **Bathtub Gin** (p99). Or, you can catch some laughs at comedy headquarters like the **Upright Citizens Brigade Theatre** (p101) or the **Comedy Cellar** (p102).

For a local's day in Chelsea, see p86.

◉ Top Sights

The High Line (p84)

◯ Local Life

Chelsea Galleries (p86)

💜 Best of New York City

Drinking

Little Branch (p98)

Bathtub Gin (p99)

Boom Boom Room (p100)

Vin Sur Vingt (p98)

Vol de Nuit (p99)

Entertainment

Upright Citizens Brigade Theatre (p101)

Comedy Cellar (p102)

LGBT

Marie's Crisis (p98)

Julius Bar (p100)

Getting There

Ⓢ Subway Take the A/C/E or 1/2/3 and disembark at 14th St if you're looking for a good place to make tracks.

🚌 Bus Try the M14 or the M8 to access the westernmost areas of Chelsea and the West Village by public transportation.

Top Sights
The High Line

In the early 1900s, the area around western Chelsea was the largest industrial section of Manhattan and a set of elevated tracks were created to move freight off the cluttered streets below. The rails eventually became obsolete, and in 1999 a plan was made to convert the scarring strands of metal into a public green space. On June 9, 2009, part one of the city's most beloved urban renewal project opened with much ado, and it's been one of New York's star attractions ever since.

⊙ Map p88, C3

www.thehighline.org

Gansevoort St

⊘ 7am-7pm

Ⓢ L, A/C/E to 14th St-8th Ave, C/E to 23rd St-8th Ave, 🚌 M11 to Washington St, M11, M14 to 9th Ave, M34 to 10th Ave

Don't Miss

Public Art
In addition to being a haven of hovering green, The High Line is also an informal art space featuring a variety of installations, both site-specific and stand-alone. For detailed information about the public art on display at the time of your visit, check out www.thehighline.org/about/public-art.

Secret Staffers
As you walk along the High Line, you'll find dedicated staffers wearing shirts with the signature double-H logo who can point you in the right direction or offer you additional information about the converted rails. Group tours for children can be organized on a variety of topics, from the plant life of the high-rise park to the area's history.

The Industrial Past
It's hard to believe that The High Line – a shining example of brilliant urban renewal – was once a dingy rail line that anchored a rather unsavory district of thugs, trannies and slaughterhouses. The tracks that would one day become the High Line were commissioned in the 1930s when the municipal government decided to raise the street-level tracks after years of accidents that gave Tenth Ave the nickname 'Death Avenue.' The project drained over $150 million in funds (equivalent to around $2 billion by today's dime) and took roughly five years to complete. After two decades of effective use, a rise in truck transportation and traffic led to the eventual decrease in usage, and finally, in the 1980s, the rails became obsolete.

☑ Top Tips

▶ Start early at 30th St, wander south and exit at 14th St for a bite at Chelsea Market before exploring the West Village. If your tummy's grumbling, tackle The High Line in the reverse direction, gelato in hand.

▶ If you want to contribute financially to The High Line, become a member on the website. Members receive discounts at neighborhood establishments, such as Diane von Furstenberg's boutique and Amy's Bread in Chelsea Market.

✗ Take a Break

The High Line invites gastronomic establishments from around the city to set up vending carts and stalls for to-go items. Expect a showing of the finest coffee and ice cream establishments during the warmer months.

A cache of eateries is stashed within the brick walls of Chelsea Market (p90) at the 14th St exit of The High Line.

Local Life
Chelsea Galleries

The High Line may be the big-ticket item in this part of town, but there's plenty going on underneath the strand of green. Chelsea is home to the highest concentration of art galleries in the city – over 300 and counting. Most lie in the 20s, between Tenth and Eleventh Aves in what was once a cluster of industrial warehouses.

....

❶ Greene Naftali

Sharp, edgy and youth-oriented **Greene Naftali** (📞212-463-7770; www.green enaftaligallery.com; 526 W 26th St; ⏱10am-6pm Tue-Sat; 🚇C/E to 23rd St) has an ever-rotating display of art in all kinds of media: film/video, installation, painting, drawing and performance art. Check out the column running through the gallery's center; it's often used to display pieces.

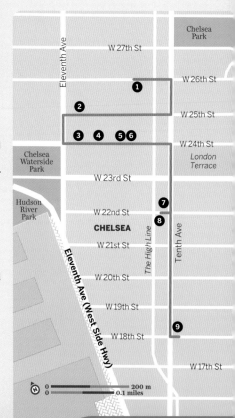

❷ Cheim & Read

Sculptures of every shape, size and material abound at **Cheim & Read** (www.cheimread.com; 547 W 25th St btwn Tenth & Eleventh Aves; ⏱10am-6pm Tue-Sat; **S**C/E to 23rd St) and monthly rotations keep the exhibits fresh – expect blazing light installations and inspired photography displays.

❸ Gagosian

Gagosian (www.gagosian.com; 555 W 24th St; ⏱10am-6pm Sat; **S**C, E to 23rd St) offers a different vibe than most of the one-off galleries, as it's part of a constellation of showrooms that spreads well across the globe. Also check out the 21st St location, which easily rivals some of the city's museums with large-scale installations.

❹ Mary Boone

Check out **Mary Boone Gallery** (www.maryboonegallery.com; 541 W 24th St; **S**C/E, 1 to 23rd St), whose owner found fame in the '80s with her eye for Jean-Michel Basquiat and Julian Schnabel – it's considered one of the main 'blue-chip' galleries in the area.

❺ Barbara Gladstone

The curator of the **Barbara Gladstone Gallery** (www.gladstonegallery.com; 515 W 24th St btwn Tenth & Eleventh Aves; ⏱10am-6pm Tue-Sat, closed weekends Jul & Aug; **S**C/E, 1 to 23rd St) has learned a thing or two after 30 years in the Manhattan art world. Ms Gladstone consistently puts together the most talked-about and well-critiqued displays around.

❻ Andrea Rosen

Another 'blue-chip' wonder, the **Andrea Rosen Gallery** (www.andrearosengallery.com; 525 W 24th St; ⏱10am-6pm Tue-Sat; **S**C/E, 1 to 23rd St) is expertly curated and often features exceptional oeuvres by the likes of Felix Gonzalez-Torres.

❼ Refuel, Spanish-Style

Wielding Spanish tapas amid closet-sized surrounds, **Tía Pol** (www.tiapol.com; 205 Tenth Ave btwn 22nd & 23rd Sts; small plates $2-16; ⏱dinner Tue-Sun; **S**C/E to 23rd St) is the real deal, as the hordes of swarming locals can attest. The red-wine options will have your tongue doing backflips, as will the array of small plates.

❽ Matthew Marks

Famous for exhibiting big names like Jasper Johns and Ellsworth Kelly, **Matthew Marks** (www.matthewmarks.com; 522 W 22nd St; ⏱10am-6pm Mon-Fri; **S**C/E to 23rd St) is a truly a Chelsea pioneer. There are three other nearby locations (on 22nd and 24th Sts) besides this one.

❾ Alexander & Bonin

Since moving to Chelsea from SoHo in 1997, the three-story **Alexander & Bonin** (www.alexanderandbonin.com; 132 Tenth Ave near 18th St; ⏱11am-6pm Tue-Sat; **S**C/E to 23rd St) has made excellent use of its airy space with a stellar roster of artists, including several prestigious Turner Prize winners.

A

Pier 66

Twelfth Ave (West Side Hwy)

Hudson River Park

B

Eleventh Ave

W 27th St

43

Chelsea Waterside Park

9

Pier 62

Pier 61

Pier 60

Pier 59

Eleventh Ave (West Side Hwy)

7

57 66

53

14

The High Line

Tenth Ave

W 26th St

W 25th St

W 24th St

W 23rd St

W 22nd St

W 21st St

W 20th St

W 19th St

W 18th St

W 17th St

W 16th St

W 15th St

C

Chelsea Park

CHELSEA

26

15 17

31

2

Ninth Ave

D

41 51

W 26th St

W 25th St

23rd St S

W 21st St 40

52 63

54

8th Ave
14th St S

Eighth Ave

Hudson River

60 62

55

33

Little W 12th St

The High Line

MEATPACKING DISTRICT

23

W 12th St

Bethune St

Washington St

Hudson River Park

West Side Hwy

W 13th St

Gansevoort St

Horatio St

Jane St

Abingdon Sq

Bank St

Perry St

Charles St

5

11

29

39

20

WEST VILLAGE

18

61

12

W 11th St

W 10th St

Christopher St

Barrow St

Morton St

Greenwich St

Bleecker St

Eighth Ave

Hudson St

Seventh Ave
Broadway
Madison Sq Park
Madison Ave

For reviews see

◉	Top Sights	p84
◎	Sights	p90
✖	Eating	p93
🍷	Drinking	p98
🎭	Entertainment	p101
🛍	Shopping	p105

1

0   500 m
0   0.25 miles

23rd St   23rd St   23rd St   23rd St   23rd St

◉8   ☎38

**FLATIRON
DISTRICT**   E 22nd St

🔒65   E 21st St   Park Ave S

E 20th St   **GRAMERCY
PARK**

Gramercy Park

E 20th St

🍴37   Fifth Ave   E 19th St   Second Ave

18th St   E 18th St

⑤   E 17th St   Irving Pl   Third Ave

**UNION
SQUARE**   E 16th St   Stuyvesant
Sq

Union Sq   E 15th St

14th St   6th Ave-
14th St   14th St-Union Sq   3rd Ave

⑤   ⑤   E 14th St   ⑤   E 14th St   E 14th St

3

W 13th St   E 13th St   **EAST
VILLAGE**

W 12th St   10◎   25✖   🔒64   E 12th St   🔒56

30   Greenwich Ave   W 11th St   E 11th St   E 11th St

44   University Pl   ◎6   Fourth Ave

21   W 10th St   E 10th St

36   W 9th St   **8th St-NYU**   **Astor Pl**   Stuyvesant St   E 9th St

48   58   W 8th St   E 8th St ⑤   ⑤◎4   St Marks Pl

34   MacDougal St   E 8th St   Astor Pl   Lafayette St   E 7th St   Second Ave

59   **Christopher St-
Sheridan Sq**   Washington Sq N   Greene St   Waverly Pl   Cooper
Sq   E 6th St

28   ⑤   **Christopher Park**
Washington Pl   ◎1 ◎ **Washington
Sq Park**   Broadway   E 5th St

22✖   **W 4th St-Washington Sq**   E 4th St

**GREENWICH
VILLAGE**   32   45   Washington Sq S   W 4th St   Mercer St   **NOHO**

New York University   Great Jones St

Minetta   42   W 3rd St   Bond St   Bowery   E 2nd St

46   La   19 35   Sullivan St   Thompson St   LaGuardia Pl   Bleecker St   Bleecker St   E 1st St

Commerce
St   27   **Broadway-
Lafayette St**   **Lower East Side-
2nd Ave**

St Lukes Pl   Leroy St   Downing St   50   16   47

James J
Walker Park   W Houston St   ⑤ **E Houston St**

Sights

Washington Square Park

SQUARE

1 Map p88, F4

What was once a potter's field and a square for public executions is now the unofficial town square of the Village. It plays host to lounging New York University (NYU) students, fire-eating street performers, curious canines and their owners, and legions of speed-chess pros. Encased in perfectly manicured brownstones and gorgeous twists of modern architecture (all owned by NYU), Washington Sq Park is one of the most beautiful garden spaces in the city – especially as you are welcomed by the iconic Stanford White Arch on the north side of the green. (www.washingtonsquareparkcouncil.org; Fifth Ave at Washington Sq N; **S** A/C/E, B/D/F/V to W 4th St-Washington Sq, N/R/W to 8th St-NYU)

Chelsea Market

MARKET

2 Map p88, C3

In a shining example of redevelopment and preservation, the Chelsea Market has taken a former factory of cookie giant Nabisco (creator of the Oreo) and turned it into an 800ft-long shopping concourse that caters to foodies. And that's only the lower part of a larger, million-sq-ft space that occupies a full city block – upstairs you'll find the current home of several TV channels, including the Food Network, Oxygen Network and NY1, the local news channel. (www.chelseamarket.com; 75 Ninth Ave at 15th St; ⏱7am-9pm Mon-Sat, 10am-8pm Sun; **S** A/C/E to 14th St, L to 8th Ave)

New York University

UNIVERSITY

3 Map p88, G4

In 1831, Albert Gallatin, formerly Secretary of the Treasury, founded an intimate center of higher learning open to all students, regardless of race or class background. He'd scarcely recognize the place today, which has swelled to a student population of more than 54,000. For a unique experience, sign up for a one-day class – from American history to photography – offered by the School of Professional Studies and Continuing Education. (NYU; 📞212-998-4636; www.nyu.edu; information center 50 W 4th St; **S** A/C/E, B/D/F/V to W 4th St-Washington Sq, R/W to 8th St-NYU)

Astor Place

SQUARE

4 Map p88, G4

This square is named after the Astor family, who built an early New York fortune on beaver pelts and lived on Colonnade Row, just south of the square. Originally Astor Pl was the home of the Astor Opera House (now gone), which attracted the city's wealthy elite for regular performances in the mid-1800s. Today the square is largely known as the home of the Village Voice and the Cooper Union design institute. (8th St btwn Third & Fourth Aves; **S** R/W to 8th St-NYU, 6 to Astor Pl)

Understand

The History of Washington Square Park

Although quite ravishing today, Washington Sq Park has a long and sordid history before finally blossoming into the public space we see today (thanks largely to a $16 million renovation that began in 2007).

Early History
When the Dutch settled Manhattan, they gave what is now the park to their freed black slaves. The land was between the Dutch and Native settlements, so, in a way, the area acted as a buffer between enemies.

At the turn of the 19th century, the municipality of New York purchased the land for use as a burial ground straddling the city's limit. At first, the cemetery was mainly for indigent workers, but the space quickly reached capacity during an outbreak of yellow fever. Over 20,000 bodies remain buried under the park today.

By 1830, the grounds were used for military parades, and then quickly transformed into a park for the wealthy elite who were constructing lavish townhouses along the surrounding streets.

Stanford White Arch
The iconic Stanford White Arch, colloquially known as the Washington Square Arch, dominates the park with its 72ft of beaming white Dover marble. Originally designed in wood to celebrate the centennial of George Washington's inauguration in 1889, the arch was so popular that it was replaced with stone six years later and adorned with statues of the general in war and peace. In 1916, artist Marcel Duchamp climbed to the top of the arch by its internal stairway and declared the park the 'Free and Independent Republic of Washington Square.'

Freedom of Speech
Once it was clear that the park was here to stay, it became a haven for beatniks and political outcry, especially when urban planners sought to change the shape and usage of the space. Locals protested, and the shape has remained largely unchanged since the 1800s.

The political tradition continues even today and Barack Obama led a rally here in 2007 to drum up support for his presidential bid. Turnout was, unsurprisingly, overwhelming.

Local Life

Robert Hammond on The High Line

Co-founder and executive director of Friends of The High Line Robert Hammond shares his High Line (p84) highlights: 'What I love most about The High Line are its hidden moments, like at the Tenth Ave cut-out near 17th St, most people sit on the bleachers, but if you turn the other way, you can see the Statue of Liberty far away in the harbor. Architecture buffs will love looking down 18th St, and up on 30th is my favorite moment – a steel cut-out where you can see the cars underneath.'

Pier 45   OUTDOORS

 5   Map p88, C5

Known to many as the Christopher St Pier, this is an 850ft-long finger of concrete, spiffily renovated with a grass lawn, flowerbeds, an outdoor cafe, tented shade shelters and a stop for the New York Water Taxi. It's a magnet for downtowners of all stripes, from local families with toddlers in daylight to mobs of young gays looking to cruise. (Christopher St at Hudson River; S 1 to Christopher St-Sheridan Sq)

Grace Church   CHURCH

6   Map p88, G4

This Gothic Revival Episcopal church, designed in 1843 by James Renwick Jr, was made of marble quarried by prisoners at 'Sing Sing,' the state peni-

tentiary 30 miles away. After years of neglect, Grace Church is being spiffed up in a major way. Now it's a National Landmark, whose elaborate carvings, towering spire and verdant, and groomed yard are sure to stop you in your tracks as you make your way down this otherwise ordinary stretch of the Village. (✆212-254-2000; www.gracechurchnyc.org; 802 Broadway at 10th St; ⏰10am-5pm, services daily; S R/W to 8th St-NYU, 6 to Astor Pl)

Chelsea Art Museum   MUSEUM

7   Map p88, B2

Occupying a three-story red-brick building dating from 1850, this popular museum stands on land once owned by writer Clement Clarke Moore (author of the famous poem 'A Visit from St Nicholas'). Its focus is on post-war abstract expressionism, especially by national and international artists, and its permanent collection includes works by Antonio Corpora, Laszlo Lakner, Jean Arp and Ellen Levy. (✆212-255-0719; www.chelseaartmuseum.org; 556 W 22nd St; adult/child $8/free; ⏰noon-6pm Tue, Wed, Fri & Sat, to 8pm Thu; S C/E to 23rd St)

Chelsea Hotel   HISTORIC BUILDING

8   Map p88, E1

It's probably not any great shakes as far as hotels go – and besides, it mainly houses long-term residents – but as a place of mythical proportions, the Chelsea Hotel is top of the line. The red-brick hotel, featuring ornate iron balconies and no fewer than seven plaques declaring its literary landmark status, has played a major role in pop-culture history. (☎212-243-3700; 222 W 23rd St btwn Seventh & Eighth Aves; **S**1, C/E to 23rd St)

Chelsea Piers Complex SPORTS

 9 · Map p88, B2

This massive waterfront sports center caters to the athlete in everyone. You can set out to hit a bucket of golf balls at the four-level driving range, ice skate on the complex's indoor rink or rent in-line skates to cruise along the new bike path on the Hudson River Park – all the way down to Battery Park. The complex also has a jazzy bowling alley, Hoop City for basketball, a sailing school for kids, batting cages, a huge gym facility with an indoor pool (day passes for nonmembers are $50), indoor rock-climbing walls – the works. (☎212-336-6000; www.chelseapiers.com; Hudson River at end of W 23rd St; **S**C/E to 23rd St)

Forbes Collection MUSEUM

10 · Map p88, F3

These galleries, located in the lobby of the headquarters of Forbes magazine, house rotating exhibits and curios from the personal collection of the late publishing magnate Malcolm Forbes. The eclectic mix of objects on display includes Fabergé eggs, toy boats, early versions of Monopoly and over 10,000 toy soldiers. (☎212-206-5548; www.forbesgalleries.com; 62 Fifth Ave at

12th St; admission free; ⏰10am-4pm Tue-Sat; **S**L, N/Q/R/W, 4/5/6 to 14th St-Union Sq)

Downtown Boathouse KAYAKING

 11 · Map p88, D5

New York's most active public boathouse offers free walk-up 20-minute kayaking (including equipment) in the protected embayment in the Hudson River on weekends and some weekday evenings. (☎646-613-0740; www.downtownboathouse.org; Pier 40, near Houston St; tours free; ⏰9am-6pm Sat & Sun mid-May–mid-Oct, some weekday evenings mid-Jun–mid-Sep; **S**1 to Houston St)

New York Trapeze School SPORTS

Fulfill your circus dreams, like Carrie did on *Sex and the City*, flying trapeze to trapeze in this open-air tent by the river near Downtown Boathouse (see 11 · Map p88; D5). It's open from May to September, on Pier 40. The school also has an indoor facility open year-round. Check the website for daily class times. (www.newyork.trapezeschool.com; Pier 40 at West Side Hwy; classes $47-65, 5-week course $270; **S**1 to Houston St)

Eating

RedFarm FUSION $$

 12 · Map p88, D4

Savvy Sino fusion is this cottage-style restaurant's signature on its flavorful dishes. A recent chart-topper on the best lists of many foodies, RedFarm earns our devotion for preparing

ALEX SEGRE/ALAMY ©

Chelsea Market (p90)

mouthwatering mains (rib steak!) without a hint of pretension. Besides the heavily touted mixed-bag recipes, RedFarm also sports some of the best drinks in town – the Suntory Old-Fashioned is one of the finest scotch cocktails out there. (☎212-792-9700; www.redfarmnyc.com; 529 Hudson St btwn 10th & Charles Sts; mains $14-39; 🕒5pm-12:30am Mon-Thu, to midnight Fri, 11am-2:30pm & 5pm-midnight Sat, 11am-2:30pm & 5-11pm Sun; [S]A/C/E, B/D/F, M to W 4th St, 1/2 to Christopher St-Sheridan Sq, 1/2/3 to 14th St)

Tartine

FRENCH **$$**

13 🍴 Map p88, D4

Tartine is the corner bistro of your French-ified dreams: wobbly stacks of chairs and tables, pink steaks and escargot, found treasures nailed to wooden walls, and a good-cop-bad-cop duo of waitresses who indiscriminately bounce dishes and diners around the teeny-tiny room. It's BYO, and staff will gladly uncork your bottle for some covert street-side sips while you wait for your table. (☎212-229-2611; www.tartinecafenyc.com; 253 W 11th St btwn 4th St & Waverly Pl; mains $10-24; 🕒9am-10:30pm Mon-Sat, to 10pm Sun; [S]1/2/3 to 14th St, 1/2 to Christopher St-Sheridan Sq, L to 8th Ave)

Cookshop

MODERN AMERICAN **$$**

14 🍴 Map p88, C2

A brilliant brunching pit stop before (or after) tackling the verdant High

Line across the street, Cookshop is a lively place that knows its niche and does it oh so well. Excellent service, eye-opening cocktails (good morning Bloody Maria!), a perfectly baked breadbasket and a selection of inventive egg mains make this a favorite in Chelsea on a Sunday afternoon. Dinner is a sure-fire win as well. (212-924-4440; www.cookshopny.com; 156 Tenth Ave btwn 19th & 20th Sts; mains $14-33; lunch & dinner; L to 8th Ave, A/C/E to 14th St, A/C/E to 23rd St)

Le Grainne
FRENCH $$

15 Map p88, C2

Tap the top of your French onion soup as you dream of that Pollyanna ingenue Amélie cracking open her crème brûlée. Le Grainne transports the senses from the busy blocks of Chelsea to the backstreets of Paris. The tin-topped eatery really excels at lunch time, when baguette sandwiches and savory crepes are scarfed down amid cramped quarters; come for dinner to breath in the wafting garlic as heartier pastas are tossed in the kitchen. (646-486-3000; www.legrainne cafe.com; 183 Ninth Ave btwn 21st & 22nd Sts; mains $9.50-27; 8am-midnight Mon-Sun; A/C/E, 1/2 to 23rd St, A/C/E to 14th St)

Tomoe
SUSHI $$

16 Map p88, F5

Slap-dash scrawls and scribbles on the wall about credit-card restrictions and house specials are oddly juxtaposed with elegant California rolls (the size of hockey pucks!) and impossibly tender strips of sashimi resting on wasabi-tinged clouds of rice. Known with half-mocking affection as 'Garbage Sushi' due to the large dumpster outside that partially hides the facade, Tomoe has somehow missed the critics' reviews, making it everyone's favorite sushi spot for people in the know. (212-777-9346; www.tomoesushi. com; 172 Thompson St btwn Houston & Bleecker Sts; sushi roll from $4.50, combo platter $19.95; 5-11pm Mon-Sat, 1-3pm Tue-Sat, 5-10pm Sun; A/C/E to Spring St, N/R to Prince St, B/D/F, M to Broadway-Lafayette St)

Billy's Bakery
BAKERY $

17 Map p88, D2

NYC's *Sex and the City*–fueled cupcake craze has come and gone, but Billy's is still cranking out its four-bite bits of heaven. Red velvet and banana cream top the recipe list, and a clutch of retro-style pastries are imagined by the I-don't-care-what-I'm-wearing hipsters in the back. Why buy one

Local Life
Eighth Ave Brunch
If you're a dude looking to meet (or at least look at) other dudes, but the cruise-y bar scene isn't your style, then opt for the weekend brunch scene along Eighth Ave. You'll spot piles of friendly Chelsea boys drinking their hangovers off in tight jeans and even tighter T-shirts.

Local Life

Eating at Chelsea Market

Boutique bakeries fill the renovated hallways of this foodie haven (p90). **Eleni's** (Map p88, C3; Chelsea Market; S A/C/E to 14th St, L to 8th Ave) is of special note – Eleni Gianopulos was one of the first tenants here and her expertly designed cookies are a big hit. Also worth a stop is **Sarabeth's** (Map p88, C3; www.sarabeths.com; Chelsea Market; S A/C/E to 14th St, L to 8th Ave), where flour and dough are whipped into perfect dessert recipes. Sweet tooths will fawn over the icy outpost of **l'Arte Del Gelato** (Map p88, C3; www.lartedelgelato.com; Chelsea Market; S A/C/E to 14th St, L to 8th Ave). Gelato is made fresh every day – the perfect snack for The High Line.

when six fit oh so perfectly into their cute little boxes. (☑ 212-647-9956; www.billysbakerynyc.com; 184 Ninth Ave btwn 21st & 22nd Sts; cupcakes $3; ⏲ 8:30am-11pm Mon-Thu, to midnight Fri & Sat, 9am-10pm Sun; S A/C/E, 1/2 to 23rd St, A/C/E to 14th St)

Spotted Pig   PUB $$

18 Map p88, D4

This Michelin-starred gastro-pub is a favorite of Villagers, serving a hearty, upscale blend of mains from Italy and the UK. Two floors are bedecked in old-timey souvenirs that serve to make the experience both casual and refined. It doesn't take reservations, so there is often a wait for a table.

Brunch and lunch are less packed, so you can usually get a seat straight away. (☑ 212-620-0393; www.thespottedpig.com; 314 W 11th St at Greenwich St; mains $14-30; ⏲ lunch & dinner; 🖋 🖼; S A/C/E to 14th St, L to 8th Ave)

Minetta Tavern   BISTRO $$

19 Map p88, F5

Book in advance, or come early to snag a table on a weeknight, because Minetta Tavern is pretty much always packed to the rafters. The snug red-leather banquettes, dark-paneled walls with black-and-white photos, classic checkered floors, tin ceilings and flaring yellow bistro lamps will lure you in. The flavor-filled bistro fare – pan-seared marrow bones, roasted chicken, crisp fries and big burgers, and mustn't-miss French dip sandwiches – will have you wishing you lived upstairs. (☑ 212-475-3850; www.minettatavernny.com; 113 MacDougal St; mains $17-34; ⏲ dinner daily, brunch Sat & Sun; S A/C/E, B/D/F/V to W 4th St)

Café Cluny   BISTRO $$

20 Map p88, D4

As the name might suggest, Café Cluny brings the whimsy of Paris to the West Village, with woven bistro-style bar chairs, light wooden upholstery and a selection of joie-de-vivre-inducing platters like *steak frites*, mixed green salads and roasted chicken. (☑ 212-255-6900; www.cafecluny.com; 284 W 12th St; mains $10-32; ⏲ 8am-11pm Mon, to midnight Tue-Fri, 9am-midnight Sat, to 11pm Sun; S L to 8th Ave, A/C/E, 1/2/3 to 14th St)

Taïm

ISRAELI $

21 🍴 Map p88, E4

Not all Middle Eastern fare is alike, and this tiny falafel joint proves it with its smoothies, salads and sass – and its falafel, which ranges from the traditional type to those spiced up with roasted red pepper or hot harissa. Whichever fried balls you choose, you'll get them stuffed into pita with creamy tahini sauce and a generous dose of Israeli salad. Or you can try them all in a platter that gets you three tasty dips. (☎212-691-1287; 222 Waverly Pl btwn Perry & W 11th Sts; mains $5-9.50; 🕒lunch & dinner; [S]1/2/3 to 14th St)

Tertulia

TAPAS $$$

22 🍴 Map p88, E4

A favorite of Gwyneth Paltrow, Tertulia offers perfected Spanish tapas in cozy surrounds with plenty of blonde-wood bar seating and exposed brick. Waiters tend to patrons with the utmost care, offering thoughtful suggestions from both the small-plates menu and the wine list. Tiny portions and pricier vino means the bill can add up quickly – you've been warned. (☎646-559-9909; www.tertulianyc.com; 359 Sixth Ave; small plates $5-19; [S]A/C/E, B/D/F, M to W 4th St, 1/2 to Christopher St-Sheridan Sq, 1/2 to Houston St)

Barbuto

MODERN AMERICAN $$

23 🍴 Map p88, C4

Occupying a cavernous garage space with sweeping see-through doors that roll up and into the ceiling during the warmer months, Barbuto slaps together a delightful assortment of new American faves like roast chicken and moist risotto. There's a cluster of photography studios upstairs, so you might spot some models and artsy types filing by. (☎212-924-9700; www.barbutonyc.com; 775 Washington St btwn 12th & Jane Sts; mains $18-25; [S]L to 8th Ave, A/C/E to 14th St, 1/2 to Christopher St-Sheridan Sq)

Joe's Pizza

PIZZERIA $

24 🍴 Map p88, E5

Joe's is the Meryl Streep of pizza parlors, collecting dozens of awards and accolades over the last three decades while safely cementing its reputation as one of the top spots for a slice in NYC. No-frills pies are served up indiscriminately to students, tourists and celebrities alike (everyone's stopped by for a bite, from Kirsten Dunst to Bill Murray). (☎212-366-1182; www.joespizzanyc.com; 7 Carmine St btwn Sixth Ave & Bleecker St; slices from $2.75; 🕒10am-4:30am Mon-Sun; [S]A/C/E, B/D/F, M to W 4th St, 1/2 to Christopher St-Sheridan Sq, 1/2 to Houston St)

Souen

ASIAN $$

25 🍴 Map p88, G3

A paradigm of pure food, Souen delivers a traditional Japanese macrobiotic diet to eager diners who come to clear their minds and cleanse. Pure grains are reputed to have curative properties – just make sure to chew a lot (as the waitstaff will often remind you)!

(📞212-627-7150; www.souen.net; 28 E 13th St btwn 5th Ave & University Pl; mains $8-23.50; ⏱10am-11pm Mon-Sat, to 10pm Sun; Ⓢ4/5/6, L, N/Q/R to Union Sq-14th St)

Co
PIZZERIA $$

26 Map p88, D1

Masterfully prepared pizza is served in bright, wooden surrounds that feel like a Scandinavian cafeteria. Expect a faithful reproduction of the trademark Neapolitan thin crust pies topped with an assortment of fresh-from-the-farm items like fennel and buffalo mozzarella. Salads of artichoke, beet or radicchio – as well as global wines and a sprinkling of sweets – round out the offerings. (📞212-243-1105; 230 Ninth Ave at 24th St; pizza $9-18; ⏱dinner Mon, lunch & dinner Tue-Sun; Ⓢ C/E to 23rd St)

Drinking

Little Branch
COCKTAIL BAR

27 Map p88, E5

If it weren't for the casual bouncer dressed in slacks and suspenders, you'd never guess that a charming bar lurked behind the boring brown door positioned at the odd triangular intersection. When you get the go-ahead to enter, you'll find a basement bar that feels like a wonder kickback to Prohibition times. Squeaky tunes waft overhead as locals clink glasses and sip inventive, old-timey cocktails. (📞212-929-4360; 22 Seventh Ave S at Leroy St; Ⓢ1 to Houston St)

Marie's Crisis
BAR

28 Map p88, E4

Aging Broadway queens, wide-eyed out-of-town gay boys, giggly tourist girls and various other fans of musical theater assemble around the piano here and take turns belting out campy numbers, often joined by the entire crowd. It's old-school fun, no matter how jaded you were when you went in. (📞212-243-9323; 59 Grove St btwn Seventh Ave S & Bleecker St; ⏱4pm-4am; Ⓢ1 to Christopher St-Sheridan Sq)

Art Bar
BAR

29 Map p88, D3

A decidedly bohemian crowd favors Art Bar, which doesn't look like much up front (oval booths crowded too close to the wooden bar), but has a bit more going on in the back. Grab your beer or one of the house specials (usually martinis) and head for the couches, placed under a huge *Last Supper* mural featuring Jimmy Dean and Marilyn Monroe, among others. (📞212-727-0244; 52 Eighth Ave near Horatio St; ⏱4pm-4am, happy hour 4-7pm; Ⓢ L to 8th Ave-14th St, A/C/E to 14th St)

Vin Sur Vingt
WINE BAR

30 Map p88, E3

A cozy spot just off Seventh Ave's bustle, Vin Sur Vingt is a thin wine bar with a strip of bar seating and a quaint row of two-seat tables, perfect for a first date. Warning: if you come for a pre-dinner drink, you'll inevitably be charmed into staying through

Marie's Crisis

dinner as you munch on the excellent selection of bar bites. Reasonably priced vino keeps the locals coming back for seconds. (📞212-924-4442; www. vinsur20nyc.com; 201 W 11th St btwn Seventh Ave & Waverly Pl; ⏰5pm-2am Mon-Fri, 11am-2am Sat, to midnight Sun; Ⓢ1/2/3 to 14th St, 1/2 to Christopher St-Sheridan Sq, L to 8th Ave)

Bathtub Gin   BAR

31 🚇 Map p88, D2

Amid New York City's serious obsession with speakeasy-styled hangouts, Bathtub Gin manages to poke its head above the crowd with its super-secret front door, which doubles as a wall for an unassuming cafe. Inside, chill seating, soft background beats and kindly staff make it a great place to sling

back bespoke cocktails with friends. (📞646-559-1671; www.bathtubginnyc.com; 132 Ninth Ave btwn 18th & 19th Sts; ⏰6pm-1:30am Sun-Tue, to 3:30am Wed-Sat; Ⓢ A/C/E to 14th St, L to 8th Ave, A/C/E to 23rd St)

Vol de Nuit   PUB

32 🚇 Map p88, F4

Even all the New York University students can't ruin this: a cozy Belgian beer bar, with a few dozen zonkers like Lindemans Framboise (strawberry beer!) and *frites* (fries) to share at the front patio seats, the lounge, the communal wood tables or under the dangling red lights at the bar. (📞212-982-3388; 148 W 4th St; Ⓢ A/C/E, B/D/F/V to W 4th St-Washington Sq)

Boom Boom Room

LOUNGE

33 🍸 Map p88, C3

With smooth beige surrounds, softer music and plenty of room to swig your top-shelf tipple, the Boom Boom Room is strictly VIP and the favored hangout for the vogue elite (and *Vogue* elite) – expect models, their photographer and the occasional celeb sighting. Come early and book ahead – that's the only way to gain access if you're not a cornerstone of New York's social scene. (☎212-645-4646; 848 Washington St btwn 13th & Little W 12th Sts; 🕘10pm-4am Wed-Thu, 11pm-4am Fri & Sat; [S] L to 8th Ave, 1/2/3, A/C/E to 14th St)

Le Bain

DANCE CLUB

This sweeping rooftop venue sits at the tragically hip Standard Hotel along with Boom Boom Room (see **33** 🍸 Map p88; C3). Le Bain sees a garish parade of party promoters who do their thang on any day of the week. Have you seen those Stefon sketches on Saturday Night Live? If not, brace yourself for plumes of pot smoke on the turf-laced balconies, make-out sessions in the jet-black bathrooms, a giant Jacuzzi built right into the dance floor, and an ambassador from every walk of life in New York getting wasted on pricy snifters. Best. Night. Ever. (☎212-645-4646; 848 Washington St btwn 13th & Little W 12th Sts; 🕘10pm-4am Wed-Thu, 11pm-4am Fri & Sat; [S] L to 8th Ave, 1/2/3, A/C/E to 14th St)

Kettle of Fish

BAR

34 🍸 Map p88, E4

Step into this dimly lit spot, full of couches and plump chairs, and prepare to stay for a while because the crowd is simply beguiling. It's a dive bar, a sports bar and a gay bar in one, and everyone mixes happily with each other. There are stacks of board games, such as Monopoly and checkers, which patrons are encouraged to play, as well as darts. The owner is a Green Bay Packers fan, so expect raucous activity on game days. (☎212-414-2278; www.kettleoffishnyc.com; 59 Christopher St near Seventh Ave; 🕘3pm-4am Mon-Fri, 2pm-4am Sat & Sun; [S] 1 to Christopher St-Sheridan Sq)

124 Old Rabbit Club

BAR

35 🍸 Map p88, F5

You'll wanna pat yourself on the back when you a) find the darn place, and b) gain access to this speakeasy-style joint (hint: look for the '124' and ring the buzzer). Once you're here, grab a seat at the dimly lit bar and reward yourself with a quenching stout or one of the dozens of imported brews. (☎212-254-0575; 124 MacDougal St; [S] A/C/E, B/D/F, M to W 4th St, 1/2 to Christopher St-Sheridan Sq, 1/2 to Houston St)

Julius Bar

GAY

36 🍸 Map p88, E4

One of the infamous originals – in fact, it's the oldest operating gay bar in New York City – Julius is a dive bar through and through. The only hint of its homo roots is the clientele, which is a mixed bag of faithful locals and the occasional newbie. It's refreshingly unpretentious and just steps away from the better-known Stonewall and Duplex. (☎212-243-1928; 159 W 10th St at Waverly Pl; S A/C/E, B/D/F, M to W 4th St, 1/2/3 to 14th St, 1/2 to Christopher St-Sheridan Sq)

G Lounge GAY

39 Map p88, E2

Glossy and unpretentious, this gay bar is as straight-friendly as they come, and it's really all about the music. DJs rotate daily, but Tuesday is always BoyBox night. Check out the website to find out who's spinning while you're in town. For heavy drinking and dancing with no cover, you can't beat G – although you may have to wait in line to get in. Dress at G Lounge is refreshingly casual. Cash only. (☎212-929-1085; www.glounge.com; 223 W 19th St btwn Seventh & Eighth Aves; ⏱4pm-4am; S1 to 18th St)

Barracuda GAY

38 Map p88, E1

This longtime favorite holds its own even as newer, slicker places come and go. That's because it's got a simple, winning formula: affordable cocktails, a cozy rec-room vibe and free entertainment from some of the city's top drag queens. (☎212-645-8613; 275 W 22nd St at Seventh Ave; S C/E to 23rd St)

Cubbyhole LESBIAN, GAY

39 Map p88, D3

A tiny hideaway festooned with brightly patterned bar stools and strings of colorful lights, this no-attitude neighborhood watering hole has that truly rare mix of lesbians and gay men who are out to make friends rather than hit the road with the first trick they find. It's got a great jukebox, friendly bartenders and plenty of regulars. (☎212-243-9041; 281 W 12th St; S A/C/E to 14th St, L to 8th Ave)

Rawhide GAY

40 Map p88, D2

Brand your behind with a rainbow flag and jump into Rawhide, one of the last reminders of Chelsea's grittier days. Beefy bartenders serve a mixed bag of queens, though it traditionally attracts a leather crowd. (☎212-242-9332; 212 Eighth Ave btwn 20th & 21st Sts; S A/C/E, 1/2 to 23rd St, 1/2 to 18th St)

Entertainment

Upright Citizens Brigade Theatre COMEDY

41 Map p88, D1

Pros of comedy sketches and outrageous improvisations reign at this popular 74-seat venue, which gets drop-ins from casting directors. Getting in is cheap, and so is the beer (from $2 a can). You may recognize pranksters on stage from late-night

TERRENCE JENNINGS/CORBIS ©

Mos Def performs at Blue Note

comedy shows. Admission is free Wednesdays after 11pm, when newbies take the reins. Check the website for popular classes on sketch and improv, now spilling over to an annex location on W 30th St. (☎212-366-9176; www.ucbtheatre.com; 307 W 26th St btwn Eighth & Ninth Aves; cover charage $5-8; [S] C/E to 23rd St)

Comedy Cellar

COMEDY

42 ★ Map p88, F5

This long-established basement club in Greenwich Village features mainstream material and a good list of regulars (eg Colin Quinn, SNL's Darrell Hammond, Wanda Sykes), plus the occasional high-profile drop-in, such as Dave Chappelle. (☎212-254-3480; www.comedycellar.com; 117 MacDougal St btwn W 3rd & Bleecker Sts; cover charge $20; 🕒shows start approx 9pm Sun-Fri, 7pm & 9:30pm Sat; [S] A/C/E, B/D/F/V to W 4th St-Washington Sq)

Sleep No More

THEATER

43 ★ Map p88, B1

After a smashing success in London, British theater company Punchdrunk has reimagined its evocative performance installation in NYC. The installation is held in a series of Chelsea warehouses that have been redesigned to look like an abandoned hotel. It's a choose-your-own adventure kind of experience where audience members are free to wander the grounds and interact with the actors who perform a variety of scenes that range from the bizarre to the risqué. (www.sleepnomorenyc.com; McKittrick Hotel, 530 W 27th St; ⏰7pm-midnight Mon-Sat; **S**C/E to 23rd St)

Village Vanguard

JAZZ

44 ⭐ Map p88, E4

Possibly the city's most prestigious jazz club, the Vanguard has hosted every major star of the past 50 years. It started as a home to spoken-word performances and occasionally returns to its roots, but most of the time it's just smooth, sweet jazz all night long. Mind your step on the steep stairs and close your eyes to the signs of wear and tear – acoustically, you're in one of the greatest venues in the world. (📞212-255-4037; www.villagevanguard.com; 178 Seventh Ave at 11th St; **S**1/2/3 to 14th St)

Blue Note

JAZZ

45 ⭐ Map p88, F5

This is by far the most famous (and expensive) of the city's jazz clubs. Most shows are $20 at the bar, $35 at a table, but prices can rise for the biggest jazz stars, and a few outside the normal jazz act (um, Doobie Brothers' Michael McDonald, anyone?). Go on an off night and be quiet – all attention is on the stage! (📞212-475-8592; www.bluenote.net; 131 W 3rd St btwn Sixth Ave & MacDougal St; **S**A/C/E, B/D/F/V to W 4th St-Washington Sq)

 Local Life

West 4th Street Basketball Courts

Also known as 'the Cage,' this small **basketball court** (Map p88, F4; Sixth Ave btwn 3rd & 4th Sts; ⏰hours vary; **S**A/C/E, B/D/F/V to W 4th St-Washington Sq) stands enclosed within chain-link fencing and is home to some of the best streetball in the country. Though it's more touristy than its counterpart, Rucker Park in Harlem, that's also part of its charm. Games held here draw massive, excitable crowds, who often stand 10-deep to hoot and holler for the skilled, competitive guys who play here. Prime time is summer, when the W 4th St Summer Pro-Classic League hits the scene.

Cherry Lane Theater

THEATER

46 ⭐ Map p88, E5

A theater with a distinctive charm hidden in the West Village, Cherry Lane has a long and distinguished history. It was started by poet Edna St Vincent Millay and has given a voice to numerous playwrights and actors over the years. Today, it remains true to its mission of creating 'live' theater that's accessible to the public. Readings, plays and spoken-word performances rotate frequently. (📞212-989-2020; www.cherrylanetheater.com; 38 Commerce St; ⏰hours vary; **S**1 to Christopher St-Sheridan Sq)

Angelika Film Center

CINEMA

47 ⭐ Map p88, G5

Angelika Film Center specializes in foreign and independent films and has some quirky charms (the rumble of the subway, long lines and occasionally bad sound). But its roomy cafe is a great place to meet friends and the beauty of its Stanford White–designed, beaux arts building is undeniable. (☏212-995-2000; www. angelikafilmcenter.com; 18 W Houston St at Mercer St; tickets $10-14; 🐾; Ⓢ B/D/F/V to Broadway-Lafayette St)

Smalls Jazz Club

JAZZ

48 ⭐ Map p88, E4

Living up to its name, this cramped but appealing basement jazz den offers a grab-bag collection of jazz acts who take the stage nightly. Cover for the evening is $20 (including a free drink Sunday through Thursday), with a come-and-go policy if you need to duck out for a slice. (☏212-283-9728; www.smallsjazzclub.com; 183 W 10th St at Seventh Ave; cover charge $20; Ⓢ 1 to Christopher St-Sheridan Sq)

Duplex

CABARET, KARAOKE

Right next door to Kettle of Fish (see 34 Map p88; E4), cabaret, karaoke and campy dance moves are par for the course at the legendary Duplex. Pictures of Joan Rivers line the walls, and the performers like to mimic her sassy form of self-deprecation, while getting in a few jokes about audience members as well. It's a fun and

unpretentious place, and certainly not for the bashful. (☏212-255-5438; www.theduplex.com; 61 Christopher St; cover charge $10-20; ⊗4pm-4am; Ⓢ 1 to Christopher St-Sheridan Sq)

IFC Center

CINEMA

49 ⭐ Map p88, E5

This art-house cinema in New York University–land has a great cafe and a solidly curated lineup of new independents, cult classics and foreign films. Catch shorts, documentaries, '80s revivals, director-focused series, weekend classics and frequent special series, such as midnight screenings of holiday classics at Christmas. (☏212-924-7771; www.ifccenter.com; 323 Sixth Ave at 3rd St; Ⓢ A/C/E, B/D/F/V to W 4th St-Washington Sq)

Le Poisson Rouge

LIVE MUSIC

50 ⭐ Map p88, F5

This newish high-concept art space (complete with dangling fish aquarium) hosts a highly eclectic lineup, with the likes of Deerhunter, Marc Ribot, Lou Reed and Laurie Anderson performing in past years. Aside from the main (high-tech) concert space, there's also an art gallery and a bar-cafe open during the day. (☏212-505-3474; www. lepoissonrouge.com; 158 Bleecker St; Ⓢ A/C/E, B/D/F/V to W 4th St-Washington Sq)

Magnet Theater

COMEDY

51 ⭐ Map p88, D1

Magnet Theater has a jam-packed schedule, which features tons of comedy in several incarnations (mostly improv) and lures crowds of rowdy youngsters. Our favorite is the musical improv, but you can't go wrong with the sketch-comedy workshops. (☎212-244-8824; www.magnettheater.com; 254 W 29th St btwn Seventh & Eighth Aves; 🕒6:30-11pm Tue-Wed, to midnight Thu & Fri, to 1am Sat, 6-11pm Sun; [S]1/2 to 28th St, A/C/E to 23rd St, 1/2/3 to 34th St-Penn Station)

Atlantic Theater Company

THEATER

52 ★ Map p88, D2

Founded by David Mamet and William H Macy in 1985, the Atlantic Theater Company is a pivotal anchor for New York City's off-Broadway community. It has hosted many Tony Award and Drama Desk winners over the last 25-plus years. (☎212-691-5919; www.atlantictheater.org; 336 W 20th St btwn Eighth & Ninth Aves; 🕒10am-6pm Mon-Fri, 8-10pm Tue-Sat, 2-4pm Sat, 3-5pm & 7-9pm Sun; [S]A/C/E to 23rd St, A/C/E to 14th St, 1/2 to 18th St)

Kitchen

DANCE

53 ★ Map p88, C2

lA loft-like experimental space in west Chelsea that also produces edgy theater, readings and music performances, Kitchen is where you'll find new, progressive pieces and works-in-progress from local movers and shakers. (☎212-255-5793; www.thekitchen.org; 512 W 19th St btwn Tenth & Eleventh Aves; [S]A/C/E to 14th St, L to 8th Ave)

Shopping

Barneys Co-op

FASHION, ACCESSORIES

54 🔒 Map p88, D2

The edgier, younger, less expensive version of Barneys has (relatively) affordable deals at this expansive, loft-like space, with a spare, very selective inventory of clothing for men and women, plus shoes and cosmetics. The biannual warehouse sale (February and August) packs the place, with both endless merchandise and mobs of customers. (☎212-593-7800; 236 W 18th St; 🕒11am-8pm Mon-Fri, to 7pm Sat, noon-6pm Sun; [S]1 to 18th St)

Yoyamart

CHILDREN

55 🔒 Map p88, D3

Although it's ostensibly geared toward the younger set, Yoyamart is a fun place to browse for adults – even if you're not packing a child or two.

☑ Top Tip

Lost Like a Local

It's perfectly acceptable to arm yourself with a map (or rely on your smartphone) to get around the West Village's charming-but-challenging side streets. Even some locals have a tricky time finding their way! Just remember that 4th St makes a diagonal turn north – breaking away from usual east–west street grid – and you'll quickly become a Village pro.

Sure, you'll find adorable apparel for babies and toddlers, but there are also cuddly robots, Gloomy Bear gloves, plush ninjas, build-your-own-ukulele kits, CD mixes and various anime-style amusement. (☎212-242-5511; www.yoyashop.com; 15 Gansevoort St; ⏰11am-7pm Mon-Sat, noon-6pm Sun; 🚇A/C/E to 14th St, L to 8th Ave)

Strand Book Store   BOOKS

56 Map p88, G3

Book fiends (or even those who have casually skimmed one or two) shouldn't miss New York's most loved and famous bookstore. In operation since 1927, the Strand sells new, used and rare titles, spreading an incredible 18 miles of books (over 2.5 million of them) among three labyrinthine floors. Check out the staggering number of reviewers' copies in the basement, or sell off your own tomes before you get back on the plane, as the Strand buys or trades books at a side counter on weekdays. (☎212-473-1452; www.strandbooks.com; 828 Broadway at 12th St; ⏰9:30am-10:30pm Mon-Sat, 11am-10:30pm Sun; 🚇L, N/Q/R/W, 4/5/6 to 14th St-Union Sq)

Printed Matter   BOOKS

57 Map p88, C2

Printed Matter is a wondrous little two-room shop dedicated to limited-edition artist monographs and strange little zines. Here you will find nothing carried by mainstream bookstores. Instead, trim little shelves hide call-to-arms manifestos, critical essays about comic books, flip books that reveal Jesus' face through barcodes and how-to guides written by prisoners. (☎212-925-0325; 195 Tenth Ave btwn 21st & 22nd Sts; ⏰11am-6pm Tue & Wed, to 7pm Thu-Sat; 🚇C/E to 23rd St)

Bonnie Slotnick Cookbooks   BOOKS

Bonnie, the kindly owner of this great cookbook shop just near Julius Bar (see 36 Map p88, E4), dotes on her customers, who are searching for the perfect cooking tome. Stocked to the ceiling with shelf after shelf of the best recipes on earth, the shop – bedecked like grandma's pantry – is bound to reveal some truly unique finds, like themed references (Jewish, gay, soup-specific etc) to antique wares. (☎212-989-8962; www.bonnieslotnickcookbooks.com; 163 W 10th St btwn Waverly Pl & Seventh Ave; 🚇1/2 to Christopher St-Sheridan Sq, A/C/E, B/D/F, M to W 4th St, 1/2/3 to 14th St)

Three Lives & Company   BOOKS

58 Map p88, E4

Your neighborhood bookstore extraordinaire, Three Lives & Company is a wondrous spot that's tended by a coterie of exceptionally well-read individuals, which makes a trip to the store not just a pleasure, but an adventure in the magical world of words. (☎212-741-2069; www.threelives.com; 154 W 10th St, btwn Seventh Ave & Waverly Pl; 🚇1/2 to Christopher St-Sheridan Sq, A/C/E, B/D/F, M to W 4th St, 1/2/3 to 14th St)

SPENCER PLATT/GETTY IMAGES ©

Strand Book Store

The Bathroom
BEAUTY, HOMEWARES

59 🔒 Map p88, E4

Although most New York City shops tend to be kitchen-obsessed, Colin Heywood's boutique knows that the most important room in the house (or – in NYC – the apartment) is the bathroom. Styled like an old-school apothecary, this West Village wonder offers browsers a charming collection of handmade brands, which offer products from home goods to luxury soaps. (🎵212-929-1449; http://store. inthebathroom.com; 94 Charles St btwn W 4th & Bleecker Sts; ⏲noon-8pm Mon-Fri, 11am-8pm Sat, noon-7pm Sun; 🚇1/2 to Christopher St-Sheridan Sq, A/C/E, B/D/F, M to W 4th St, 1/2/3 to 14th St)

Jeffrey New York
FASHION

60 🔒 Map p88, C3

One of the pioneers in the Meatpacking District's makeover, Jeffrey sells several high-end designer clothing lines – Versace, Pucci, Prada, Michael Kors etc – as well as accessories, shoes and some cosmetics. DJs spinning pop and indie add to the hip vibe. (🎵212-206-1272; www.jeffreynewyork.com; 449 W 14th St; ⏲10am-8pm Mon-Sat, 12:30-6pm Sun; 🚇A/C/E to 14th St, L to 8th Ave)

Greenwich Letterpress
STATIONERY

Located a few shops over from Kettle of Fish (see 34 🔒 Map p88; E4) and founded by two sisters, this cute

MARTIN KREUZER/GETTY IMAGES ©

Stella McCartney

card shop specializes in wedding announcements and other specially made letterpress endeavors. Skip the stock postcards of the Empire State Building and send your loved ones a bespoke greeting card from this stalwart stationer. (212-989-7464; www. greenwichletterpress.com; 39 Christopher St btwn Seventh Ave & Waverly Pl; 1-6pm Mon, 11am-7pm Tue-Fri, noon-6pm Sat & Sun; S1/2 to Christopher St-Sheridan Sq, A/C/E, B/D/F, M to W 4th St, 1/2/3 to 14th St)

Marc by Marc Jacobs   FASHION

61   Map p88, D4

With five small shops sprinkled around the West Village, Marc Jacobs has established a real presence in this well-heeled neighborhood. Large

front windows allow easy peek-ing – assuming there's not a sale, during which you'll only see hordes of fawning shoppers. (212-924-0026; www.marcjacobs.com; 403-405 Bleecker St; noon-8pm Mon-Sat, to 7pm Sun; SA/C/E to 14th St, L to 8th Ave)

Stella McCartney   FASHION

62   Map p88, C3

More showroom than full-fledged store, McCartney's Meatpacking outpost has a minimal selection on hand, but, oh, what a selection it is. Drapy, gauzy, muted in color yet high on femininity, the delicate, ethereal clothes shine in this pared-down set-ting. Of course, McCartney's clothes are animal-product free, in keeping with her vegan philosophy. (☎212-255-1556; www.stellamccartney.com; 429 W 14th St; 🕒11am-8pm Tue-Sat, noon-6pm Sun; [S]A/C/E, L to 8th Ave-14th St)

Nasty Pig

CLOTHING

63 🛍 Map p88, D2

T-shirts, socks and underwear bearing the store's namesake, along with a bit of rubber and leather fetish wear, makes this an ideal stop for Chelsea boys and their admirers. (☎212-691-6067; 265 W 19th St btwn Seventh & Eighth Aves; [S]A/C/E to 14th St, 1/2 to 18th St, 1/2 to 23rd St)

Forbidden Planet

COMICS

64 🛍 Map p88, G3

Indulge your inner sci-fi nerd at Forbi. Find heaps of comics, books, manga, video games and figurines (ranging from *Star Trek* to *Where the Wild Things Are*). Fellow Magic and Yu-Gi-Oh! card-game lovers play upstairs in the public sitting area. (☎212-473-1576; 840 Broadway; 🕒10am-10pm Mon-Sat, 11am-8pm Sun; [S]L, N/Q/R/W, 4/5/6 to 14th St-Union Sq)

Abracadabra

ACCESSORIES

65 🛍 Map p88, F2

It's not just a Steve Miller Band song, it's also an emporium of horror, costumes and magic. Those who like this sort of thing will be hard-pressed to leave without racking up some credit-card bills. (☎212-627-5194; 19 W 21st St btwn Fifth & Sixth Aves; [S]N/R, 4/6 to 23 St)

192 Books

BOOKS

66 🛍 Map p88, C2

Located right in the gallery district is this small indie bookstore, with sections on literature, history, travel, art and criticism. A special treat is its offerings of rotating art exhibits, during which the owners organize special displays of books that relate thematically to the featured show or artist. Weekly book readings feature acclaimed (often NY-based) authors. (☎212-255-4022; www.192books.com; 192 Tenth Ave btwn 21st & 22nd Sts; 🕒11am-7pm Tue-Sat, noon-6pm Sun & Mon; [S]C/E to 23rd St)

Explore

Union Square, Flatiron District & Gramercy

The name 'Union Square' is quite apt since this neighborhood is the union of many disparate parts of the city; it's the urban glue linking unlikely cousins. Here, you'll feel the Village vibe spilling over with the likes of quirky cafes, funky shops and dreadlocked loiterers that mingles with a distinct commercial feel, replete with crowded lunch spots and after-work watering holes.

The Sights in a Day

Start the morning amid the colorful clash of personalities in **Union Square** (p113) – businessfolk dash to their offices and buskers juggle on the stone steps. If the **Union Square Greenmarket** (p122) is on, peruse freshly plucked produce from farms in the nearby Hudson Valley.

Wander by the ravishing **Flatiron Building** (p113) with its signature triangular shape, then check out **ABC Carpet & Home** (p122) for some serious souvenir shopping. Dine on-site at **ABC Kitchen** (p115) or try a classic New York carb at **Ess-a-Bagel** (p116). Wherever you decide to dine, make sure you wash it down with a hot chocolate at **City Bakery** (p116).

Take a sunset stroll around **Gramercy Park** (p114), then swing by the gourmet market at **Eataly** (p122) and take the elevator to the top to indulge in pork shoulder and hand-crafted brews at **Birreria** (p115), the lofted beer garden. If you're looking to class things up, go for a multi-course meal at **Eleven Madison Park** (p117), then end the night with a classic cocktail at **Raines Law Room** (p118).

♥ Best of New York City

Fine Dining
Birreria (p115)
Eataly (p122)

Local Eats
Ess-a-Bagel (p116)
City Bakery (p116)

LGBT
Boxers NYC (p120)

Shopping
ABC Carpet & Home (p122)

Parks
Madison Square Park (p114)
Gramercy Park (p114)

Getting There

S Subway A slew of subway lines converge below Union Square station, shuttling passengers up Manhattan's East Side on the 4, 5 and 6 lines, straight across to Williamsburg on the L, or up and over to Queens on the N, Q and R lines.

🚌 Bus The M14 and the M23 provide east–west service along 14th St and 23rd St respectively.

Union Sq

Sights

Union Square SQUARE

1  Map p112, B4

Union Sq is like the Noah's Ark of New York, rescuing at least two of every kind from the curling seas of concrete. In fact, one would be hard-pressed to find a more eclectic cross-section of locals gathered in one public place. Here, amid the tapestry of stone steps and fenced-in foliage, it's not uncommon to find denizens of every ilk: suited businessfolk gulping fresh air during their lunch breaks, dreadlocked loiterers tapping beats on their tabla, skateboarding punks flipping tricks on the southeastern stairs, rowdy college kids guzzling student-priced eats and throngs of protesting masses chanting fervently for various causes. (www.unionsquarenyc.org; 17th St btwn Broadway & Park Ave S; S L, N/Q/R/W, 4/5/6 to 14th St-Union Sq)

Flatiron Building LANDMARK

2  Map p112, B3

Built in 1902, the 20-story Flatiron Building, designed by Daniel Burnham, has a uniquely narrow triangular footprint that resembles the prow of a massive ship, and a traditional beaux arts limestone facade, built over a steel frame, which gets more complex and more beautiful the longer you stare at it. Best viewed from the traffic island north of 23rd St between

Broadway and Fifth Ave, this unique structure dominated the plaza back in the skyscraper era of the early 1900s. In fact, it was the world's tallest building until 1909. (Broadway cnr Fifth Ave & 23rd St; S N/R, 6 to 23rd St)

Madison Square Park   PARK

3 Map p112, B3

This park defined the northern reaches of Manhattan until the island's population exploded after the Civil War. It has enjoyed a rejuvenation in the past few years thanks to a renovation and re-dedication project. Now locals unleash their dogs here in the popular dog-run area and workers

enjoy lunches – which can be bought from the hip, on-site Shake Shack – while perched on the shaded benches or sprawled on the wide lawn. (www. nycgovparks.org; 23rd to 26th Sts btwn Fifth & Madison Aves; 6am-1am; S N/R, 6 to 23rd St)

Gramercy Park   PARK

4 Map p112, C3

This gorgeous, English-style park was created by Samuel Ruggles in 1831 after he drained the swamp in this area and laid out streets in a colonial style. It's one of the most inspired moments of calm in the city. It's a private park, so you can't enter, but it's

Understand
The Immortal Flatiron

The construction of the Flatiron Building (originally known as the Fuller Building) coincided with the proliferation of mass-produced picture postcards – the partnership was kismet. Even before its completion, there were images of the soon-to-be tallest tower circulating the globe, creating much wonder and excitement.

Publisher Frank Munsey was one of the building's first tenants. From his 18th-floor offices, he published *Munsey's Magazine*, which featured the writings of short-story writer William Sydney Porter, whose pen name was 'O Henry.' His musings, the paintings of John Sloan and the photographs of Alfred Stieglitz best immortalized the Flatiron back in the day – along with a famous comment by actress Katharine Hepburn, who said in an interview that she'd like to be admired as much as the grand old building.

Like many of New York City's monumental homages to civic progress, the Flatiron Building is still fully functional and houses an assortment of private businesses. Plans are underway to transform the building into a luxurious five-star hotel, but progress is on permanent hold until the final tenants willingly vacate the premises.

well worth peering through the iron gates. (E 20th St btwn Park & Third Aves; $\boxed{S}$6 to 23rd St)

Eating

Birreria AMERICAN $$

5 Map p112, A3

The crown jewel of Italian gourmet market Eataly is its rooftop beer garden tucked betwixt the Flatiron's corporate towers. A beer menu of encyclopedic proportions offers drinkers some of the best brews on the planet (watch out though – some bottles cost more than a main!). The signature pork shoulder is your frosty one's soul mate; big bellies should tack on a heaping side of farm-fresh mushrooms. (www.eatalyny.com; 200 Fifth Ave at 23rd St; mains $15-24; ⏱11:30am-midnight Sun-Wed, to 1am Thu-Sat; $\boxed{S}$F, N/R, 6 to 23rd St)

ABC Kitchen MODERN AMERICAN $$

A culinary avatar of the wildly wonderful home goods department store ABC Carpet & Home (see 26 🔒 Map p112; B4), ABC Kitchen's trim, cottage-like surrounds is neatly tucked behind the ballroom chandeliers and oriental drapery out front. Plates are as eclectic as the fairy-tale decor – though you'll never go wrong with an organic appetizer and one of the scrumptious whole-wheat pizzas. (☎212-475-5829; www.abckitchennyc.com; 35 E 18th St btwn Broadway & Park Ave; small plates $9-15;

Local Life
Food Trucks & Carts
The Union Sq and Flatiron areas have designated parking spaces for some of the best food trucks and carts in town. Head to the southwest corner of 14th St and Third Ave to check out trucks hawking their edible wares. The halal food cart at 28th St and Madison Ave has garnered quite a cult following – some say it's the tastiest one in town.

⏱5:30-10pm Sun-Thu, to 11:30pm Fri & Sat, last reservations half-hour prior; $\boxed{S}$L, N/Q/R, 4/5/6 to Union Sq)

Casa Mono TAPAS $$

6 Map p112, C4

Another winner from Mario Batali and Chef Andy Nusser, Casa Mono has a great, long bar where you can sit and watch your *pez espada a la plancha* (pan-grilled swordfish) and *gambas al ajillo* (shrimp in garlic) take a grilling. Or grab one of the wooded tables and nosh on tapas with *jerez* (sherry) from the bottles lining the walls. For a cheese dessert, hop next door to Bar Jamon, also owned by Batali; you may have to squeeze in – the place is communal and fun. (☎212-253-2773; www.casamononyc.com; 52 Irving Pl btwn 17th & 18th Sts; small plates $9-20; ⏱noon-midnight; $\boxed{S}$4/5/6, N/R/Q, L to Union Sq)

CHRIS GOODNEY/BLOOMBERG/GETTY IMAGES ©

Eleven Madison Park

Ess-a-Bagel

DELI $

7 🍴 Map p112, D3

It's simply impossible to resist the billowy tufts of sesame-scented smoke that waft out onto First Ave. Inside, crowds of lip-smacked locals yell at the bagel mongers for their classic New York snack topped with generous gobs of cream cheese. And those gaudy, jewel-dripping chandeliers jammed into the Styrofoam ceiling? You stay classy, Ess-a-Bagel. (☎212-260-2252; www.ess-a-bagel.com; 359 First Ave at 21st St; bagels from $1; 🕐6am-9pm Mon-Fri, to 5pm Sat & Sun; [S]L, N/Q/R, 4/5/6 to Union Sq)

City Bakery

BAK

8 🍴 Map p112, A4

A happy marriage between gourm entrees and cafeteria service, City Bakery is best known for its scrum tious drip coffee (look how they p the milk in first – yum!) and worl famous homemade hot chocolate crowned by a plump marshmallo the shape of a fairy's pillow. (☎212 366-1414; www.thecitybakery.com; 3 W 18 St btwn Fifth & Sixth Aves; hot chocolate cafeteria lunch per pound $14 ; 🕐7:30am Mon-Fri, 8am-7pm Sat, 10am-6pm Sun; [S]L, N/Q/R, 4/5/6 to 14th St-Union Sq)

Shake Shack

BURGERS **$**

9 Map p112, B3

Part of chef Danny Meyer's gourmet burger chainlet, Shake Shack whips up hyper-fresh burgers, crinkle-cut fries and a rotating line-up of frozen custards. Veg-heads can dip into the crisp Portobello burger. Lines are long, but worth it. (212-989-6600; www.shakeshack.com; cnr 23rd St & Madison Ave; hamburger from $3.50; ⏱lunch & dinner; R/W to 23rd St)

BaoHaus

TAIWANESE **$**

10 Map p112, D5

Blink and you'll miss this hole-in-the-wall and bastion of food-related pun-dom. Three-bite *bao* (Taiwanese pocket sandwiches) are whipped up in seconds by the sociable staffers. Go for the signature Chairman Bao (har har) – a thick slice of pork belly hugged by a cloudlike bun. (646-669-8889; www.baohausnyc.com; 238 E 14th St near Second Ave; bao from $3; ⏱11am-midnight Sun-Thu, 11.30am-4am Fri & Sat; L, N/Q/R, 4/5/6 to Union Sq)

Bite

SANDWICHES **$**

11 Map p112, C5

A sweet play on words ('bite' or 'bayit' means 'house' in Hebrew), this tribute to the hummus homeland is a no-frills snacking spot that whips up light, Mediterranean-inspired fare amid wood-paneled surrounds. Go for one of the pressed paninis – the eggplant pesto is a veggie's dream –

and wash it down with a muddy, home-brewed coffee. (212-677-3123; www.bitenyc.com; 211 E 14th St btwn Second & Third Aves; sandwiches $7.50; ⏱8am-noon Mon-Sat, 11am-9pm Sun; L, N/Q/R, 4/5/6 to Union Sq)

Eleven Madison Park

FRENCH **$$$**

12 Map p112, B3

An art deco wonder often overlooked in this star-studded town, Eleven Madison Park is welcoming enough to bring children into fine dining and delicious enough to please even the most discerning diner. The menu includes dishes such as muscovy duck with honey sauce, wild salmon with horseradish crust and fennel risotto, halibut mi-cuit (half-cooked) with carrots, and seasonal surprises. (212-889-0905; www.elevenmadisonpark.com; 11 Madison Ave btwn 24th & 25th Sts; four-course dinner $125; ⏱lunch & dinner; N/R, 6 to 23rd St)

 Local Life
Curry Hill

The four-block section north of Union Sq and Gramercy, traditionally known as Murray Hill, is sometimes referred to as Curry Hill – a nod to the numerous Indian restaurants and shops that proliferate here. Starting around E 28th St and flowing north on Lexington Ave to about E 33rd St, you'll find some of the finest Indian eateries in town – and most at bargain prices.

Nuela
PERUVIAN $$

13 🍴 Map p112, A3

Though the smooth lipstick reds and reflective black decor is somewhat reminiscent of a Shanghai bordello, Nuela's over-sleek surrounds can be easily forgiven with generous portions of fresh-from-the-sea ceviches, brilliantly battered potato wedges and frothy, meringue-topped pisco sours. (☎212-929-1200; www.nuelany.com; 43 W 24th St btwn Broadway & Sixth Ave; ceviches $10-18, mains $25-35; 🕒5:30-9pm Sun & Mon, to 10pm Tue-Thu, to 11pm Fri & Sat; [S]F, N/R, 6 to 23rd St)

Maialino
ITALIAN $$

14 🍴 Map p112, C3

Danny Meyer's done it again – take your taste buds on a Roman holiday at Maialino, sampling exquisite iterations of Italian peasant fare created from the greenmarket produce from down the street in Union Sq. You can come for a fresh cup of breakfast brew, but the lunchtime prix fixe (at a reasonable $35) should not be passed up. (☎212-777-2410; www.maialinonyc.com; 2 Lexington Ave at 21st St; mains $15-36; 🕒breakfast, lunch & dinner; [S]4/5, N/R to 23rd St)

Boqueria Flatiron
TAPAS $$

15 🍴 Map p112, A4

A holy union between Spanish-style tapas and market-fresh fare, Boqueria has wooed the after-work crowd with a brilliant assortment of smooth wines that wash down a selection of small plates showcasing the spectrum of recipes one can whip up using aged cheese, from-the-farm ham and organic vegetables. (☎212-343-4255; www.boquerianyc.com/flatiron.html; 53 W 19th St btwn Fifth & Sixth Aves; 🕒noon-midnight; [S]N/R/W to 23rd St)

Drinking

Raines Law Room
COCKTAIL BAR

16 🍷 Map p112, A4

A sea of velvet drapes and overstuffed leather lounge chairs, tin-tiled ceilings, the perfect amount of exposed brick and expertly crafted cocktails using perfectly aged spirits – these guys are about as serious as a mortgage payment when it comes to amplified atmosphere. Walk through the unassuming entrance and let Raines Law Room transport you to a far more sumptuous era. (www.raineslawroom.com; 48 W 17th St btwn Fifth & Sixth Aves; [S]F/M to 14th St, L to 6th Ave, 1/2 to 18th St)

Beauty Bar
THEME BAR

17 🍷 Map p112, D5

A kitschy favorite since the mid-'90s, this homage to old-fashioned beauty parlors pulls in a cool local crowd with its gritty soundtrack, nostalgic vibe and around $10 manicures (with a free Blue Rinse margarita thrown in) between Wednesday and Sunday. (☎212-539-1389; 531 E 14th St btwn Second & Third Aves;

Coffee at Maialino

⏱5pm-4am Mon-Fri, 7pm-4am Sat-Sun; Ⓢ L to 3rd Ave)

Rolf's Bar & Restaurant
THEME BAR

18 Map p112, C3

During the six weeks before Christmas, Rolf's transforms itself from a standard-fare German bar into a whimsical tribute to the yuletide season that falls somewhere between Santa's workshop and an *Addams Family* holiday party, with bulbous ornaments and hundreds of dolls that stare at you blankly while you swig your pint. (☎212-477-4750; www.rolfsnyc.com; 281 Third Ave btwn 21st & 22nd Sts;

⏱noon-4am; Ⓢ N/R, 4/6 to 23rd St, 4/6 to 28th St)

Crocodile Lounge
LOUNGE

19 Map p112, D5

Williamsburg comes to Manhattan! The Brooklyn success story Alligator Lounge – 20-something hideout with free pizza – has set up a 14th St outpost hauling in East Villagers seeking free dinner, some Skee-Ball and a few unusual microbrews on tap. (☎212-477-7747; 325 E 14th St btwn First & Second Aves; Ⓢ L to 1st Ave)

HUW JONES/LONELY PLANET IMAGES ©

Union Square Greenmarket (p122)

Boxers NYC

GAY

20 Map p112, A3

Dave & Busters meets David Bowie at this self-proclaimed gay sports bar in the heart of the Flatiron District. There's football on the TV, buffalo wings at the bar and topless wait staff keeping the pool cues polished. The drag theme on Mondays keeps everyone keenly aware that Boxers has a different definition of 'bromance.' (☎212-255-5082; www.boxersnyc.com; 37 W 20th St, btwn Fifth & Sixth Aves; **S**F, N/R, 6 to 23rd St)

Nowhere

GAY

21 Map p112, D5

Dark, dank and rife with flannel-clad fellas in super-skinny jeans: Nowhere is everything your local gay dive bar should be. The booze is priced for the '99%' and there's a pizza joint nearby, which keeps crowds hanging out 'til the wee hours of the morn. (☎212-477-4744; 322 E 14th St; **S**L, N/Q/R, 4/5/6 to Union Sq)

Splash Bar

GAY

22 Map p112, A4

As megaclubs come and go, this staple (found near Chelsea's eastern border with the Flatiron District) has become hotter than ever. It's a multilevel club that balances both a lounge and dance-club vibe, thanks to a mix of hang-out spaces, an unrivaled lineup of DJs, great special events and performances, and some of the most smokin' bartenders around. (☎212-691-0073; www.splashbar.com; 50 W 17th St btwn Fifth & Sixth Aves; ⏰5pm-4am Wed-Sat; §L to 6th Ave, F/V to 14th St)

71 Irving Place   CAFE

23 ☕ Map p112, C4

No one takes their coffee more seriously than Irving Farm, a quaint cafe just steps away from the peaceful Gramercy Park. Hand-picked beans are lovingly roasted on a farm in the Hudson Valley (about 90 miles from NYC) and imbibers can tell – this is one of the smoothest cups of joe you'll find in Manhattan. (Irving Farm Coffee Company; www.irvingfarm.com; 71 Irving Pl btwn 18th & 19th Sts; ⏰7am-10pm Mon-Fri, 8am-10pm Sat & Sun; §4/5/6, N/Q/R to 14th st-Union Sq, 4/6 to 23rd St)

Entertainment

Fuerza Bruta   PERFORMING ARTS

24 ⭐ Map p112, B4

Defying the laws of gravity and the theater-going experience in general, Fuerza Bruta is sensory overload on steroids as a visceral world of sound and fury is unleashed upon unwitting audience members. You've gotta see it to believe it. (Daryl Roth Theatre, 101 E 15th St at Union Sq; tickets $79-89, rush tickets $27; ⏰shows 8pm Wed-Fri, 7pm & 10pm Sat, 7pm Sun; §L, N/Q/R/W, 4/5/6 to 14th St-Union Sq)

Understand

Metronome

A walk around Union Sq reveals almost a dozen notable pieces of art – there's Rob Pruitt's 10ft homage to Andy Warhol and the imposing equestrian statue of George Washington. But on the south side of the square sits a massive art installation that either earns confused stares or simply gets overlooked by passersby. A symbolic representation of the passage of time, *Metronome* has two parts: a digital clock with a puzzling display of numbers and a wandlike apparatus with smoke puffing out of concentric rings. We'll let you ponder the latter while we give you the skinny on what exactly the winking orange digits denote. The 14 numbers must be split into two groups of seven. The seven from the left tell the current time (hour, minute, second, tenth-of-a-second) and the seven from the right are meant to be read in reverse order: they represent the remaining amount of time in the day.

Union Square Theater

THEATER

25 ★ Map p112, B4

The coolest thing about the Union Square Theater is that it's built in what used to be Tammany Hall, the seat of the most corrupt Democratic political machine that's ever ruled the city. Now the theater outrages the public in other ways, by hosting searing works like *The Laramie Project* and the side-splittingly funny (and un-PC) puppet show *Stuffed and Unstrung* (not for children). Campy musicals also pop up sometimes. (☎212-674-2267; www.nytheater.com; 100 E 17th St at Union Sq; [S] L, N/Q/R/W, 4/5/6 to 14th St-Union Sq)

Shopping

ABC Carpet & Home

HOMEWARES

26 🛍 Map p112, B4

Home designers and decorators stroll to ABC Carpet & Home to brainstorm ideas. Set up like a museum on six floors, ABC is filled with all sorts of furnishings, small and large, including easy-to-pack knickknacks, designer jewelry, global gifts, and more bulky antique furnishings and carpets. Come Christmas season the shop is a joy to behold: the decorators here go all out with lights and other wondrous touches. (☎212-473-3000; www.abccarpetandhome.com; 888 Broadway at 19th St; 🕘10am-7pm Mon-Wed & Fri, to 8pm Thu, 11am-7pm Sat, noon-6pm Sun; [S] L, N/Q/R/W, 4/5/6 to 14th St-Union Sq)

> ☑ Top Tip
>
> **Traffic on 14th Street**
>
> Human traffic can be overwhelming in Union Sq, especially along 14th St. If you're in a rush, or trying to hoof it on foot, then switch over to 13th St and you'll cover a lot more ground in much less time.

Union Square Greenmarket

MARKET

27 🛍 Map p112, B4

The Union Square Greenmarket is arguably the most famous greenmarket in NYC. It attracts many of the city's top chefs to its stalls – to finger aromatic greens, fresh yellow corn and deep-orange squashes. (17th St btwn Broadway & Park Ave S; 🕘10am-6pm Mon, Wed, Fri & Sat; [S] L, N/Q/R/W, 4/5/6 to 14th St-Union Sq)

Eataly

FOOD & DRINK

A 50,000-sq-ft tribute to the dolce vita, Mario Batali's food-filled wonderland is a New York–ified version of those dreamy Tuscan markets you find in Diane Lane films. Decked stem to stern with gourmet edibles, Eataly is a must for a picnic lunch – though make sure to leave room for some pork shoulder at the rooftop beer garden, Birreria (see **5** 🍴 Map p112, A3). (www.eatalyny.com; 200 Fifth Ave at 23rd St; [S] F, N/R, 6 to 23rd St)

Produce at Eataly

Idlewild Books

BOOKS

28 🔒 Map p112, A4

Idlewild is a great shopping destination when planning or even daydreaming about travel. Books are divided by region, and cover guidebooks as well as fiction, travelogues, history, cookbooks and other stimulating fare for delving into a country. The big windows overlooking the street, high ceilings and world globe display (all for sale) add to the charm. (☎212-414-8888; www.idlewildbooks.com; 12 W 19th St btwn Fifth & Sixth Aves; ⏰11:30am-8pm Mon-Fri, noon-7pm Sat & Sun; ⓢL, N/Q/R/W, 4/5/6 to 14th St-Union Sq)

Books of Wonder

BOOKS

29 🔒 Map p112, A4

Chelsea folks adore this small, fun-loving bookstore devoted to children's and young-adult titles. It's a great place to take the kids on a rainy day, especially when a kids' author is giving a reading or a storyteller is on hand. (☎212-989-3270; www.booksofwonder.com; 18 W 18th St btwn Fifth & Sixth Aves; ⏰10am-7pm Mon-Sat, 11am-6pm Sun; 👶; ⓢF/V, L to 6th Ave-14th St)

Midtown

Midtown is the home of the NYC found on postcards: flashing lights, Times Sq billboards, glittering Broadway theaters, canyons of sky-scrapers, endless streams of concrete roadways and bustling crowds that rarely thin. Scores of competitively priced hotels make it a great place to start and end your day during your New York foray.

The Sights in a Day

Midtown is big, bold and best seen on foot, so slice it up and enjoy it bit by bit. The top end of Fifth Ave (around the 50s) makes for a fabled introduction. It's here that you'll find glam icons like **Tiffany & Co** (p150) and the Plaza Hotel, not to mention the incredible **Museum of Modern Art** (p130). You could easily spend an entire day at the latter, ogling masterpieces, eating, drinking, catching a film and shopping for books and design objects.

Drop by Koreatown for lunch – **Hangawi** (p138) is a great choice – then wander betwixt the city's signature skyscrapers, including the **Chrysler Building** (p134), **Rockefeller Center** (p134) and the almighty **Empire State Building** (p128).

Bright and blinding **Times Square** (p126) is most spectacular at night. You'll find a TKTS Booth here selling cut-price Broadway tickets. The queues are usually shortest after 5.30pm. Catch a Broadway show, such as **Book of Mormon** (p145), then splurge on dinner at **Le Bernardin** (p137) before dancing away the calories in Hell's Kitchen, best known for its kickin' bars and gay scene, including **Industry** (p142).

 Top Sights

Times Square (p126)

Empire State Building (p128)

Museum of Modern Art (p130)

Best of New York City

Entertainment

Book of Mormon (p145)

Chicago (p145)

Wicked (p146)

Playwrights Horizons (p146)

Museums

Museum of Modern Art (p130)

Architecture

Empire State Building (p128)

Chrysler Building (p134)

Grand Central Terminal (p134)

Getting There

S Subway Midtown's main interchange stations are Times Sq–42nd St, Grand Central–42nd St and 34th St–Herald Sq.

Bus Useful for the western and eastern parts of Midtown. Routes include the 11 (northbound on Tenth Ave and southbound on Ninth Ave) and the M15 (northbound on First Ave and southbound on Second Ave).

Top Sights
Times Square

Love it or hate it, the intersection of Broadway and Seventh Ave (better known as Times Sq) is New York City's hyperactive heart: a restless, hypnotic torrent of glittering lights, bombastic billboards and raw urban energy. It's not hip, fashionable or in-the-know, and it couldn't care less. It's too busy pumping out iconic, mass-marketed NYC – yellow cabs, golden arches, soaring skyscrapers and razzle-dazzle Broadway marquees.

Map p132, D4

www.timessquare.com

Broadway at Seventh Ave

[S] N/Q/R, S, 1/2/3, 7 to Times Sq-42nd St

Don't Miss

New Year's Eve Everyday

Over one million people gather in Times Sq every New Year's Eve (NYE) to watch an illuminated Waterford Crystal ball descend at midnight – a mere 90-second spectacle that is arguably one of NYC's greatest anticlimaxes. Thankfully, you don't have to endure the crowds and cold to experience this short-lived thrill: the **Times Square Visitor Center** (Map p132, D3; 📱212-484-1222; www.timessquarenyc.org; 1560 Broadway btwn 46th & 47th Sts; ⏰8am-8pm; Ⓢ N/Q/R, S, 1/2/3, 7 to Times Sq-42nd St) offers a simulated NYE light show every 20 minutes year-round, as well as a close-up look at the Centennial Dropping Ball used in 2007.

Broadway

New York's Theater District covers an area stretching from 40th St to 54th St between Sixth and Eighth Aves, with dozens of Broadway and off-Broadway theaters that show everything from blockbuster musicals to new and classic drama. Unless there's a specific show you're after, the best – and most affordable – way to score tickets in the area is at the **TKTS Booth** (Map p132, D3; www.tdf.org/tkts; Broadway at W 47th St; ⏰3-8pm Wed-Sun, 2-8pm Tue, also 10am-2pm Tue-Sat, 11am-3pm Sun during matinee performances; Ⓢ N/Q/R, S, 1/2/3, 7 to Times Sq-42nd St), where you can line up and get same-day half-price tickets for top shows.

Views From the TKTS Booth

The TKTS Booth is an attraction in itself, with its illuminated roof of 27 ruby-red steps rising a panoramic 16ft above 47th St. Needless to say, the view across Times Sq from the top is a crowd-pleaser, so good luck finding a spot to rest.

☑ Top Tips

▶ If you must have your 15 seconds of fame, look for the giant monitor above the Forever 21 store at 1540 Broadway. The screen features a fashion model who, every now and then, takes a Polaroid of the crowd, shakes it out and zooms in on it. Ready for your close-up?

✗ Take a Break

For a panoramic overview over the square, order a drink at the Renaissance Hotel's **R Lounge** (Map p132, D3; www.rloungetimessquare.com; Two Times Square, 714 Seventh Ave at 48th St; ⏰11am-midnight Sun & Mon, to 1am Tue & Wed, to 2am Thu-Sat; Ⓢ N/Q/R to 49th St), which offers floor-to-ceiling glass windows of the neon-lit spectacle. It might not be the best-priced sip in town, but with a view like this, who's counting? Warp back in time with classic drinks at Rum House (p143), located in the Hotel Edison, a New York institution.

Top Sights
Empire State Building

The Chrysler Building may be prettier and One World Trade Center may now be taller, but the queen bee of the New York skyline remains the Empire State Building. It's Hollywood's tallest star, enjoying more than its fair share of close-ups in around one hundred films, from *King Kong* to *Independence Day*. No other building screams New York quite like it, and heading up to the top is as quintessential an experience as pastrami, rye and pickles at Katz's.

Map p18, E5

www.esbnyc.com

350 Fifth Ave at 34th St

adult/child $22/16, incl 102nd floor $37/31

🕗8am-2am

Ⓢ B/D/F/M, N/Q/R to 34th St-Herald Sq

Don't Miss

Observation Decks

The Empire State Building has two observation decks. The open-air 86th-floor deck offers an alfresco experience, with coin-operated telescopes for close-up glimpses of the metropolis in action. Further up, the enclosed 102nd-floor deck is New York's highest – at least until the opening of the observation deck at One World Trade Center in mid-2014. Needless to say, the views over the city's five boroughs (and five neighboring states, weather permitting) are quite simply exquisite. Both decks are especially spectacular at sunset, when the city dons its nighttime cloak in dusk's afterglow.

Light Shows

Since 1976, the building's top 30 floors have been floodlit in a spectrum of colors each night, reflecting seasonal and holiday hues. Famous combos include red, pink and white for Valentine's Day; green for St Patrick's Day; red and green for Christmas; and lavender for Gay Pride weekend in June. For a full rundown of the color schemes and meanings, check the website.

Astounding Statistics

The statistics of Gotham's most iconic tower are astounding: 10 million bricks, 60,000 tons of steel, 6400 windows and 328,000 sq ft of marble. Built on the original site of the Waldorf-Astoria, construction took a record-setting 410 days, using seven million hours of labor. Coming in at 102 stories, it's 1472 ft from top to bottom.

☑ Top Tips

▶ Alas, your passage to heaven will involve a trip through purgatory: the queues to the top are notorious. Getting here very early or very late will help you avoid delays – as will buying your tickets online ahead of time, where an extra $2 purchase charge is well worth the hassle it will save you.

▶ On the 86th floor between 10pm and 1am from Thursday to Saturday, the twinkling sea of lights below is accompanied by a live saxophone soundtrack (yes, requests are taken).

✕ Take A Break

Escape the maddening swarms of tourists and head to Koreatown, just a couple of blocks over, for some late-night grub after your sunset skyline viewing. Swing by darling dining destination Hangawi (p138) or try Gahm Mi Oak (p141) for midnight munchies.

Top Sights
Museum of Modern Art

Superstar of the modern art scene, the Museum of Modern Art's (MoMA) booty makes many other collections look...well...endearing. There are more A-listers here than at an Oscars after party: Van Gogh, Matisse, Picasso, Warhol, Lichtenstein, Rothko, Pollock, Bourgeois. Founded in 1929, the museum has amassed over 150,000 artworks, documenting the emerging creative ideas and movements of the late 19th century through to those of today. For art buffs, it's Valhalla. For the uninitiated, it's a thrilling crash course in all that is beautiful and addictive about art.

Map p18, E2

www.moma.org

11 W 53rd St

adult/child $25/free

⊙10:30am-5:30pm Sat-Mon, Wed & Thu, to 8pm Fri

S E/M to 5th Ave-53rd St

Museum of Modern Art exterior (architects: Yoshio Taniguchi and Kohn Pedersen Fox)

Don't Miss

Collection Highlights

MoMA's permanent collection spans four levels. Many of the big hitters are on the last two levels, so tackle the museum from the top down before the fatigue sets in. Must-sees include Van Gogh's *The Starry Night*, Cézanne's *The Bather*, Picasso's *Les Demoiselles d'Avignon* and Henri Rousseau's *The Sleeping Gypsy*, not to mention iconic American works like Warhol's *Campbell's Soup Cans* and *Gold Marilyn Monroe*, Lichtenstein's equally poptastic *Girl With Ball* and Hopper's haunting *House by the Railroad*.

Abby Aldrich Rockefeller Sculpure Garden

With architect Yoshio Taniguchi's acclaimed reconstruction of the museum in 2004 came the restoration of the Sculpture Garden to the original, larger vision of Philip Johnson's 1953 design. Johnson described the space as a 'sort of outdoor room,' and on warm, sunny days, it's hard not to think of it as a soothing, alfresco lounge. Famous works include Aristide Maillol's *The River*, which sits among scupltures from greats including Auguste Rodin, Alexander Calder and Henry Moore.

Film Screenings

Not only a palace of visual art, MoMA screens an incredibly well-rounded selection of celluloid gems from its collection of over 22,000 films, including the works of the Maysles Brothers and every Pixar animation film ever produced. Expect anything from Academy-nominated documentary shorts and Hollywood classics to experimental works and international retrospectives. Best of all, your museum ticket will get you in for free.

☑ Top Tips

▶ To maximize your time and create a plan of attack, download the museum's floor plan and visitor guide from the website beforehand.

✕ Take A Break

Don't miss one of the museum's carefully curated dining experiences. For communal tables and a super-casual vibe, nosh on Italian-inspired fare at **Cafe 2** (⏱11am-5pm Sat-Mon, Wed & Thu, to 7.30pm Fri;). For table service, à la carte options and Danish design, opt for **Terrace Five** (⏱11am-5pm Sat-Mon, Wed & Thu, to 7.30pm Fri). If you're after a luxe feed, book a table at fine-dining **Modern** (☎212-333-1220; www.themodernnyc.com; 3-/4-course lunch $55/70, 4-course dinner $98; ⏱restaurant lunch Mon-Fri, dinner Mon-Sat, bar 11.30am-10.30pm Mon-Thu, to 11pm Fri & Sat, to 9.30pm Sun), whose Michelin-starred menu serves up decadent, French-American creations.

A

West End Ave

W 60th St
W 59th St

B

Amsterdam Ave
Fordham University

Columbus Ave

W 58th St
W 57th St
W 56th St
W 55th St
W 54th St
W 53rd St
W 52nd St
W 51st St
W 50th St
W 49th St
W 48th St
W 47th St
W 46th St
W 45th St
W 44th St
W 43rd St

Tenth Ave
Ninth Ave

Time Warner Center

17 ✕

C

59th St-
Columbus Circle
Columbus Circle

D

Central Park

Center Dr

Central Park S

Broadway

57th St-
7th Ave S

57th St

32 ☆
13 ✕
40 ☆

7th Ave S

Seventh Ave

(Avenue of the Americas)

30 🚇

22 ✕

26 ☆

14 ✕
11 ✕

NYC & Company i

10 ✕

50th St S

50th St S

35 ☆
38 S

49th St S

47th-50th Sts-
Rockefeller Center S

33 ☆
34

Worldwide Plaza

THEATER DISTRICT

Eighth Ave

39 ☆

29 ☆

NYC & i Company

24 ✕

20 ✕
37 ☆

TIMES SQUARE

Hudson River Park

Twelfth Ave (West Side Hwy)

Dewitt Clinton Park

Eleventh Ave

HELL'S KITCHEN

W 42nd St
W 41st St
W 40th St

Pier 83

Pier 81

Lincoln Tunnel

42nd St
Port Authority S

31 ☆
36 ☆

Times Square ◉

42nd St-
Bryant Park S

42nd St-
Times Sq S

Port Authority Bus Terminal

Tenth Ave

Greenwich St

Ninth Ave

W 41st St

Bryant Park S

W 39th St
W 38th St
W 37th St
W 36th St
W 35th St

Eighth Ave

GARMENT DISTRICT

Seventh Ave

Broadway

Sixth Ave

50 🔒

34th St-
Penn Station S

HERALD SQUARE

51 🔒

Herald Sq

34th St-
Herald Sq S

For reviews see	
◉ Top Sights	p126
◎ Sights	p134
🍴 Eating	p137
🍷 Drinking	p142
☆ Entertainment	p144
🔒 Shopping	p149

W 34th St S
49 🔒
W 33rd St

42 ☆
Penn Station 🚇
W 32nd St

16

W 31st St

0 _____ 500 m
0 _____ 0.25 miles

Sights

Chrysler Building NOTABLE BUILDING

1 Map p132, F4

The 77-floor Chrysler Building makes most other skyscrapers look like uptight geeks. It was designed by William Van Alen in 1930 and is a dramatic fusion of art deco and Gothic aesthetics, adorned with stern steel eagles and topped by a spire that screams Bride of Frankenstein. The building was originally constructed as the headquarters for Walter P Chrysler and his automobile empire. More than 80 years on, Chrysler's ambitious $15-million statement remains one of New York City's most poignant symbols. (Lexington Ave at 42nd St; ☺lobby 8am-6pm Mon-Fri; ⓈS, 4/5/6, 7 to Grand Central-42nd St)

Grand Central Terminal NOTABLE BUILDING

2 Map p132, F3

Threatened by the debut of rival Penn Station (the majestic original, not the current eyesore), shipping and railroad magnate Cornelius Vanderbilt set to work on transforming his 19th-century Grand Central Depot into a 20th-century showpiece. The fruit of his envy is Grand Central Terminal, New York City's most breathtaking beaux arts building. More than just a station, Grand Central is an enchanted time machine, its swirl of chandeliers, marble, and historic bars and restaurants a porthole into an era where train travel and romance were not mutually exclusive. (www.grandcentralterminal.com; 42nd St at Park Ave; ☺5:30am-2am; ⓈS, 4/5/6, 7 to Grand Central-42nd St)

Take a Break Don't miss a drink at the **Campbell Apartment** (www.hospitalityholdings.com; 15 Vanderbilt Ave at 43rd St; ☺noon-1am Mon-Thu, to 2am Fri, 2pm-2am Sat, 3pm-midnight Sun; ⓈS, 4/5/6, 7 to Grand Central-42nd St).

Rockefeller Center NOTABLE BUILDING

3 Map p132, E2

This 22-acre 'city within a city' debuted at the height of the Great Depression. Taking nine years to build, it was America's first multi-use retail, entertainment and office space – a modernist sprawl of 19 buildings (14 of which are the original art deco structures), outdoor plazas and big-name tenants. Developer John D Rockefeller Jr may have sweated over the cost (a mere $100 million), but it was all worth it – the Center was declared a National Landmark in 1987. (www.rockefellercenter.com; Fifth to Sixth Aves & 48th to 51st Sts; ☺24hr, times vary for individual businesses; ⓈB/D/F/M to 47th-50th Sts-Rockefeller Center)

Radio City Music Hall NOTABLE BUILDING

4 Map p132, D2

Ladies and gentleman, boys and girls, welcome to the one and only Radio City Music Hall. This spectacular art

Understand
Midtown Skyscrapers: The Best of the Rest

Midtown's skyline is more than just the Empire State and Chrysler Buildings, with enough other beauties to satisfy the wildest of high-rise dreams. Celebrate all things phallic with three of Midtown's finest.

Lever House
Upon its debut, 21-story **Lever House** (Map p132, F2; 390 Park Ave btwn 53rd & 54th Sts; Ⓢ E, M to Fifth Ave-53rd St) was the height of cutting-edge. The UN Secretariat Building was the only other skyscraper to feature a glass skin, an innovation that would redefine urban architecture. The building's form was equally bold: two counter-posed rectangular shapes consisting of a slender tower atop a low-rise base. The open courtyard features marble benches by Japanese-American sculptor Isamu Noguchi, while the lobby exhibits contemporary art specially commissioned for the space.

Hearst Tower
Foster & Partners' **Hearst Tower** (Map p132, C1; 949 Eighth Ave btwn 56th & 57th Ave; Ⓢ A/C, B/D, 1 to 59th St-Columbus Circle) is one of New York's most creative works of contemporary architecture. Its diagonal grid of trusses evokes a jagged glass-and-steel honeycomb, best appreciated up close and from an angle. The tower rises above the hollowed-out core of John Urban's 1928 cast-stone Hearst Magazine Building, itself originally envisioned as a skyscraper. The 46-floor structure is also one of the city's greenest creations: around 90% of its structural steel is from recycled sources. In the lobby you'll find Riverlines, a mural by Richard Long.

Bank of America Tower
While striking for its crystal shape and piercing, 255ft spire, the **Bank of America Tower** (Map p132, D4; Sixth Ave btwn 42nd & 43rd Sts; Ⓢ B/D/F/M to 42nd St-Bryant Park) hit the headlines for its green credentials. The stats are impressive: a clean-burning, on-site cogeneration plant providing around 65% of the tower's annual electricity requirements; CO_2-detecting air filters that channel filtered air where needed; and even destination-dispatch elevators designed to avoid empty car trips. Designed by Cook & Fox Architects, it was awarded 'Best Tall Building in America' by the Council on Tall Buildings & Urban Habitat awards in 2010.

Local Life
America Today

While New York bursts with superlative artworks, some are too easy to miss. An outstanding example is Thomas Hart Benton's *America Today*, an epic, multipanel mural in the lobby of the **AXA Equitable Building** (Map p132, D2; 1290 Sixth Ave btwn 51st & 52nd Sts; ⏱11am-6pm Mon-Fri, noon-5pm Sat; Ⓢ B/D/F/M to 47th-50th Sts-Rockefeller Center).

Painted between 1930 and 1931, its intense color and rhythm are an energy-packed ode to American industry, progress and optimism during the Jazz Age. The panels capture a range of scenes, from the stoic toil of steel industry workers to the wild hedonism of dance-hall culture.

deco diva is a 5901-seat movie palace and was the brainchild of vaudeville producer Samuel Lionel 'Roxy' Rothafel. Roxy was never one for understatement, launching his venue on 23 December 1932 with an over-the-top extravaganza that included a Symphony of the Curtains (starring... you guessed it...the curtains) and the high-kick campness of precision dance troupe the Roxyettes (mercifully renamed the Rockettes). (www. radiocity.com; 1260 Sixth Ave at 51st St; tours adult/child $22.50/16; ⏱tours 11am-3pm; Ⓢ B/D/F/M to 47th-50th Sts-Rockefeller Center)

New York Public Library   CULTURAL BUILDING

5 ◎ Map p132, E4

Loyally guarded by 'Patience' and 'Fortitude' (the famous marble lions overlooking Fifth Ave), this beaux arts show-off is one of NYC's best free attractions. When dedicated in 1911, New York's flagship library ranked as the largest marble structure ever built in the US. To this day, its Rose Main Reading Room will steal your breath with its lavish, coffered ceiling. (Stephen A Schwarzman Building; www.nypl. org; Fifth Ave at 42nd St; ⏱10am-6pm Mon & Thu-Sat, to 8pm Tue & Wed, 1-5pm Sun, guided tours 11am & 2pm Mon-Sat, 2pm Sun; 📶; Ⓢ B/D/F/M to 42nd St-Bryant Park, 7 to Fifth Ave)

St Patrick's Cathedral   CHURCH

6 ◎ Map p132, E2

America's largest Catholic cathedral is a vision in neo-Gothic. Built at a cost of nearly $2 million during the Civil War, the building did not originally include the two front spires – those were added in 1888. Highlights include the Louis Tiffany–designed altar and Charles Connick's stunning Rose Window, the latter gleaming above a 7000-pipe church organ. (www. saintpatrickscathedral.org; Fifth Ave btwn 50th & 51st Sts; ⏱6.30am-8.45pm; Ⓢ B/D/F/M to 47th-50th Sts-Rockefeller Center)

Bryant Park
PARK

7 👁 Map p132, E4

European coffee kiosks, alfresco chess games, summer film screenings and winter ice-skating: it's hard to believe that this leafy oasis was dubbed 'Needle Park' in the '80s. Nestled behind the show-stopping New York Public Library building, it's a handy spot for a little time-out from the Midtown madness. (www.bryantpark.org; 42nd St btwn Fifth & Sixth Aves; ⏲7am-midnight Mon-Sat, to 11pm Sun May-Sep, 7am-10pm Sun-Thu, to midnight Fri & Sat Nov-Feb, 7am-7pm Mar, 7am-10pm Apr & Oct; 📶; [S] B/D/F/M to 42nd St-Bryant Park, 7 to Fifth Ave)

United Nations
NOTABLE BUILDING

8 👁 Map p132, H3

Welcome to the headquarters of the United Nations (UN), a worldwide organization overseeing international law, international security and human rights. While the soaring, Le Corbusier–designed Secretariat building is off-limits, 60-minute guided tours do take in the General Assembly, where the annual convocation of member nations takes place every fall, as well as exhibitions about the UN's work and artworks given by member states. (☎212-963-8687; www.un.org/tours; First Ave at 46th St; guided tour adult/child $16/11, children under 5yr not admitted; ⏲tours 9:45am-4:45pm Mon-Fri, 10am-4:15pm Sat & Sun, closed Sat & Sun Jan & Feb; 📶; [S] S, 4/5/6, 7 to Grand Central-42nd St)

Museum of Sex
MUSEUM

9 👁 Map p132, E5

From vintage vibrators to homosexual necrophilia in the mallard duck, 'MoSex' explores the world of sex in culture and nature. One long-running exhibition, *Action: Sex and the Moving Image,* examines representations of sex in mainstream cinema and pornography, while the permanent collection showcases everything from vintage blow-up dolls and homemade copulation machines to anti-onanism devices. (www.museumofsex.com; 233 Fifth Ave at 27th St; adult/child $17.50/$15; ⏲11am-8pm Sun-Thu, to 9pm Fri & Sat; [S] N/R to 23rd St)

Eating

Le Bernardin
SEAFOOD **$$$**

10 🍴 Map p132, D2

The interiors may have been slightly sexed-up for a 'younger clientele' (the stunning storm-themed triptych is by Brooklyn artist Ran Ortner), but triple Michelin-starred Le Bernardin remains a luxe, fine-dining holy grail. At the helm is celebrity chef Eric Ripert, whose deceptively simple-looking seafood often borders on the transcendental. (☎212-554-1515; www.le-bernardin.com; 155 W 51st St btwn Sixth & Seventh Aves; prix fixe lunch/dinner $75/125, tasting menus $145-190; ⏲lunch Mon-Fri, dinner Mon-Sat; [S] 1 to 50th St, B/D/E to 7th Ave)

Danji

KOREAN $$

11 🍴 Map p132, C2

Young-gun chef Hooni Kim has captured tastebuds with his Michelin-starred Korean 'tapas.' Served in a snug-and-slinky contemporary space, his drool-inducing creations are divided into 'traditional' and 'modern' options. Though the highlights are many, the celebrity dish is the sliders, a duo of bulgogi beef and spiced pork belly, each dressed with scallion vinaigrette and served on butter-grilled buns. Head in early or prepare to wait. (www.danjinyc.com; 346 W 52nd St; plates $7-20; 🕒lunch Mon-Fri, dinner Mon-Sat; [S]C/E to 50th St)

Hangawi

KOREAN $$

12 🍴 Map p132, E5

Sublime, flesh-free Korean is the draw at high-achieving Hangawi. Leave your shoes at the entrance and slip into a soothing, zen-like space of meditative music, soft low seating and clean, complex flavored dishes. Showstoppers include the leek pancakes and a seductively smooth tofu claypot in ginger sauce. (☎212-213-0077; www.hangawirestaurant.com; 12 E 32nd St btwn Fifth & Madison Aves; mains $17-25; 🕒lunch Mon-Sat, dinner daily; [S]B/D/F/M, N/Q/R to 34th St-Herald Sq)

Burger Joint

BURGERS $

13 🍴 Map p132, D1

With only a small neon burger as your clue, this speakeasy burger hut loiters

Understand

A Brief History of Times Square

At the turn of last century, Times Sq (p126) was known as Longacre Sq, an unremarkable intersection far from the city's commercial epicenter of Lower Manhattan. This changed with a deal between subway pioneer August Belmont and New York Times publisher Adolph Ochs. Heading construction of the city's first subway line (from Lower Manhattan to the Upper West Side and Harlem), Belmont realized that a business hub along 42nd St would maximize profit and patronage on the route. He then approached Ochs, who had recently turned around the fortunes of the *New York Times*, arguing that moving the newspaper's operations to the intersection of Broadway and 42nd St would be a win-win for Ochs. Not only would an in-house subway station mean faster distribution of the newspaper, but the influx of commuters to the square would mean more sales right outside its headquarters. Belmont even convinced New York Mayor George B McClellan Jr to rename the square in honor of the broadsheet.

KEVIN CLOGSTOUN/LONELY PLANET IMAGES ©

Chrysler Building (p134)

behind the curtain in lobby of the Le Parker Meridien hotel. If you find it, you'll stumble onto a thumping scene of graffiti-strewn walls, retro booths, and attitude-loaded staff slapping up beef-n-patty brilliance. (www.parkermeridien.com/eat4.php; Le Parker Meridien, 119 W 56th St; burgers $7; [S] F to 57th St)

Totto Ramen

JAPANESE $

14 🍴 Map p132, C2

Good things come to those who wait. Like tiny Totto. Write your name and number of guests on the clipboard by the door and wait for your (cash-only) ramen revelation. We recommend that you skip the chicken and go for the pork, which sings in dishes like miso ramen (with fermented soybean paste, egg, scallion, bean sprouts, onion and homemade chili paste). (www.tottoramen.com; 366 W 52nd St; ramen $9.50-12.50; ⏰ lunch Mon-Sat, dinner Mon-Sun; [S] C/E to 50th St)

The Smith

AMERICAN $$

15 🍴 Map p132, G2

Its name aglow in bold red neon, the Smith has sexed-up dining in the far eastern throws of Midtown with its industrial-chic interior, buzzing bar and well-exectued brasserie grub. With much of the food made from scratch on-site, the emphasis is on regional produce, retro American and Italian-inspired flavors, and slick and personable service. (www.thesmithnyc.com; 956 Second Ave at 51st St; mains $17-29;

Local Life

Koreatown

For kimchi and karaoke, it's hard to beat **Koreatown** (Map p132, E5; 31st to 36th Sts & Broadway to Fifth Ave; **S** B/D/F/M, N/Q/R to 34th St-Herald Sq). Mainly concentrated on 32nd St, with some spillover into the surrounding streets south and north of this strip, it's a Seoulful mix of Korean-owned restaurants, shops, salons and spas. Authentic BBQ is available around the clock at many of the spots on 32nd St, some with microphone, video screen and Manic Monday at the ready.

⊙7:30am-midnight Mon-Wed, to 1am Thu-Fri, 10am-1am Sat, to midnight Sun; **S** 6 to 51st St)

John Dory Oyster Bar SEAFOOD $$$

16 ✗ Map p132, D5

This loud, vibey seafood favorite sits just off the Ace Hotel lobby. Only hotel guests can book, so head in early for clever, tapas-style creations like sea urchin with pomegranate and black pepper, or chorizo-stuffed squid with smoked tomato. Between 5pm and 7pm, $15 gets you six oysters or clams and a glass of sparkling vino or ale. (www.thejohndory.com; 1196 Broadway at 29th St; small plates $9.50-25 ; ⊙noon-midnight; **S**N/R to 28th St)

A Voce ITALIAN $$$

17 ✗ Map p132, C1

Inside the swanky Time Warner mall, light, airy and modern A Voce combines sweeping views of Central Park with high-end interpretations of Italian classics. Think caramelized onion-filled ravioli with foie gras, balsamic and breadcrumbs; or grilled swordfish with chickpeas, broccoli and a sucker-punch *nduja* (spicy salami spread) vinaigrette. The well-versed wine list includes almost 20 drops by the glass. Book ahead. (☎212-823-2523; www.avocerestaurant.com; 10 Columbus Circle at 59th St; prix fixe lunch Mon-Fri $29, dinner mains $25-39; ⊙lunch & dinner daily, brunch Sat & Sun; **S**A/C, B/D, 1 to 59th St-Columbus Circle)

Social Eatz FUSION $

18 ✗ Map p132, G2

American comfort food gets an Asian twist at this hip, '70s-inspired diner. Celebrate inter-racial harmony with Korean beef tacos, St Louis pork ribs with *gochujang*-spiked BBQ sauce or Korean spiced slaw. Topping them all is the mighty Bibimbap Burger, voted America's best by prolific foodie website Eater. Well-priced and super tasty, this spot is a justifiable hit. (www.socialeatz.com; 232 E 53rd St btwn Second & Third Aves; burgers $8-11, salads $6-7; **S**E/M to Lexington Ave-53rd St)

El Parador Cafe MEXICAN $$

19 ✗ Map p132, G5

Back in the day, the far-flung location of this Mexican stalwart (serving here since 1970) was much appreciated by philandering husbands. The shady regulars may have gone, but the old-school charm remains, from the beveled candleholders and dapper Latino waiters, to the satisfying south-of-the-border standbys. (📞212-679-6812; www.elparadorcafe.com; 325 E 34th St; mains $18-29; 🕐noon-midnight, closed Sun Aug; 🚇6 to 33rd St)

Marseille
FRENCH, MEDITERRANEAN **$$**

20 Map p132, C3

A nostalgic fusion of theatrical lighting, sweeping curves and mirrored panels, this Hell's Kitchen gem looks somewhere between an old cinema lobby and an art deco brasserie. At once buzzing and romantic, it's a fabulous spot to kick back with a spiced pear martini and nibble on flavor-packed French-Med fare. (www.marseillenyc.com; 630 Ninth Ave at 44th St; mains $19-28.50; 🕐lunch & dinner; 🚇A/C/E to 42nd St-Port Authority)

Sarge's Deli
DELI **$$**

21 Map p132, F5

Sarge's is the underdog of historic Manhattan delis, leaving the tourists to its more famous rivals. It's like a scene from a '70s sitcom: brown vinyl booths filled with weathered cabbies, loud-mouthed businessmen and neurotic couples. Eavesdrop 24/7 over a pastrami sandwich, blintzes and matza ball chicken soup, but leave room for the pornographically good strawberry cheesecake – one slice is enough for two. (www.sargesdeli.com; 548 Third Ave btwn 36th & 37th Sts; mains $15-26; 🕐24hr; 🚇6 to 33rd St)

Bocca di Bacco
ITALIAN **$$**

22 Map p132, C2

With its art-slung walls and rustic interior, this electric restaurant/wine bar combo is Hell's Kitchen's take on the classic Italian enoteca. Sit at the bar for vino and impromptu conversation, or book a table for a more private tête-à-tête. Fueling the conversation is a repertoire of beautifully prepared Italian dishes, from soulful zuppe (soups) to sublime meats and seafood mains. (📞212-265-8828; www.boccadibacconyc.com; 828 Ninth Ave btwn 54th & 55th Sts; mains $16-24; 🕐dinner Mon-Sun; 🚇A/B, C/D, 1 to 59th St-Columbus Circle)

Gahm Mi Oak
KOREAN **$$**

23 Map p132, E5

If you're craving *yook hwe* (raw beef and Asian pear matchsticks) at 3am, this Koreatown savior has you covered. The shtick here is authenticity, shining through in dishes like the house specialty *sul long tang* (a milky broth of ox bones, boiled for 12 hours, and pimped with brisket and scallion). Korean wise man say *sul long tang* cure evil hangover. (43 W 32nd St btwn Broadway & Fifth Ave; dishes $10-22; 🕐24hr; 🚇N/Q/R, B/D/F/M to 34th St-Herald Sq)

El Margon
CUBAN **$**

24 Map p132, D3

It's still 1973 at this ever-packed Cuban lunch counter, where orange Laminex and greasy goodness never

PJ Clarke's

went out of style. Go for gold with its legendary cubano sandwich (a pressed panino jammed with rich roast pork, salami, cheese, pickles, mojo and mayo). Not only is it obscenely good, it's the city's best hangover cure. (136 W 46th St btwn Sixth & Seventh Aves; sandwiches from $4, mains $9; S B/D/F/M to 47-50th Sts-Rockefeller Center)

Drinking

Top of the Strand COCKTAIL BAR

25 Map p132, E4

For that 'Oh my God, I'm in New York' feeling, head to the Strand hotel's rooftop bar, order a martini (extra dirty) and drop your jaw (discreetly). Sporting slinky cabanas and a sliding glass roof, its view of the Empire State Building is unforgettable. (www.topofthes trand.com; Strand Hotel, 33 W 37th St btwn Fifth & Sixth Aves; ; S B/D/F/M to 34th St)

Industry GAY

26 Map p132, C2

What was once a parking garage is now the hottest gay bar in Hell's Kitchen – a slick 4000-sq-ft watering hole with handsome lounge areas, a pool table and a stage for top-notch drag divas. Head in between 4pm and 9pm for the two-for-one drinks special, or squeeze in later to party with the eye-candy party hordes. Cash only. (www.industry-bar.com; 355 W 52nd St btwn Eighth & Ninth Aves; ⏰4pm-4am; S C/E, 1 to 50th St)

Lantern's Keep

COCKTAIL BAR

27 Map p132, E3

Can you keep a secret? If so, cross the lobby of the Iroquois hotel and slip into this dark, intimate cocktail salon. Its speciality is pre-Prohibition libations, shaken and stirred by passionate, personable mixologists. If you're feeling spicy, request a Groom's Breakfast, a fiery melange of gin, hot sauce, Worcestershire sauce, muddled lime, cucumber, and salt and pepper. (☎212-453-4287; www.thelanternskeep.com; Iroquois Hotel, 49 W 44th St; ☺5pm-midnight Tue-Sat; Ⓢ B/D/F/M to 42nd St-Bryant Park)

PJ Clarke's

BAR

28 Map p132, F2

Another bastion of old New York, this lovingly worn wooden saloon has been straddling the scene since 1884. Buddy Holly proposed to his fiancée here and Old Blue Eyes pretty much owned table 20. Choose a jukebox tune, order a round of crab cakes and settle in with a come-one-and-all crowd of collar-and-tie colleagues, college students and nostalgia-longing urbanites. (www.pjclarkes.com; 915 Third Ave at 55th St; Ⓢ E/M to Lexington Ave-53rd St)

Rum House

COCKTAIL BAR

29 Map p132, C3

Not along ago, this was Hotel Edison's crusty old piano bar. Enter the capable team from Tribeca bar Ward III, who ripped out the green carpet, polished up the coppertop bar and revived this slice of old NYC. You'll still find a nightly pianist, but he's accompanied by well-crafted drinks and an in-the-know medley of whiskeys and rums. (www.edisonrumhouse.com; 228 W 47th St btwn Broadway & Eighth Ave; ☺11am-4am Mon-Sun; Ⓢ N/Q/R to 49th St)

Stumptown Coffee

CAFE

Hipster baristas in fedora hats brewing killer coffee? No, you're not in Williamsburg, you're at the Manhattan outpost of Portland's most celebrated coffee roaster. The queue is a small price to pay for proper espresso in Midtown, so count your blessings. It's standing-room only, though weary

Local Life
A Perfect Night out on Broadway

Broadway's biggest name – Tony Award winner Nikki M James, star of *Book of Mormon* – gives us her top picks for a perfect night out: 'When I have friends in town, I always send them to **Becco** (Map p132, C3; www.becco-nyc.com; 355 W 46th St; Ⓢ N/Q/R, S, 1/2/3, 7 to Times Sq-42nd St) after the show – they do a great Italian meal and, if you call in advance, they're very accommodating of larger parties. Afterwards, swing by Don't Tell Mama (p147) to check out some fun, offbeat cabaret. Or, class things up at **Print** (Map p132, A3; 653 11th Ave at 48th St; Ⓢ C/E to 50th St) for the city views and great drinks.'

Local Life

Brill Building & Music Row

The **Brill Building** (Map p132, D2; Broadway at 49th St) might look unassuming, but this 1930s veteran was a one-stop shop for artists in the 1960s, who could craft a song, cut a demo and (hopefully) convince a producer without ever leaving the building. Among the legends who did were Carole King, Bob Dylan, Joni Mitchell and Paul Simon. A few legacies live on, from sheet-music megastore **Colony** (Map p132, D3; www.colonymusic.com; 1619 Broadway; 🕒9am-1am Mon-Sat, 10am-midnight Sun; [S]N/Q/R to 49th St) to music outfitter **Rudy's Music** (Map p132, D3; www.rudysmusic.com; 169 W 48th St at Seventh Ave; 🕒closed Sun; [S]N/Q/R to 49th St) on W 48th St, a street once dubbed Music Row.

punters might find a seat in the adjacent Ace Hotel lobby near the John Dory Oyster Bar (see **16** 🍴 Map p132; D5). (www.stumptowncoffee.com; 18 W 29th St btwn Broadway and Fifth Ave; 🕒6am-8pm Mon-Sun; [S]N/R to 28th St)

Robert — COCKTAIL BAR

30 🍸 Map p132, C1

Perched on the 9th floor of the Museum of Arts & Design, '60s-inspired Robert is technically a high-end, modern-American restaurant. While the food is satisfactory, it's a bit overpriced, so head in late afternoon or post-dinner, find a sofa and gaze out over Central Park with a MAD Manhattan (Bourbon, Blood Orange Vermouth and liquored cherries). Magic. (www.robertnyc.com; Museum of Arts & Design, 2 Columbus Circle btwn Eighth Ave & Broadway; [S]A/C, B/D, 1 to 59th St-Columbus Circle)

Entertainment

Jazz at Lincoln Center — JAZZ

Perched high atop the Time Warner Center, Jazz at Lincoln Center together with A Voce (see **17** 🍴 Map p132; C1) consists of three state-of-the-art venues: the midsized Rose Theater, the panoramic, glass-backed Allen Room and the intimate, atmospheric Dizzy's Club Coca-Cola. It's the last one you're likely to visit given its regular, nightly shows. The talent is often exceptional, as are the dazzling Central Park views. (☎tickets to Dizzy's Club Coca-Cola 212-258-9595, tickets to Rose Theater & Allen Room 212-721-6500; www.jazzatlincolncenter.org; Time Warner Center, Broadway at 60th St; [S]A/C, B/D, 1 to 59th St-Columbus Circle)

Signature Theatre — THEATER

31 ★ Map p132, B4

Now in its new Frank Gehry–designed home – complete with three theaters, bookshop and cafe – Signature Theatre devotes entire seasons to the body of work of its playwrights-in-residence. To date, featured dramatists have included Tony Kushner, Edward Albee, Athol Fugard and Kenneth Lonergan. (☎tickets 212-244-7529; www. signaturetheatre.org; 480 W 42nd St btwn Ninth & Tenth Aves; Ⓢ A/C/E to 42nd St-Port Authority Bus Terminal)

Carnegie Hall
LIVE MUSIC

32 ⭐ Map p132, D1

This legendary music hall may not be the world's biggest or grandest, but it's one of the most acoustically blessed venues around. Opera, jazz and folk greats feature in the Isaac Stern Auditorium, with edgier jazz, pop, classical and world music in the hugely popular Zankel Hall. (☎212-247-7800; www. carnegiehall.org; W 57th St & Seventh Ave; Ⓢ N/Q/R to 57th St-7th Ave)

Book of Mormon
THEATER

33 ⭐ Map p132, C3

Subversive, obscene and ridiculously hilarious, this cutting musical satire is the work of *South Park* creators Trey Parker and Matt Stone and *Avenue Q* composer Robert Lopez. Winner of nine Tony Awards, it tells the story of two naive Mormons on a mission to 'save' a Ugandan village. (Eugene O'Neill Theatre; ☎tickets 212-239-6200; www. bookofmormonbroadway.com; 230 W 49th St btwn Broadway & Eigth Ave; Ⓢ N/Q/R to 49th St, 1 to 50th St, C/E to 50th St)

Chicago
THEATER

34 ⭐ Map p132, C3

This beloved Bob Fosse/Kander & Ebb classic – a musical about showgirl Velma Kelly, wannabe Roxie Hart, lawyer Billy Flynn and the fabulously sordid goings-on of the Chicago

Understand
The Early Days of Broadway

The Broadway of the 1920s was well-known for its lighthearted musicals, commonly fusing vaudeville and music hall traditions, and producing classic tunes like George Gershwin's *Rhapsody in Blue* and Cole Porter's *Let's Misbehave*. At the same time, Midtown's theater district was evolving as a platform for new American dramatists. One of the greatest was Eugene O'Neill. Born in Times Sq at the long-gone Barrett Hotel (1500 Broadway) in 1888, the playwright debuted many of his works here, including Pulitzer Prize winners *Beyond the Horizon* and *Anna Christie*. O'Neill's success on Broadway paved the way for other American greats like Tennessee Williams, Arthur Miller and Edward Albee. This surge of serious talent led to the establishment of the annual Tony Awards in 1947, Broadway's answer to Hollywood's Oscars.

underworld – has made a great come-back. This version, revived by director Walter Bobbie, is seriously alive and kicking. (Ambassador Theater; 🎫tickets 212-239-6200; www.chicagothemusical.com; 219 W 49th St btwn Broadway & Eighth Ave; **S**N/Q/R to 49th St, 1, C/E to 50th St)

Wicked

THEATER

35 ⭐ Map p132, C2

A whimsical, mythological and extravagantly produced prequel to *The Wizard of Oz*, this pop-rock musical – a stage version of Gregory Maguire's 1995 novel – gives the story's witches a turn to tell the tale. Its followers are an insanely cultish crew, attending frequent performances and launching all sorts of fan clubs, fansites and obsessive blogs to keep themselves occupied. (Gershwin Theatre; 🎫tickets 212-586-6510; www.wickedthemusical.com; 221 W 51st St btwn Broadway & Eighth Ave; **S**B/D/F/M to 47th-50th Sts-Rockefeller Center)

Top Tip
The Ticket Lottery

Show up around two hours before a Broadway show and put your name in the lottery to score front-row seats. *Book of Mormon*, for example, gives away around 20 tickets every night for $32. It's not easy to get tickets, but it can be a lot of fun hanging out with other fans, especially in good weather.

Playwrights Horizons

THEATER

36 ⭐ Map p132, B4

An excellent place to catch what could be the next big thing, this veteran 'writers' theater' is dedicated to fostering contemporary American works. Notable past productions include *Saved*, a musical by Michael Friedman based on the quirky film, as well as *I Am My Own Wife* and *Grey Gardens*, both of which moved on to Broadway. (🎫tickets 212-279-4200; www.playwrightshorizons.org; 416 W 42nd St btwn Ninth & Tenth Aves; **S**A/C/E to 42nd St-Port Authority Bus Terminal)

Birdland

JAZZ, CABARET

37 ⭐ Map p132, C3

Off Times Sq, it's got a slick look, not to mention the legend – its name dates from bebop legend Charlie Parker (aka 'Bird'), who headlined at the previous location on 52nd St, along with Miles, Monk and just about everyone else (you can see their photos on the walls). Covers run from $20 to $50 and the line-up is always stellar. (🎫212-581-3080; www.birdlandjazz.com; 315 W 44th St btwn Eighth & Ninth Aves; admission $10-50; ⏱club from 7pm, shows around 8:30pm & 11pm; ; **S**A/C/E to 42nd St-Port Authority Bus Terminal)

Caroline's on Broadway

COMEDY

38 ⭐ Map p132, D2

You may recognize this big, bright, mainstream classic from comedy specials filmed here on location. It's a top spot to catch US comedy big guns

Billboards at Times Sq

and sitcom stars, but for something a little more subversive, don't miss the late-late Friday night show *The Degenerates*. (☎212-757-4100; www.carolines.com; 1626 Broadway at 50th St; Ⓢ N/Q/R to 49th St, 1 to 50th St)

Don't Tell Mama

CABARET

39 ⭐ Map p132, C3

Piano bar and cabaret venue extraordinaire, Don't Tell Mama is an unpretentious little spot that's been around for more than 25 years and has the talent to prove it. Its regular roster of performers aren't big names, but true lovers of cabaret who give each show their all and don't mind a little singing help from the audience sometimes. (☎212-757-0788; www.

donttellmamanyc.com; 343 W 46th St; 2-drink minimum; ⊙4pm-1am; Ⓢ N/Q/R, S, 1/2/3, 7 to Times Sq-42nd St)

City Center

DANCE

40 ⭐ Map p132, D2

This Moorish, red-domed wonder almost went the way of the wrecking ball in 1943, but was saved by preservationists, only to face extinction again when its major ballet companies departed for the Lincoln Center. Today, it hosts dance troupes including the Alvin Ailey and American Dance Theater, theater productions, and the New York Flamenco Festival in February or March. (☎212-581-1212; www.nycitycenter.org; 131 W 55th St btwn Sixth & Seventh Aves; Ⓢ N/Q/R to 57th St-7th Ave)

Understand
TV Tapings

If you want to be part of a live studio audience for a TV taping, NYC is the place to do it. Just follow the following instructions. For more show ticket details, visit the websites of individual TV stations or try www.tvtickets.com.

Saturday Night Live Known for being difficult to get into. Try your luck in the fall lottery by sending an email to snltickets@nbcuni.com in August. Or line up by 7am the day of the show on the 49th St side of Rockefeller Plaza for standby tickets.

Late Show with David Letterman Request tickets online at www.cbs.com/lateshow or submit a request in person by showing up at the theater (1697 Broadway between 53rd and 54th Sts) between 9:30am and 12:30pm Monday to Friday, and 10am and 6pm Saturday and Sunday. Try for a standby ticket by calling ☎212-247-6497 at 11am on the day of the taping.

Daily Show with Jon Stewart Reserve tickets at least three months ahead at www.thedailyshow.com/tickets. If the day of taping you want is filled, try emailing requesttickets@thedailyshow.com.

Oak Room   CABARET

41 ⭐ Map p132, D3

Glam up, order a martini and get the Dorothy Parker vibe at this famous piano bar. Famed for launching the careers of Harry Connick Jr, Diana Krall and Michael Feinstein, its Sunday brunch often sees jazz veteran Barbara Carroll grace the piano. (www.algonquinhotel.com; Algonquin Hotel, 59 W 44th St btwn Fifth & Sixth Aves; Ⓢ B/D/F/V to 42nd St-Bryant Park)

Madison Square Garden   LIVE MUSIC

42 ⭐ Map p132, C5

NYC's major performance venue – part of the massive complex housing Penn Station and the WaMu Theater – hosts big-arena performers, from Kanye West to Madonna. It's also a sports arena, with New York Knicks, New York Liberty and New York Rangers games, as well as boxing matches and events like the Annual Westminster Kennel Club Dog Show. (www.thegarden.com; Seventh Ave btwn 31st & 33rd Sts; Ⓢ 1/2/3 to 34th St-Penn Station)

Therapy   GAY

Industry may be the street's new hot shot, but this multilevel, contemporary space was the first gay man's lounge-club to draw throngs to Hell's Kitchen. It still draws the crowds with its nightly shows (from music to comedy) and decent fare Sunday to Friday (burgers, hummus, salads). Drink monikers team with the theme: Oral Fixation and Size Queen, to name a few. Located near Totto Ramen (see **14** ❌ Map p132; C2). (www.therapy-nyc.com; 348 W 52nd St btwn Eighth & Ninth Aves; **S** C/E, 1 to 50th St)

Shopping

Barneys
DEPARTMENT STORE

43 🔒 Map p132, E1

Serious fashionistas shop at Barneys, well-known for its spot-on collections of in-the-know labels like Holmes & Yang, Kitsuné, Miu Miu and Derek Lam. For less expensive deals (geared to a younger market), check out Barneys Co-op on the 7th and 8th floors, then head to Fred's on the 9th floor for a well-earned prosecco. (www.barneys.com; 660 Madison Ave at 61st St; **S** N/Q/R to 5th Ave-59th St)

Bergdorf Goodman
DEPARTMENT STORE

44 🔒 Map p132, E1

Not merely loved for its Christmas windows (the city's best), BG gets the approval of the fashion cognoscenti for its exclusive labels and all-round fabulousness. Reinvent yourself with threads from the likes of John Varvatos, Marc Jacobs and Etro, then complete the picture with a lust-inducing booty of handbags, shoes, jewelry, cosmetics and homewares. The men's store is across the street.

(www.bergdorfgoodman.com; 754 Fifth Ave btwn 57th & 58th Sts; **S** N/Q/R to 5th Ave-59th St, F to 57th St)

Bloomingdale's
DEPARTMENT STORE

45 🔒 Map p132, F1

Fresh from a major revamp, epic 'Bloomie's' is something like the Metropolitan Museum of Art to the shopping world: historic, sprawling, overwhelming and packed with bodies, but you'd be sorry to miss it. Raid the racks for clothes and shoes from a who's who of US and global designers, including an increasing number of 'new-blood' collections. Refuel pitstops include a branch of cupcake heaven Magnolia Bakery. (www.bloomingdales.com; 1000 Third Ave at E 59th St; ⏱10am-8:30pm Mon-Fri, to 7pm Sat, 11am-7pm Sun; 🛜; **S** 4/5/6 to 59th St, N/Q/R to Lexington Ave-59th St)

MoMA Design & Book Store
BOOKS, GIFTS

The flagship store at the Museum of Modern Art (see ◉ Map p132; E2) is a savvy spot to souvenir-shop in one fell swoop. Aside from stocking must-have books (from art and architecture tomes to pop culture-readers and kids' picture books), you'll find art prints and posters, edgy homewares, jewelry, bags and one-of-a-kind knick-knacks. For furniture, lighting and MUJI merchandise, head to the MoMA Design Store across the street. (www.momastore.org; 11 W 53rd St btwn Fifth & Sixth Aves; **S** E/M to 5th Ave-53rd St)

○ Local Life

Garment District

The famed **Garment District** (Map p132, D3; Seventh Ave btwn 34th St & Times Sq; S N/Q/R, S, 1/2/3 & 7 to Times Sq-42nd St) is where you'll find a huge selection of fabrics, sequins and lace. Check out the sidewalk when you hit Seventh and 39th St and you'll catch the Fashion Walk of Fame, honoring the likes of Betsey Johnson, Marc Jacobs, Halston and other fashion visionaries. It's on the same corner as Claes Oldenburg's sculpture of the world's largest button, held upright by a 31ft-tall steel needle.

Saks Fifth Ave   DEPARTMENT STORE

46 🔒 Map p132, E2

Complete with beautiful vintage elevators, Saks' 10-floor flagship store fuses old-world glamor with solid service and must-have labels. Go luxe with the likes of Escada, Kiton and Brunello, or opt for younger, edgier, more affordable labels like Scotch & Soda, Vince and Rag & Bone. There's a decent selection of cosmetics and homewares, and its January sale is legendary. (www.saksfifthavenue.com; 611 Fifth Ave at 50th St; S B/D/F/M to 47th-50th Sts-Rockefeller Center, E/M to 5th Ave-53rd St)

Tiffany & Co   JEWELRY, HOMEWARES

47 🔒 Map p132, E1

This fabled jeweler, with its trademark clock-hoisting Atlas over the door, has won countless hearts with its luxe diamond rings, watches, silver Elsa Peretti heart necklaces, crystal vases and glassware. Swoon, drool, but whatever you do, don't harass the elevator attendants with tired 'Where's the breakfast?' jokes. (www.tiffany.com; 727 Fifth Ave; S F to 57th St)

FAO Schwarz   CHILDREN

48 🔒 Map p132, E1

The toy store giant, where Tom Hanks played footsy piano in the movie *Big*, is number one on the NYC wish list of most visiting kids. Why not indulge them? The magical (over-the-top consumerist) wonderland, with dolls up for 'adoption,' life-size stuffed animals, gas-powered kiddie convertibles, air-hockey sets and much more, might even thrill you, too. (www.fao.com; 767 Fifth Ave; S 4/5/6 to 59th St, N/Q/R to 5th Ave-59th St)

B&H Photo-Video   ELECTRONICS

49 🔒 Map p132, C5

Visiting NYC's most popular camera shop is an experience in itself – it's massive and crowded, and bustling with black-clad (and tech-savvy) Hasidic Jewish salesmen bussed in from communities in distant Brooklyn neighborhoods. Your chosen item is dropped into a bucket, which then moves up and across the ceiling to the purchase area (which requires a second queue). (www.bhphotovideo.com; 420 Ninth Ave btwn 33th & 34th Sts; ⊘9am-7pm Mon-Thu, to 1pm Fri, 10am-6pm Sun; S A/C/E to 34th St-Penn Station)

Drama Book Shop
BOOKS

50 [🛍] Map p132, C4

Broadway fans will find treasures in print at this expansive bookstore, which has taken its theater (both plays and musicals) seriously since 1917. Staffers are good at recommending worthy selections, which span the classics to current hits. Check the website for regular events, which include talks with playwrights. (www.dramabookshop.com; 250 W 40th St btwn Seventh & Eighth Aves; ⏲11am-7pm Mon-Wed, Fri & Sat, to 8pm Thu; [S] A/C/E to 42nd St-Port Authority Bus Terminal)

Macy's
DEPARTMENT STORE

51 [🛍] Map p132, D5

The world's largest department store covers most bases, with clothing, furnishings, kitchenware, sheets, cafes, hair salons and even a branch of the Metropolitan Museum of Art gift store. It's more 'mid-priced' than 'exclusive,' with affordable mainstream labels and big-name cosmetics. Plus, riding the creaky wooden elevators between the 8th and 9th floors on the Broadway side is a must-do NYC experience. (www.macys.com; 151 W 34th St at Broadway; [S] B/D/F/M, N/Q/R to 34th St-Herald Sq)

Argosy
BOOKS

52 [🛍] Map p132, F1

Since 1925, this landmark used-book store has stocked fine antiquarian items such as leatherbound books, old maps, art monographs and other classics picked up from high-class estate sales and closed antique shops. Interesting extras including autographed publicity stills from classic TV shows like *MASH*. Prices range from costly to clearance. (www.argosybooks.com; 116 E 59th St; ⏲10am-6pm Mon-Fri year-round, to 5pm Sat Sep–mid-May; [S] 4/5/6 to 59th St, N/Q/R to Lexington Ave-59th St)

Dylan's Candy Bar
FOOD & DRINK

53 [🛍] Map p132, F1

Willy Wonka has nothing on this three-level feast of giant swirly lollipops, crunchy candy bars, glowing jars of jelly beans, softball-sized cupcakes and a luminescent staircase embedded with scrumptious, unattainable candy. Stay away on weekends to avoid being pummeled by small, sugar-crazed kids. There's a cafe for hot chocolate, espresso, ice cream and other pick-me-ups on the 2nd floor. (www.dylanscandybar.com; 1011 Third Ave at 60th St; ⏲10am-9pm Mon-Thu, to 10pm Fri & Sat, 11am-9pm Sun; [S] N/Q/R to Lexington Ave-59th St)

Explore

Upper East Side

High-end boutiques line Madison Ave and sophisticated mansions run parallel along Fifth Ave, which culminates in an architectural flourish called Museum Mile – one of the most cultured strips in the city, if not the world. It's here that you'll find the gigantic Metropolitan Museum of Art holding court with its faithful siblings – Guggenheim, Whitney and Frick – in orbit.

The Sights in a Day

☼ A day on the Upper East Side can easily be devoted to the Big Apple's clutch of world-class museums – it's a great neighborhood to explore on days with unfavorable weather. Start at the **Metropolitan Museum of Art** (p154), the mothership of museums. You could very well spend the entire day here, but its best to cut yourself off after two hours if you're going to fit in the opulent **Frick Collection** (p161) and the stunning **Neue Galerie** (p162).

☼ Join the 'ladies who lunch' crowd with a late bite at **Via Quadronno** (p165) or **Café Sabarsky** (p165), then recaffeinate at **Sant Ambroeus** (p165) before filling the afternoon with a medley of contemporary wonders, starting at the **Guggenheim Museum** (p158) and finishing at the **Whitney Museum of American Art** (p161).

☾ Return to the Met for a round of pre-dinner drinks at the **Metropolitan Museum Roof Garden Café & Martini Bar** (p167), then gorge on burgers served on saucers at **JG Melon** (p165). For a taste of classic New York cabaret, try for seats at **Feinstein's at the Regency** (p169).

 Top Sights

Metropolitan Museum of Art (p154)

Guggenheim Museum (p158)

💜 **Best of New York City**

Local Eats

William Greenberg Desserts (p166)

Via Quadronno (p165)

Museums

Metropolitan Museum of Art (p154)

Guggenheim Museum (p158)

Frick Collection (p161)

Neue Galerie (p162)

Museum of the City of New York (p163)

Architecture

Whitney Museum of American Art (p161)

Temple Emanu-El (p163)

Getting There

S Subway The sole subway lines here are the 4/5/6, which travel north and south on Lexington Ave.

🚌 Bus The M1/2/3/4 buses make the scenic drive down Fifth Ave along Central Park. The M15 can be handy for getting around the far east side.

Top Sights
Metropolitan Museum of Art

This sprawling encyclopedic museum, founded in 1870, houses one of the biggest art collections in the world. Its permanent collection has more than two million individual objects, from Egyptian temples to American paintings. Known colloquially as 'The Met,' the museum attracts almost six million visitors a year to its 17 acres of galleries – making it the largest single-site attraction in New York City. (Yup, you read that right: 17 acres.) In other words, plan on spending some time here. It is BIG.

Map p18, A2

www.metmuseum.org

1000 Fifth Ave at 82nd St

adult/child $25/free

⏱9:30am-5:30pm Tue-Thu & Sun, to 9pm Fri & Sat

Ⓢ4/5/6 to 86th St

Greek art at the Metropolitan Museum of Art

Don't Miss

Egyptian Art

The museum has an unrivaled collection of ancient Egyptian art, some of which dates back to the Paleolithic era. Located to the north of the Great Hall, the 39 Egyptian galleries open dramatically with one of the Met's prized pieces: the Mastaba Tomb of Perneb (c 2300 BC), an Old Kingdom burial chamber crafted from limestone. From here, a web of rooms is cluttered with funerary stele, carved reliefs and fragments of pyramids. These eventually lead to the Temple of Dendur (Gallery 131), a sandstone temple to the goddess Isis that resides in a sunny atrium gallery with a reflecting pool.

European Paintings

On the museum's 2nd floor, the European Paintings' galleries display a stunning collection of masterpieces. This includes more than 1700 canvases from the roughly 500-year-period starting in the 13th century, with works by every important painter from Duccio to Rembrandt. On the north end, in Gallery 615, is Vermeer's tender 17th-century painting *A Maid Asleep*. Gallery 608, to the west, contains a luminous 16th-century altar by Renaissance master Raphael. And in a room stuffed with works by Zurbarán and Murillo (Gallery 618), there is an array of paintings by Velázquez, the most extraordinary of which depicts the dashing Juan de Pareja.

Art of the Arab Lands

The New Galleries for the Art of the Arab Lands, Turkey, Iran, Central Asia, and Later South Asia are comprised of 15 incredible rooms that showcase the museum's extensive collection of art from the Middle East and Central and South

☑ Top Tips

▶ A desk inside the Great Hall has audio tours in several languages ($7), while docents offer guided tours of specific galleries. These are free with admission. Check the website or information desk for details.

▶ The museum crowds can often be overbearing. If you're looking for a bit of calm, it's best to avoid the Met on weekends at all costs.

✗ Take a Break

In the warmer months (April to October), wander up to the roof garden for brilliant views of Central Park and its abutting skyscrapers. You'll also find the Roof Garden Café & Martini Bar (p167), the best place in the museum for a sip — especially at sunset.

Asia. In addition to garments, secular decorative objects and manuscripts, you'll find treasures such as a 12th-century ceramic chess set from Iran (Gallery 453). There is also a superb array of Ottoman textiles (Gallery 459), a medieval-style Moroccan court (Gallery 456) and an 18th-century room from Damascus (Gallery 461).

American Wing

In the museum's northwest corner, the recently revamped American galleries showcase a wide variety of decorative and fine art from throughout US history. These include everything from colonial portraiture to Hudson River School masterpieces to John Singer Sargent's unbearably sexy *Madame X* (Gallery 771) – not to mention Emanuel Leutze's massive canvas of *Washington Crossing the Delaware* (Gallery 760).

Greek & Roman Art

The 27 galleries devoted to classical antiquity are another Met must, some of which are dramatically illuminated by natural daylight. From the Great Hall, a passageway takes viewers through a barrel-vaulted room flanked by the chiseled torsos of Greek figures. This spills right into one of the Met's loveliest spaces: the airy Roman sculpture court (Gallery 162), full of marble carvings of gods and historical figures. The statue of a bearded Hercules from AD 68–98 is particularly awe-inspiring.

Roof Garden

One of the best spots in the entire museum is the roof garden, which features rotating sculpture installations by contemporary and 20th-century artists. (Sol Lewitt, Jeff Koons and Andy Goldsworthy have all shown here.) But its best feature is the views it offers of the city and Central Park. The roof garden is open from April to October.

Metropolitan Museum of Art

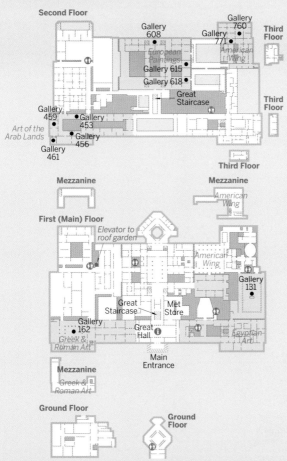

Top Sights
Guggenheim Museum

A sculpture in its own right, architect Frank Lloyd Wright's building almost overshadows the collection of 20th-century art within. Completed in 1959, the inverted ziggurat structure was initially derided by some critics, but the swishing spirals of white quickly became a beloved architectural icon, featuring on countless postcards, TV programs and films.

Map p18, A1

www.guggenheim.org

1071 Fifth Ave at 89th St

adult/child $18/free

⊙10am-5:45pm Sun-Wed & Fri, to 7:45pm Sat

Ⓢ4/5/6 to 86th St

Don't Miss

Permanent Collection Galleries

Although the Museum of Modern Art has garnered a reputation in New York City for having a more robust collection of oeuvres, the Guggenheim is very much a heavy hitter as well, boasting a variety of art from the 20th and 21st centuries. Hanging on the white-washed walls are works by the likes of Kandinsky, Picasso, Chagall, Jackson Pollock, Van Gogh, Monet, Magritte and Degas. Much of the Guggenheim's art is made up of several personal collections, including those of Justin Thannhauser, Peggy Guggenheim and the Robert Mapplethorpe Foundation, which generously bequeathed 200 photographs, making the museum the single-most important public repository of his work.

Exterior Views of the Facade

An architectural marvel from the outside and within, the Guggenheim didn't always garner the praise it does today. In fact, in 1959, when it opened, the structure was savaged by the *New York Times*, which lambasted it as 'a war between architecture and painting in which both come out badly maimed.' Beyond early criticism, the edifice itself was a logistical nightmare to build. Construction was delayed for almost 13 years due to budget constraints, the outbreak of WWII and outraged neighbors who weren't all that excited to see an architectural spaceship land in their midst. Construction was completed in 1959, after both Wright and Guggenheim had passed away.

INTERIOR OF THE SOLOMON R. GUGGENHEIM MUSEUM, NEW YORK ©THE SOLOMON R. GUGGENHEIM FOUNDATION.

☑ Top Tips

▶ The line to get in to the museum can be brutal at any time of the year. You'll save a lot of time if you purchase your tickets in advance on the website.

▶ Admission is by donation between 5:45pm and 7:45pm on Saturdays.

✗ Take a Break

There are two good on-site food options: **Wright** (☏ 212-427-5690; www. thewrightrestaurant.com; mains $21-27; ⊙ 11:30am-3:30pm Fri-Wed), at ground level, a space-age eatery serving steamy risotto and classic cocktails, and **Cafe 3** (www.gug genheim.org; sandwiches $8; ⊙ 10:30am-5pm Fri & Sun-Wed, to 7pm Sat), on the 3rd floor, which offers sparkling views of Central Park and excellent coffee and light snacks.

Jacqueline Kennedy Onassis Reservoir

86th St Transverse

Guggenheim Museum

Metropolitan Museum of Art

79th St Transverse

Central Park

Conservatory Water

72nd St Transverse

The Mall

65th St Transverse

The Pond

Central Park S

YORKVILLE

Carl Schurz Park

UPPER EAST SIDE

John Jay Park

Rockefeller University

Roosevelt Island

East River

Franklin D Roosevelt Dr

East End Ave

York Ave

First Ave

Second Ave

Third Ave

Lexington Ave

Park Ave

Madison Ave

Fifth Ave

East Dr

E 93rd St
E 92nd St
E 91st St
E 90th St
E 89th St
E 88th St
E 87th St
E 86th St
E 85th St
E 84th St
E 83rd St
E 82nd St
E 81st St
E 80th St
E 79th St
E 78th St
E 77th St
E 76th St
E 75th St
E 74th St
E 73rd St
E 72nd St
E 71st St
E 70th St
E 69th St
E 68th St
E 67th St
E 66th St
E 65th St
E 64th St
E 63rd St
E 62nd St
E 61st St
E 60th St
E 59th St

86th St
68th St-Hunter College
77th St
Lexington Ave-63rd St
Lexington Ave-59th St
5th Ave-59th St
59th St

Roosevelt Island Tramway Station

Queensboro-59th St Bridge

500 m
0.25 miles

For reviews see

◉	Top Sights	p154
◎	Sights	p161
✖	Eating	p164
⊖	Drinking	p167
☆	Entertainment	p169
⊕	Shopping	p170

Whitney Museum of American Art (architects: Marcel Breuer and Hamilton P Smith)

Sights

Whitney Museum
of American Art   MUSEUM

1 ◎ Map p160, B3

The Whitney makes no secret of its mission to provoke, which starts with its imposing Brutalist building, a structure that houses works by 20th-century masters Edward Hopper, Jasper Johns, Georgia O'Keeffe and Mark Rothko. In addition to rotating exhibits, there is a biennial on even years, an ambitious survey of contemporary art that rarely fails to generate controversy. (☎212-570-3600, 800-944-8639; www.whitney.org; 945 Madison Ave cnr 75th St; adult/child $18/free;

⊙11am-6pm Wed, Thu, Sat & Sun, 1-9pm Fri; §6 to 77th St)

Frick Collection   GALLERY

2 ◎ Map p160, A4

This spectacular art collection sits in a mansion built by prickly steel magnate Henry Clay Frick, one of the many such residences that made up Millionaires' Row. The museum has 12 splendid rooms that display masterpieces by Titian, Vermeer, Gilbert Stuart, El Greco and Goya. The Oval Room is graced by Jean-Antoine Houdon's stunning figure *Diana the Huntress*. The museum is generally not crowded and feels refreshingly intimate. Children under 10 are not admitted. (📞212-288-0700; www.frick.org; 1 E 70th St at Fifth Ave; admission $18, by donation 11am-1pm Sun; ⏱10am-6pm Tue-Sat, 11am-5pm Sun; 🚇6 to 68th St-Hunter College)

Neue Galerie
MUSEUM

3 ◎ Map p160, A2

This restored Carrère and Hastings mansion from 1914 is a resplendent showcase for German and Austrian art, featuring works by Paul Klee, Ernst Ludwig Kirchner and Egon Schiele. In pride of place on the 2nd floor is Gustav Klimt's golden 1907 portrait of Adele Bloch-Bauer – which was acquired for the museum by cosmetics magnate Ronald Lauder for a whopping $135 million. This is a small but beautiful place with winding staircases and wrought-iron banisters. Children under 12 are not admitted. (📞212-628-6200; www.neuegalerie.org; 1048 Fifth Ave cnr E 86th St; admission $20, 6-8pm 1st Fri of every month free; ⏱11am-6pm Thu-Mon; 🚇4/5/6 to 86th St)

Local Life
Road Runners

The long-time club and organizer of the New York City Marathon, **New York Road Runners Club** (Map p160, A1; www.nyrrc.org; 9 E 89th St btwn Madison & Fifth Aves; ⏱10am-8pm Mon-Fri, to 5pm Sat, to 3pm Sun; 🚇4/5/6 to 86th St), coordinates runs throughout the year, including a midnight fun run on New Year's Eve.

Jewish Museum
MUSEUM

4 ◎ Map p160, A1

This New York City gem is tucked into a French-Gothic mansion from 1908, which houses 30,000 items of Judaica, as well sculpture, paintings and decorative arts. The museum is well regarded for its thoughtful temporary exhibits, featuring retrospectives on influential figures such as Chaim Soutine and sprawling examinations of socially conscious photography in New York. (📞212-423-3200; www.jewishmuseum.org; 1109 Fifth Ave at 92nd St; adult/child $12/free, 11am-5:45pm Sat free; ⏱11am-5:45pm Thu-Tue, to 4pm Fri; ♿; 🚇6 to 96th St)

National Academy Museum
MUSEUM

5 ◎ Map p160, A1

Co-founded by painter/inventor Samuel Morse in 1825, the National Academy Museum is comprised of an incredible permanent collection of paintings by figures such as Wil Barnet, Thomas Hart Benton and George Bellows. (The collection includes some highly compelling self-portraits.) The museum is housed in a beaux arts structure designed by architect Ogden Codman, which features a marble foyer and spiral staircase. (📞212-369-4880; www.nationalacademy.org; 1083 Fifth Ave at 89th St; adult/child $12/free; ⏱noon-5pm Wed & Thu, 11am-6pm Fri-Sun; 🚇4/5/6 to 86th St)

Temple Emanu-El SYNAGOGUE

6 Map p160, A4

Founded in 1845 as the first Reform synagogue in New York and completed in 1929, this temple is now one of the largest Jewish houses of worship in the world. An imposing Romanesque structure, it is more than 175ft long and 100ft tall, with a brilliant, hand-painted ceiling that contains details in gold. (☎212-744-1400; www.emanuelnyc.org; 1 E 65th St cnr Fifth Ave; admission free; 🕒10am-5pm Mon-Thu; [S] 6 to 68th St-Hunter College)

Museum of the City of New York MUSEUM

7 Map p160, A1

Situated in a colonial Georgian-style mansion, this local museum focuses solely on New York City's past, present and future. You'll find internet-based historical resources, lots of vintage photographs and a scale model of New Amsterdam shortly after the Dutch arrival. The 2nd-floor gallery includes entire rooms from demolished homes of New York grandees. (☎212-534-1672; www.mcny.org; 1220 Fifth Ave btwn 103rd & 104th Sts; suggested donation $20; 🕒10am-6pm; [S] 6 to 103rd St)

Asia Society & Museum MUSEUM

8 Map p160, B4

Founded in 1956 by John D Rockefeller, this cultural center is meant to strengthen Western understanding of Asia and the relationships between

Neue Galerie

Asia and the US. There are events and lectures, but the biggest draw is the museum, which shows rotating contemporary exhibits, as well as treasures – such as Jain sculptures and Nepalese Buddhist paintings. (☎212 288 6400; www.asiasociety.org; 725 Park Ave at 70th St; admission $10, 6-9pm Fri mid-Sept–Jun free; 🕒11am-6pm Tue-Sun, to 9pm Fri mid-Sept–Jun; [S] 6 to 68th St-Hunter College)

Gracie Mansion HISTORIC BUILDING

9 Map p160, D1

This Federal-style home served as the country residence of merchant Archibald Gracie in 1799. Since 1942, it has been where New York's mayors have lived – with the

Salad at Café Boulud

exception of megabillionaire Mayor Michael Bloomberg, who prefers his own plush, Upper East Side digs. The house has been added to and renovated over the years. Reservations required. (☎212-570-4773, tour reservations 311 or 212-NEW-YORK; www.nyc.gov/gracie; East End Ave at E 88th St; admission $7; 🕒tours 10am, 11am, 1pm & 2pm Wed; [S]4/5/6 to 86th St)

Cooper-Hewitt National Design Museum

MUSEUM

10 ◎ Map p160, A1

Part of the Smithsonian Institution in Washington, DC, this house of culture is the only museum in the country that's dedicated to both historic and contemporary design. The collection is housed in the 64-room mansion built by billionaire Andrew Carnegie in 1901. The museum closed in 2011 for a two-year renovation and expansion. Check the website for updates. (☎212-849-8400; www.cooperhewitt.org; 2 E 91st St at Fifth Ave; adult/child $15/free; [S]4/5/6 to 86th St)

Eating

Café Boulud

FRENCH $$$

11 🍴 Map p160, A3

Now steered by Gavin Kaysen, this Michelin-starred bistro – part of Daniel Boulud's gastronomic empire – attracts a staid crowd with its globe-trotting French cuisine. Seasonal menus include classic dishes such as coq au vin, as well as more inventive fare (scallop crudo with white miso). Foodies on a budget will be interested in the two-course, $37 prix fixe lunch. (📞 212-772-2600; www.danielnyc.com/cafe bouludny.html; 20 E 76th St at Madison Ave; mains $24-44; ⊙ breakfast, lunch & dinner; ✈; Ⓢ 6 to 77th St)

JG Melon
PUB $

12 🍴 Map p160, B3

JG's is a loud, old-school, melon-themed pub that has been serving basic burgers on tea plates since 1972. It's a local favorite for both eating and drinking (the Bloody Marys are excellent) and it gets crowded in the after-work hours. If you're feeling claustrophobic, try lunchtime instead. (📞 212-744-0585; 1291 Third Ave at 74th St; burgers $10; ⊙ 11:30am-4am; Ⓢ 6 to 77th St)

Café Sabarsky
AUSTRIAN $$

The lines get long at this popular cafe at the Neue Galerie (see 3 ⊙ Map p160; A2), which evokes opulent turn-of-the-century Vienna. But the well-rendered Austrian specialties make the wait worth it. Expect crepes with smoked trout, goulash soup and creamed spätzle (a type of German noodle). And save room for dessert: there is a long list of specialty sweets, including a divine Sacher torte (dark chocolate cake laced with apricot preserves). (www.kg-ny.com; 1048 Fifth Ave at E 86th St; mains $12-20; ⊙ breakfast, lunch & dinner; ✈ 🚺; Ⓢ 4/5/6 to 86th St)

Via Quadronno
CAFE $$

13 🍴 Map p160, A3

A little slice of Italy that looks like it's been airlifted into New York, this cozy cafe-bistro has exquisite coffee (rich, not bitter), as well as a mind-boggling selection of sandwiches – one of which is stuffed with venison prosciutto and Camembert. There are soups, pastas and a very popular daily lasagna. (📞 212-650-9880; www.viaquadronno.com; 25 E 73rd St btwn Madison & Fifth Aves; sandwiches $7-17, mains $20-26; ⊙ 8am-11pm Mon-Fri, 9am-11pm Sat, 10am-9pm Sun; ✈; Ⓢ 6 to 77th St)

Earl's Beer & Cheese
AMERICAN $

14 🍴 Map p160, B1

Chef Corey Cova's comfort-food outpost channels a hipster hunting vibe, complete with buck's head on the wall. Rest assured that these aren't warmed-over American classics. Basic grilled cheese is a paradigm shifter, served with pork belly, fried egg and kimchi. There is also mac 'n' cheese and waffles (with foie gras), none of it like anything you've ever eaten. (www.earlsny.com; 1259 Park Ave btwn 97th & 98th Sts; grilled cheese $6-8, mains $8-17; ⊙ 4pm-midnight Tue-Fri, 11am-midnight Sat & Sun; Ⓢ 6 to 96th St)

Sant Ambroeus
CAFE $$

15 🍴 Map p160, A3

Behind a demure facade lies this dressy Milanese bistro and cafe that oozes old-world charm. Up front, a long granite counter dispenses inky espressos, pastries and tea sandwiches (think vegetable frittata and parma ham), while the elegant dining room in the back dishes up northern Italian specialties such as octopus salad and saffron risotto. (212-570-2211; www. santambroeus.com; 1000 Madison Ave btwn 77th & 78th St; tea sandwiches $8, pastries $10, mains $22-48; 8am-11pm; ; **S** 6 to 77th St)

Luke's
SEAFOOD $$

16 Map p160, C2

This place delivers one hell of a succulent lobster roll: a buttered, toasted, split-top bun stuffed with chilled lobster salad that is dabbed with a swipe of mayonnaise and a sprinkle of lemon butter. Simple and delicious. There are several other locations around town. (www.lukeslobster.com; 242 E 81st St near Second Ave; lobster roll $15; 11am-10pm Sun-Thu, to 11pm Fri & Sat; **S** 6 to 77th St)

Top Tip
In Search of Cheap Eats
The Upper East Side is ground zero for all things luxurious, especially the area that covers the blocks from 60th to 86th Sts between Park and Fifth Aves. As a general rule, if you're looking for eating and drinking spots that are easier on the wallet, head east of Lexington Ave. First, Second and Third Aves are lined with less pricey neighborhood spots.

Sandro's
ITALIAN $$

17 Map p160, C2

This neighborhood trattoria serves up fresh Roman dishes and homemade pastas by chef Sandro Fioriti. Specialties include crisp-fried artichokes and sea urchin ravioli. From 4:30pm to 6:30pm on weekdays, all pasta dishes are priced according to the closing average of the Dow Jones Index. (If the Dow closes at 11,000, your pasta will be $11.) Or as Sandro likes to say: 'When the Dow goes down, your value goes up!' (212-288-7374; www.sandros nyc.com; 306 E 81st St near Second Ave; mains $20-35; 4:30-11pm Mon-Sat, to 10pm Sun; **S** 6 to 77th St)

William Greenberg Desserts
BAKERY $

18 Map p160, A2

This pristine bakery serves up a delectable array of traditional Jewish treats, including *hamantaschen* (a triangular, jam-filled cookie), cupcakes, brownies and what has to be New York City's finest black-and-white cookie, a soft vanilla disc dipped in white sugar and dark chocolate glaze. Take-out only. (www.wmgreenbergdesserts.com; 1100 Madison Ave btwn 82nd & 83rd Sts; baked goods from $1.50; 8am-6:30pm Mon-Fri, to 6pm Sat, 10am-4pm Sun; ; **S** 4/5/6 to 86th St)

Candle Cafe
VEGAN $$

19 Map p160, B3

The moneyed yoga set piles into this attractive vegan cafe, which serves a long list of sandwiches, salads, comfort food and market-driven specials. The specialty at Candle Cafe is the house-made seitan. (Try it crusted with porcini and served with mashed potatoes and gravy – the perfect cold-day dish.) There is also a juice bar and a gluten-free menu. (☎212-472-0970; www.candlecafe.com; 1307 Third Ave btwn 74th & 75th Sts; mains $15-20; ⌚11:30am-10:30pm Mon-Sat, to 9:30pm Sun; 🥕; [S]6 to 77th St)

Yura on Madison

DELI $

20 🍴 Map p160, A1

Yura is a crisp, white emporium of yuppiedom, which sells fresh sandwiches, premade salads and excellent scones. Everything here is designed for quick eating or take-out. The ready-made box lunches are ideal for Central Park picnics. (www.yuraonmadison.com; 1292 Madison Ave cnr E 92nd St; sandwiches $6-9, box lunches $7-10; ⌚6:30am-7pm Mon-Fri, 7am-4pm Sat & Sun; 🥕👪; [S]6 to 96th St)

Drinking

Metropolitan Museum Roof Garden Café & Martini Bar

COCKTAIL BAR

21 🍷 Map p160, A2

The sort of setting you can't get enough of (even if you are a jaded local). The Metropolitan Museum of Art's roof-garden bar sits right above Central Park's tree canopy, allowing for splendid views of the park and the city skyline all around. Sunset is when you'll find fools in love – then again, it could all be those martinis. (www.metmuseum.org; 1000 Fifth Ave at 82nd St; ⌚10am-4:30pm Sun & Tue-Thu, to 8pm Fri & Sat, Martini Bar 5:30-8pm Fri & Sat May-Oct; [S]4/5/6 to 86th St)

BLOOMBERG/GETTY IMAGES ©

Bemelmans Bar

Bemelmans Bar

LOUNGE

22 🍷 Map p160, B3

Sink into a chocolate leather banquette and take in the glorious 1940s elegance of this fabled bar – the sort of place where the waiters wear white jackets, a baby grand is always tinkling and the ceiling is 24-carat gold leaf. Show up before 9:30pm if you don't want to pay a cover (per person

DAN HERRICK/LONELY PLANET IMAGES ©

Frick Collection courtyard

$15 to $30). (www.thecarlyle.com/dining/
bemelmans_bar; Carlyle Hotel, 35 E 76th St
at Madison Ave; ☻noon-2am Mon-Sat, to
12:30am Sun; **S**6 to 77th St)

Heidelberg

BEER GARDEN

23 📍 Map p160, C2

Beer, schnapps and schnitzel. This
old-school German beer garden
supplies the trifecta of Teutonic pleasure – as well as servers decked out
in Bavarian costume. Feeling thirsty?
You can order your Spaten in a 2L
Stiefel (glass boot). Hokey-good fun.
Ein Prosit! (www.heidelbergrestaurant.
com; 1648 Second Ave btwn 85th & 86th Sts;
☻11:30am-10pm Sun-Thu, to 11pm Fri & Sat;
S4/5/6 to 86th St)

Luke's Bar & Grill

PUB

24 📍 Map p160, C3

This laid-back local hangout offers a
respite from Red Bull and ridiculous
drink prices, with an inexpensive
selection of beers and solid pub grub,
including burgers and salads. There's
also a weekend brunch. Cash only.
(www.lukesbarandgrill.com; 1394 Third Ave
btwn 79th & 80th Sts; ☻11:30am-1am Mon-
Fri, to 2am Sat; **S**6 to 77th St)

Iggy's

KARAOKE

25 📍 Map p160, C3

How much you love this skinny
Irish-lite pub with its 100ft long bar
depends on how badly you need to
misbehave in the Upper East Side. The

karaoke mic certainly helps the raucous regulars, who bring on a bit of a frat-house atmosphere some nights. (www.iggysnewyork.com; 1452 Second Ave; ☾noon-4am; Ⓢ6 to 77th St)

Entertainment

Feinstein's at the Regency
CABARET

26 ⭐ Map p160, B5

You'll be puttin' on the ritz at this old-school cabaret spot from crooner Michael Feinstein. The storied stage has hosted everyone from Rosemary Clooney to Vikki Carr to Tony Danza. (Yes, Tony Danza.) It's a small room, so buy tickets in advance if you want to catch the big-name Broadway acts. (www.feinsteinsattheregency.com; 540 Park Ave at 61st St; tickets $40-280; Ⓢ F to Lexington Ave-63rd St, N/Q/R to Lexington Ave-59th St)

Café Carlyle

This swanky spot sits at the Carlyle Hotel along with Bemelmans Bar (see 22 Map p160, B3) and draws top-shelf talent, from Bettye Lavette to Woody Allen, who plays his clarinet here with the Eddy Davis New Orleans Jazz Band on Mondays at 8:45pm (September through May). Bring bucks: the cover doesn't include food or drinks. (www.thecarlyle.com/dining/cafe_carlyle; 35 E 76th St at Madison Ave; cover $90-175; Ⓢ6 to 77th St)

Frick Collection
CLASSICAL MUSIC

The opulent mansion-museum Frick Collection (see 2 ◎ Map p160; A 4) also hosts Sunday concerts that bring world-renowned performers such as cellist Yehuda Hanani and violinist Thomas Zehetmair. This is a lovely, intimate space and a very special type of concert experience. (www.frick.org; 1 E 70th St at Fifth Ave; Ⓢ6 to 68th St-Hunter College)

92nd St Y
CULTURAL CENTER

27 ⭐ Map p160, B1

In addition to its wide spectrum of wonderful readings, this nonprofit cultural center hosts an excellent lecture and conversation series. Past presenters have included playwright Edward Albee, cellist Yo-Yo Ma, crooner Lou Reed and novelist Gary Shteyngart. (www.92y.org; 1395 Lexington Ave at 92nd St; 🚹; Ⓢ6 to 96th St)

Comic Strip Live
COMEDY

28 ⭐ Map p160, C2

Adam Sandler, Jerry Seinfeld and Eddie Murphy have all performed at this club. Not recently, but you're sure to find somebody stealing their acts here most nights. Seriously, folks, it'll get you out of your hotel room for a few laughs – at least until you get your bill. Is this thing on? Reservations required. (☏212-861-9386; www.comicstrip live.com; 1568 Second Ave btwn 81st & 82nd Sts; cover charge $22-28 plus 2-drink min; ☾shows 8:30pm Sun-Thu, 8:30pm, 10:30pm

& 12:30pm Fri, 8pm, 10:30pm & 12:30am Sat; S 4/5/6 to 86th St)

Shopping

Encore

CONSIGNMENT STORE

29  Map p160, A2

An exclusive consignment shop has been emptying out Upper East Side closets since the 1950s. (Jacqueline Kennedy Onassis used to sell her clothes here.) Expect to find a gently worn array of name brands such as Louboutin, Fendi and Dior. Prices are high but infinitely better than retail. (www.encoreresale.com; 1132 Madison Ave btwn 84th & 85th Sts; ⏰10:30am-6:30pm Fri-Wed, to 7:30pm Thu, noon-6pm Sun; S 4/5/6 to 86th St)

Arthritis Foundation Thrift Shop

THRIFT STORE

30  Map p160, B2

When local bargain hunters are looking for steals, this is where they head: a charity-driven Upper East Side thrift store where cheap designer frocks are known to materialize within stacks of everyday cast-offs. It's closed on weekends in July and August. (1430 Third Ave at 81st St; ⏰9:30am-6pm Mon-Wed & Sat, to 8pm Thu ; S 4/5/6 to 86th St)

Encore

MARK LENNIHAN/CORBIS ©

Michael's

CONSIGNMENT STORE

31 🛍 Map p160, B3

In operation since the 1950s, this is a vaunted Upper East Side resale shop that is strong on high-end labels, including Chanel, Gucci and Prada. Almost everything on display is less than two years old. It's pricey, but cheaper than shopping the flagship boutiques on Madison Ave. (www.michaelsconsignment.com; 2nd fl, 1041 Madison Ave btwn 79th & 80th Sts; ⏰9:30am-6pm Mon-Sat, to 8pm Thu; [S]6 to 77th St)

Crawford Doyle Booksellers

BOOKS

32 🛍 Map p160, A2

This genteel Upper East Side book shop invites browsing, with stacks devoted to art, literature and the history of New York – not to mention plenty of first editions. A wonderful place to while away a chilly afternoon. (1082 Madison Ave btwn 81st & 82nd Sts; ⏰10am-6pm Mon-Sat, noon-5pm Sun; [S]6 to 77th St)

Blue Tree

FASHION, HOMEWARES

33 🛍 Map p160, B1

A charming (and expensive) little boutique sellling a dainty array of women's clothing, Lucite objects and quirky home design items, such as pig butter dishes and metallic Harry Allen banana bowls. (www.bluetreenyc.com; 1283 Madison Ave btwn 91st & 92nd Sts; ⏰10am-6pm Mon-Fri, 11am-6pm Sat & Sun; [S]4/5/6 to 86th St)

Zitomer

BEAUTY

34 🛍 Map p160, B3

This three-story retro pharmacy carries all things European, including products that aren't exactly (ahem) FDA approved. We're not talking illicit drugs, just high-powered sunscreens and skin-care creams that are usually only available across the pond. An excellent spot to cure what ails you, or simply window shop. (www.zitomer.com; 969 Madison Ave btwn 75th & 76th Sts; ⏰9am-8pm Mon-Fri, to 7pm Sat, 10am-6pm Sun; [S]6 to 77th St)

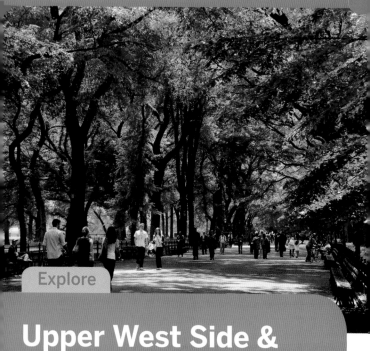

Explore

Upper West Side & Central Park

New York's antidote to the endless stretches of concrete, Central Park is a verdant escape from honking horns and sunless sidewalks. The Upper West Side lines the park with inspired residential towers, each one higher than the next. This area is most notably home to Lincoln Center, largely considered to hold the greatest concentration of performance spaces in town.

The Sights in a Day

Start things off at the **American Museum of Natural History** (p180), where you can zoom through outer space in the planetarium or gaze at the reassembled bones of a Tyrannosaurus Rex. Afterwards, walk over to **Zabar's** (p182) to pack a gourmet picnic for later.

When the weather's in your favor, fill the rest of the day in **Central Park** (p174). Spread a blanket on a patch of green, then take in the park's myriad sights, like the Bethesda Fountain, the Central Park Zoo and the Great Lawn. Pause for a drink at the **Loeb Boathouse** (p183), then hire a paddle boat for a quick jaunt around the lake.

As the sun begins to tuck behind the fortress of highrises lining the four corners of the park, it's time to head to **Lincoln Center** (p180) – the city's unofficial headquarters for performance pursuits – to visit the city's other 'Met,' the **Metropolitan Opera House** (p187). Enjoy a late-night dinner at one of the neighborhood's all-star eateries, such as **Dovetail** (p183).

Top Sights

Central Park (p174)

Best of New York City

Local Eats

Zabar's (p182)

Gray's Papaya (p185)

Entertainment

Lincoln Center (p180)

Film Society of Lincoln Center (p187)

Parks

Central Park (p174)

Getting There

S Subway On the Upper West Side, the 1/2/3 subway lines are good for destinations along Broadway and points west, while the B and C trains are best for points of interest and access to Central Park.

Bus The M104 bus runs north to south along Broadway and the M10 plies the scenic ride along the western edge of the park.

Top Sights
Central Park

Vast and majestic, Central Park is 843 acres filled with picturesque meadows, tranquil ponds and hidden architectural treasures. The rolling green isn't simply the space of the island that wasn't developed, it is – believe it or not – one of the biggest architectural feats in the entire city. In fact, it took over 20 years to convert the land from swamps and farms into the beautiful retreat you see today.

Map p18, D5

www.centralparknyc.org

59th & 110th Sts btwn Central Park West & Fifth Ave

⊙6am-1am

John Lennon tribute at Strawberry Fields

Don't Miss

Strawberry Fields

This tear-shaped **garden** (Map p178, D6; www.central parknyc.org/visit/things-to-see/south-end/strawberry -fields.html; Central Park, at 72nd St on the west side; 🚻; 🚇 A/C, B to 72nd St) serves as a memorial to former Beatle John Lennon. The garden is composed of a grove of stately elms and a tiled mosaic that reads, simply, 'Imagine.' Find it at the level of 72nd St on the west side of the park.

Bethesda Terrace & the Mall

The arched walkways of Bethesda Terrace, crowned by the magnificent Bethesda Fountain (at the level of 72nd St), have long been a gathering area for New Yorkers of all flavors. To the south is the Mall (featured in countless movies), a promenade shrouded in mature North American elms. The southern stretch, known as Literary Walk, is flanked by statues of famous authors.

Central Park Zoo

Officially known as the Central Park Wildlife Center (no one calls it that), this small **zoo** (Map p178, E8; www.centralparkzoo.com; Central Park, 64th St at Fifth Ave; adult/child $12/7; ⊙10am-5:30pm Apr-Nov, to 4:30pm Nov-Apr; 🚻; 🚇 N/Q/R to 5th Ave-59th St) is home to penguins, polar bears, snow leopards and red pandas. Feeding times in the sea lion and penguin tanks make for a rowdy spectacle. The attached **Tisch Children's Zoo** (Map p178, E8; www.centralparkzoo.com/animals-and-exhibits/exhibits/tisch-childrens-zoo.aspx; Central Park at 65th & 5th Ave), a petting zoo, has alpacas and mini-Nubian goats and is perfect for small children.

☑ Top Tips

▶ Free and custom walking tours are available via the **Central Park Conservancy** (www.centralparknyc.org/walkingtours), the nonprofit organization that supports park maintenance.

▶ Crosstown MTA buses at 66th, 72nd, 79th, 86th and 96th Sts take you through the park, but it's important to note that they pick up and drop off passengers at the edge of the park – not inside.

✕ Take a Break

Consider packing a picnic from the assortment of gourmet goodies at Zabar's (p182) in the heart of the Upper West Side.

Class things up at the Loeb Boathouse (p183) with a round of crab cakes and a smooth afternoon martini.

Understand
Central Park by Numbers

▶ six percent of Manhattan's total space

▶ seven bodies of water

▶ 21 playgrounds

▶ 136 acres of woodland

▶ 8968 benches

▶ 26,000 trees

▶ 38,000,000 visitors per year

▶ $528,783,552,000 value in a 2005 property appraisal

Conservatory Water & Alice in Wonderland Statue

North of the zoo at the level of 74th St is the Conservatory Water, where model sailboats drift lazily and kids scramble about on a toadstool-studded statue of Alice in Wonderland. There are Saturday story hours at the Hans Christian Andersen statue to the west of the water (11am June through September).

Great Lawn

The Great Lawn is a massive emerald carpet at the center of the park – between 79th and 86th Sts – and is surrounded by ball fields and London plane trees. (This is where Simon & Garfunkel played their famous 1981 concert.) Immediately to the southeast is the Delacorte Theater, home to an annual Shakespeare in the Park festival, as well as Belvedere Castle (p180), a lookout.

The Ramble

South of the Great Lawn, between 72nd and 79th Sts, is the leafy Ramble, a popular birding destination (and legendary gay pick-up spot). On the southeastern end is the Loeb Boathouse (p180), home to a waterside restaurant that offers rowboat and bicycle rentals.

Jacqueline Kennedy Onassis Reservoir

The reservoir takes up almost the entire width of the park at the level of 90th St and serves as a gorgeous reflecting pool for the city skyline. It is surrounded by a 1.58-mile track that draws legions of joggers in the warmer months. Nearby, at Fifth Ave and 90th St, is a statue of New York City Marathon founder Fred Lebow peering at his watch.

Conservatory Garden

If you want a little peace and quiet (as in, no runners, cyclists or boom boxes), the six-acre Conservatory Garden serves as one of the park's official quiet zones. And it's beautiful to boot: bursting with crabapple trees, meandering boxwood and, in the spring, lots of flowers. It's located at 105th St off Fifth Ave. Otherwise, you can catch maximum calm (and maximum bird life) in all areas of the park just after dawn.

Alice in Wonderland statue (sculptor: José De Creeft)

North Woods & Blockhouse

The North Woods, on the west side between 106th and 110th Sts, is home to the park's oldest structure, the Blockhouse, a military fortification from the War of 1812.

Summer Happenings in Central Park

During the warm months, Central Park is home to countless cultural events, many of which are free. The two most popular are Shakespeare in the Park (p222), which is managed by the Public Theater, and **SummerStage** (www.summerstage.org; admission free), a series of free concerts. Check out the websites for more information.

Sights

Lincoln Center
CULTURAL CENTER

1 Map p178, C8

This stark arrangement of gleaming Modernist temples contains some of Manhattan's most important performance spaces: Avery Fisher Hall (home to the New York Philharmonic), David H Koch Theater (site of the New York City ballet) and the iconic Metropolitan Opera House, whose interior walls are dressed with brightly saturated murals by painter Marc Chagall. Various other venues are tucked in and around the 16-acre campus, including a theater, two film screening centers and the renowned Juilliard School. (☎212-875-5456, tours 212-875-5350; www.lincolncenter.org; Columbus Ave btwn 62nd & 66th Sts; public plazas free, tours adult/child $15/8; 🕒performance hours vary, tours 10:30am & 4:30pm; 👪; [S]1 to 66th St-Lincoln Center)

American Museum of Natural History
MUSEUM

2 Map p178, C5

Founded in 1869, this classic museum contains a veritable wonderland of more 30 million artifacts, including lots of menacing dinosaur skeletons, as well as the Rose Center for Earth & Space, with its cutting-edge planetarium. From October through May, the museum is home to the Butterfly Conservatory, a glass house featuring 500-plus butterflies from all over the world. The museum is a hit with kids, and as a result, it's swamped on weekends. Early on a weekday is the best time to go. (☎212-769-5100; www.amnh.org; Central Park West at 79th St; adult/child $16/9, interactive exhibits $14-24; 🕒10am-5:45pm, Rose Center to 8:45pm Fri, Butterfly Conservancy Oct-May; 👪; [S]B, C to 81st St-Museum of Natural History, 1 to 79th St)

Loeb Boathouse
CYCLING

3 Map p178, E6

Central Park's boathouse has a fleet of 100 rowboats plus three kayaks available for rent from April to November. In the summer, there is also a Venetian-style gondola that seats up to six (per 30 minutes $30). Bicycles available from April to November. Rentals require an ID and credit card and are weather permitting. Helmets included. (☎212-517-2233; www.thecentralparkboathouse.com; Central Park btwn 74th & 75th Sts; boating per hr $12, bike rentals per hr $9-15; 🕒10am-dusk Apr-Nov; 👪; [S]B, C to 72nd St, 6 to 77th St)

Belvedere Castle
BIRDWATCHING

4 Map p178, D5

For a DIY birding expedition with kids, pick up a 'Discovery Kit' at Belvedere Castle in Central Park. It comes with binoculars, a bird book, colored pencils and paper – a perfect way to get the tykes excited about birds. Picture ID required. (☎212-772-0210; Central Park at 79th St; admission free; 🕒10am-5pm Tue-Sun; 👪; [S]B, C, 1/2/3 to 72nd St)

American Museum of Natural History

Nicholas Roerich Museum

MUSEUM

5 ⦿ Map p178, B1

This compelling little museum, housed in a three-story townhouse from 1898, is one of the city's best-kept secrets. It contains more than 200 paintings by the prolific Nicholas Konstantinovich Roerich (1874–1947), a Russian-born poet, philosopher and painter. His most remarkable works are his stunning depictions of the Himalayas, where he often traveled. (www.roerich.org; 319 W 107th St btwn Riverside Dr & Broadway; suggested donation $5; ⏰noon-5pm Tues-Fri, 2-5pm Sat & Sun; S1 to Cathedral Pkwy)

Wollman Skating Rink

ICE SKATING

6 ⦿ Map p178, D8

Larger than Rockefeller Center skating rink and allowing all-day skating, this rink is at the southeastern edge of Central Park and offers nice views. It's open mid-October through April. Cash only. (☎212-439-6900; www.wollmanskatingrink.com; Central Park btwn 62nd & 63rd Sts; adult Mon-Thu/Fri-Sun $11/16, child $6, skate rentals $7, lock rental $5, spectator fee $5; ⏰Nov-Mar; ♿; S F to 57 St, N/Q/R to 5th Ave-59th St)

New-York Historical Society

MUSEUM

7 👁 Map p178, C6

As the antiquated hyphenated name implies, the New-York Historical Society is the city's oldest museum. It was founded in 1804 to preserve the city's historical and cultural artifacts. Today, the collection of more than 60,000 objects is quirky and fascinating and includes everything from George Washington's inauguration chair to a 19th-century Tiffany ice cream dish (gilded, of course). (www.nyhistory.org; 2 W 77th St at Central Park West; adult/child $15/5, by donation 6-8pm, library free; ⏰10am-6pm Tue-Thu & Sat, to 8pm Fri, 11am-5pm Sun; [S]B, C to 81st St-Museum of Natural History)

Riverside Park

OUTDOORS

8 👁 Map p178, B1

A classic beauty designed by Central Park creators Frederick Law Olmsted and Calvert Vaux, this waterside spot, running north on the Upper West Side and banked by the Hudson River from 59th to 158th Sts, is lusciously leafy. Plenty of bike paths and playgrounds make it a family favorite. From late March through October (weather permitting), a rowdy waterside restaurant, the West 79th Street Boat Basin Café, serves a light menu at the level of 79th St. (☎212-870-3070; www.riversideparkfund.org; Riverside Dr btwn 68th & 155th Sts; ⏰6am-1am; 👪; [S]1/2/3 to any stop btwn 66th & 157th Sts)

American Folk Art Museum

MUSEUM

9 👁 Map p178, C7

This tiny institution contains a couple of centuries' worth of folk and outsider art treasures, including pieces by Henry Darger (known for his girl-filled battlescapes) and Martín Ramírez (producer of hallucinatory caballeros on horseback). There is also an array of wood carvings, paintings, hand-tinted photographs and decorative objects. There are guitar concerts on Wednesdays and free music on Fridays. (www.folkartmuseum.org; 2 Lincoln Sq, Columbus Ave at 66th St; admission free; ⏰noon-7:30pm Tue-Sat, to 6pm Sun; [S]1 to 66th St-Lincoln Center)

Zabar's

MARKET

10 👁 Map p178, B5

A bastion of gourmet-Kosher foodieism, this sprawling local market has been a neighborhood fixture since the 1930s. And what a fixture it is: featuring a heavenly array of cheeses, meats, olives, caviar, smoked fish, pickles, dried fruits, nuts and baked goods, including pillowy fresh-out-of-the-oven knishes (Eastern European–style potato dumplings wrapped in dough). While street vendors sell knishes all over New York, most are of the frozen-industrial variety and have all the flavor of freeze-dried hockey pucks. Zabar's is the place to try the real deal. (www.zabars.com; 2245 Broadway at 80th St; ⏰8am-7:30pm Mon-Fri, to 8pm Sat, 9am-6pm Sun; [S]1 to 79th St)

Eating

Dovetail
MODERN AMERICAN $$$

11 Map p178, C6

Everything about this Michelin-starred restaurant is simple, from the decor (exposed brick, bare tables) to the uncomplicated seasonal menus focused on bracingly fresh produce and quality meats (think pistachio-crusted duck with sunchokes, dates and spinach). On Mondays, chef John Fraser has a three-course vegetarian tasting menu that is winning over carnivores with dishes like crisp cauliflower in jerk spice. (www.dovetailnyc. com; 103 W 77th St cnr Columbus Ave; tasting menu/Monday vegetarian menu $85/46, mains $34-55; dinner daily, brunch Sun; A/C, B to 81st St-Museum of Natural History, 1 to 79th St)

Fatty Crab
MALAYSIAN $

12 Map p178, B6

A brick-lined, industrial chic spot steered by chef Zakary Pelaccio serves winning Malaysian-influenced specialties. Start with sweet and sticky Julan Alor chicken wings, follow up with shrimp and pork wontons and then dig into the Dungeness crab with chili sauce. Don't forget to request extra napkins and an ice cold beer to wash it all down. (www.fattycrab.com; 2170 Broadway btwn 76th & 77th Sts; Fatty Dog $12, mains $16-29; noon-11pm Mon-Wed, to midnight Thu-Sat, to 10pm Sun; 1 to 79th St)

Café Luxembourg
FRENCH $$$

13 Map p178, B7

This quintessential French bistro is generally crowded with locals and it's no mystery why: the setting is elegant, the staff is friendly, and there's an outstanding menu to boot. The classics – salmon tartare, cassoulet and *steak frites* – are all deftly executed, and its proximity to Lincoln Center makes it a perfect pre-performance dinner destination. There is a lighter lunch menu and it serves eggy dishes at brunch. (www.cafeluxembourg.com; 200 W 70th St btwn Broadway & West End Ave; lunch mains $16-34, dinner mains $25-34; breakfast, lunch & dinner daily, brunch Sun; 1/2/3 to 72nd St)

Loeb Boathouse
AMERICAN $$$

Perched on the northeastern tip of the Central Park Lake, the Loeb Boathouse (see 3 Map p178; E6), with its views of the Midtown skyline in the distance, provides one of New York's most idyllic spots for a meal. That said, what you're paying for is the setting. While the food is generally good (the crabcakes are the standout), the service is often indifferent. To experience the location without having to lay out the bucks, a better bet is to hit the adjacent Bar & Grill, where you can still get crabcakes and excellent views. (212-517-2233; www.thecentral parkboathouse.com; Central Park Lake, Central Park at 74th St; mains $22-44; lunch daily & brunch Sat & Sun year-round, dinner daily Apr-Nov; A/C, B to 72nd St, 6 to 77th St)

Kefi

GREEK $$

14 🍴 Map p178, C5

A homey, whitewashed eatery run by chef Michael Psilakis channels a sleek taverna vibe while dispensing excellent rustic Greek dishes. Expect favorites like spicy lamb sausage, sheep-milk dumplings and grilled octopus. The platter featuring four types of spreads is delicious, as is the flat pasta with braised rabbit. The wine list features a comprehensive selection of Greek vintages (from $22 per bottle). (www.kefirestaurant.com; 505 Columbus Ave btwn 84th & 85th Sts; lunch mains $9-18, dinner mains $11-18; ⏲lunch & dinner daily, brunch Sat & Sun; 👪; [S]B, C to 86th St)

Barney Greengrass

DELI $$

15 🍴 Map p178, C4

Self-proclaimed 'King of Sturgeon' Barney Greengrass serves up the same heaping dishes of eggs and salty lox, luxuriant caviar, and melt-in-your mouth chocolate babkas that first made it famous when it opened a century ago. Pop in to fuel up in the morning or for a quick lunch. There are rickety tables set amid the crowded produce aisles. (www.barneygreengrass.com; 541 Amsterdam Ave at 86th St; mains $9-18, bagel with cream cheese $5; ⏲8:30am-4pm Tues-Fri, to 5pm Sat & Sun; 👪; [S]1 to 86th St)

Peacefood Cafe

VEGAN $$

16 🍴 Map p178, C5

This bright and airy vegan haven run by Eric Yu dishes up a popular fried seitan panini (served on homemade focaccia and topped with cashew, arugula, tomatoes and pesto), as well as an excellent quinoa salad. There are daily raw specials, organic coffees and delectable bakery selections. Healthy and good. (☎212-362-2266; www.peacefoodcafe.com; 460 Amsterdam Ave at 82nd St; paninis $13, mains $10-17; ⏲lunch & dinner; 🥕; [S]1 to 79th St)

Salumeria Rosi Parmacotto

ITALIAN $$

17 🍴 Map p178, C6

This is an intimate little meat-loving nook, where you can dip into tasting plates that feature cheeses, salumi, slow-roasted pork loin, sausages, cured hams and every other piece of the pig you care to imagine. There are other tasty Tuscan-inspired offerings too, including homemade lasagna, savory leek tart, escarole-anchovy salad and hand-rolled sweet-potato gnocchi. (☎212-877-4800; www.salumeriarosi.com; 284 Amsterdam Ave at 73rd St; mains $11-14; ⏲11am-11pm; [S]1/2/3 to 72nd St)

PJ Clarke's

PUB $$

18 🍴 Map p178, C8

Right across the street from Lincoln Center, this red-checker-tablecloth spot has a buttoned-down crowd, friendly bartenders and solid eats. If you're in a rush, belly up to the bar for a Black Angus burger and a Brooklyn Lager. A raw bar offers fresh Long Island Little Neck and Cherry Stone clams, as well as jumbo shrimp

Peacefood Cafe

cocktails. (☎212-957-9700; www.pjclarkes.com/lincoln-square-location.php; 44 W 63rd St cnr Broadway; burgers $10-14, mains $18-40; ⏰11:30am-1am; [S]1 to 66th St-Lincoln Center)

Fairway SELF-CATERING $

19 🍴 Map p178, B6

Like a museum of good eats, this incredible grocery spills its lovely mounds of produce into its sidewalk bins, seducing you inside with international goodies, fine cooking oils, nuts, cheeses, prepared foods and, upstairs, an organic market and cafe. (www.fairwaymarket.com/store-upper-west-side; 2127 Broadway at 75th St; ⏰6am-1am; [S]1/2/3 to 72nd St)

Gray's Papaya HOT DOGS $

20 🍴 Map p178, C7

It doesn't get more New York than bellying up to this classic stand-up joint in the wake of a beer bender. The lights are bright, the color palette is 1970s and the hot dogs are unpretentiously good. (A sign on the wall says, 'Best Damn Frankfurter You Ever Ate.') (☎212-799-0243; 2090 Broadway at 72nd St; hot dog $2; ⏰24hr; [S]A/B/C, 1/2/3 to 72nd St)

Absolute Bagels BAKERY $

21 🍴 Map p178, B1

This popular neighborhood bagel joint has 16 varieties of hot, chewy, hand-rolled bagels – and myriad cream cheeses to top them with (including the tofu variety). (☎ 212-932-2052; 2788 Broadway btwn 107th & 108th Sts; bagel $1; ⏰ 6am-9pm Mon-Sat, to 8pm Sun; **S** 1 to Cathedral Parkway-110th St)

Drinking

Malachy's
PUB

22 Map p178, C6

Giving new meaning to the word 'dive,' this crusty local holdout has a long bar, a line-up of regulars and a bartender with a sense of humor. In other words: the perfect place for daytime drinking. There's a cheap menu if you're feeling lucky. (www.malachys.com; 103 W 72nd St btwn Amsterdam & Columbus Aves; ⏰ noon-4am; **S** B/C, 1/2/3 to 72nd St)

Barcibo Enoteca
WINE BAR

23 Map p178, C7

Just north of Lincoln Center, this casual chic marble-table spot is ideal for sipping, with a long list of vintages from all over Italy, including 40 different varieties sold by the glass. There is a short menu of small plates and light meals. The staff is knowledgeable: ask for recommendations. (www.barciboenoteca.com; 2020 Broadway cnr 69th St; ⏰ 4:30pm-2am; **S** 1/2/3 to 72nd St)

Dead Poet
BAR

24 Map p178, C5

A skinny, mahogany-paneled pub has been a neighborhood favorite for over a decade, with a mix of locals and students nursing pints of Guinness. There are cocktails named after dead poets, including a Jack Kerouac margarita ($12) and a Pablo Neruda spiced rum sangria ($9). Funny, because we always pegged Neruda as a pisco sour kind of guy. (www.thedeadpoet.com; 450 Amsterdam Ave btwn 81st & 82nd Sts; ⏰ 9am-4am Mon-Sat, noon-4am Sun; **S** 1 to 79th St)

Ding Dong Lounge
BAR

25 Map p178, C1

It's hard to be too bad-ass in the Upper West, but this former crack den turned punk bar makes a wholesome attempt by supplying graffiti-covered bathrooms to go with its exposed-brick walls. It also, interestingly, features an array of cuckoo clocks. It's popular with Columbia students and guests from nearby hostels for its beer-and-a-shot combo (only $6). (www.dingdonglounge.com; 929 Columbus Ave btwn 105th & 106th Sts; **S** B, C, 1 to 103rd St)

Sip
COCKTAIL BAR

26 Map p178, C1

This quirky storefront decked out in bright tile and red leather serves as coffeehouse by day and friendly little cocktail lounge by night. The mixologists here produce various signature drinks, including, appropriately enough, a cappuccino martini. There are tapas, too, including small plates of chorizo and cheeses. (www.sipbar.com; 998 Amsterdam Ave btwn 109th & 110th Sts; ⏰ 10:30am-4am; **S** 1 to Cathedral Parkway-110 St)

Entertainment

Metropolitan Opera House
OPERA

27 ⭐ Map p178, C8

New York's premier opera company, the Metropolitan Opera is the place to see classics such as *Carmen, Madame Butterfly* and *Macbeth*, not to mention Wagner's *Ring Cycle*. The Opera also hosts premieres and revivals of more contemporary works, such as Peter Sellars' *Nixon in China*, which played here in 2011. The season runs from September to April. (www.metopera.org; Lincoln Center, 64th St at Columbus Ave; **S**1 to 66th St-Lincoln Center)

Film Society of Lincoln Center
CINEMA

28 ⭐ Map p178, C7

The Film Society is one of New York's cinematic gems, providing an invaluable platform for a wide gamut of documentary, feature, independent, foreign and avant-garde art pictures. Films screen in one of two facilities at Lincoln Center: the new Elinor Bunin Munroe Film Center, a more intimate, experimental venue, or the Walter Reade Theater, with wonderfully wide, screening room-style seats. (☎212-875-5456; www.filmlinc.com; Lincoln Center, Columbus Ave btwn 62nd & 66th Sts; **S**1 to 66th St-Lincoln Center)

Local Life
Lincoln Center

This vast cultural complex is ground zero for high art in Manhattan. In addition to the venues and companies listed, the **Vivian Beaumont Theater** (Map p178, C8; ☎212-721-6500; Lincoln Center, 65th St btwn Broadway & Amsterdam Ave) and the **Mitzi E Newhouse Theater** (Map p178, C8; Lincoln Center, 65th St btwn Broadway & Amsterdam Ave) showcase works of drama and musical theater. Both of these have programming information listed on Lincoln Center's main website at www.lincolncenter.org.

New York Philharmonic
CLASSICAL MUSIC

29 ⭐ Map p178, C8

The oldest professional orchestra in the US (dating back to 1842) holds its season every year at Avery Fisher Hall. Directed by Alan Gilbert, the son of two Philharmonic musicians, the orchestra plays a mix of classics (Tchaikovsky, Mahler, Haydn) and some contemporary works, as well concerts geared toward children. Tickets run in the $33 to $83 range. If you're on a budget, check out their open rehearsals on Thursdays during the day (at the discretion of the conductor) for only $18. (www.nyphil.org; Avery Fisher Hall, Lincoln Center, cnr Columbus Ave & 65th St; ♿; **S**1 to 66 St-Lincoln Center)

New York City Ballet

DANCE

30 ⭐ Map p178, C8

This prestigious company was first directed by renowned Russian-born choreographer George Balanchine back in the 1940s. Today, the company has 90 dancers and is the largest ballet organization in the US, performing 23 weeks a year at Lincoln Center's David H Koch Theater. During the holidays, the troop is best known for its annual production of *The Nutcracker*. Depending on the ballet, ticket prices can range from $29 to $250. (📞212-870-5656, student rush tickets 212-870-7766; www.nycballet.com; David H Koch Theater, Lincoln Center, Columbus Ave at 62nd St; ♿; S1 to 66th St-Lincoln Center)

American Ballet Theatre

DANCE

This seven-decade-old traveling company presents a classic selection of ballets at the Metropolitan Opera House at Lincoln Center (see 1 Map p178; C8) every spring (generally in May). Tickets are by subscription only. The Orchestra, Parterre and Grand Tier sections offer the best views. Avoid the top tier or all you'll see are the dancers' heads. Box seats toward the rear have highly obscured views. (📞212-477-3030; www.abt.org; Lincoln Center, 64th St at Columbus Ave; S1 to 66th St-Lincoln Center)

Beacon Theatre

LIVE MUSIC

31 ⭐ Map p178, C6

This historic theater from 1929 is a perfect in-between-size venue, with 2600 seats (not a terrible one in the house) and a constant flow of popular acts, from The Cure to Paul Simon to Adele. A $15-million restoration in 2009 has left the gilded interiors – a mix of Greek, Roman, Renaissance and Rococo design elements – totally sparkling. (www.beacontheatre.com; 2124 Broadway btwn 74th & 75th Sts; S1/2/3 to 72nd St)

Cleopatra's Needle

CLUB

32 ⭐ Map p178, B3

Named after an Egyptian obelisk that resides in Central Park, this venue is small and narrow like its namesake. There's no cover, but there's a $10 minimum spend. Come early and you can enjoy happy hour, when martinis are half price. But be prepared to stay late: Cleopatra's is famous for all-night jam sessions that hit their peak around 4am. (www.cleopatrasneedley.com; 2485 Broadway btwn 92nd & 93rd Sts; ⏰4pm-late; S1/2/3 to 96th St)

Merkin Concert Hall

CLASSICAL MUSIC

33 ⭐ Map p178, C7

Just north of Lincoln Center, this 450-seat hall, part of the Kaufman Center, is one of the city's more intimate venues for classical music, as well as jazz, world music and pop. The hall hosts Tuesday matinees (a deal at $17) that highlight emerging classical solo artists. Every January, it is home to the New York Guitar Festival. (www.kaufman-center.org/mch; 129 W 67th St btwn

American Ballet Theatre and New York City Ballet dancers in Christopher Wheeldon's *Commedia*, Morphoses

Amsterdam Ave & Broadway; admission varies; **S**1 to 66th St-Lincoln Center)

Smoke   JAZZ

34 ⭐ Map p178, B1

This swank but laid-back lounge – with good stage views from plush sofas – brings out old-timers and local faves, like George Coleman and Wynton Marsalis. Most nights there's a $10 cover, plus a $20 to $30 food and drink minimum. Smoke is smoke-free but then again so is the rest of NYC. (www.smokejazz.com; 2751 Broadway btwn 105th & 106th Sts; ⏰5pm-4am; **S**1 to 103rd St)

New York City Opera   OPERA

The 'people's opera,' founded by Mayor Fiorella LaGuardia in 1944, is one of New York's more interesting companies, producing updated classics, neglected operas and new and recent work. Unfortunately, it also has profound financial troubles and, in late 2011, was experiencing all kinds of labor problems. For now, the shows are taking place in a variety of venues across the city, from Central Park to Brooklyn, though it may one day return to its original home at the Lincoln Center (see 1 ◎ Map p178, C8). (☎212-870-5630; www.nycopera.com; Lincoln Center, Columbus Ave btwn 62nd & 66th Sts)

Metropolitan Opera House (p187; architect: Wallace K Harrison)

Shopping

Greenflea   MARKET

35 🔒 Map p178, C6

One of the oldest open-air shopping spots in the city, this friendly, well-stocked flea market is a perfect activity for a lazy Upper West Side Sunday morning. You'll find a little bit of everything here, including vintage and contemporary furnishings, antique maps, custom eyewear, hand-woven scarves, handmade jewelry and so much more. Check the website for weekly vendor details. The market is also open on occasional Saturdays in warm months. (www.greenfleamarkets. com; Columbus Ave btwn 76th & 77th Sts; ⏰10am-5:30pm Sun; Ⓢ B, C to 81st St-Museum of Natural History, 1 to 79th St)

Time for Children   TOYS

36 🔒 Map p178, C5

This small store sells adorable clothes for babies and toddlers, colorful books and plush toys, block sets, handmade cards and other treasures for the under-10 gang. Bonus: feel good about your purchase. Time donates 100% of its profits to the Children's Aid Society of New York. (📞212-580-8202; www. atimeforchildren.org; 506 Amsterdam Ave btwn 84th & 85th Sts; ⏰10am-7pm Mon-Sat, 11am-6pm Sun; ♿; Ⓢ1 to 86th St)

Harry's Shoes   SHOES

37 🔒 Map p178, B5

Around since the 1930s, Harry's is a classic. It's staffed by gentlemen who measure your foot in an old-school metal contraption and then wait on you patiently, making sure the shoe fits. If your feet are killing you from all the walking, you'll find sturdy, comfortable brands (Merrel, Dansko, Birkenstock) as well as Earth, a vegan brand. (www.harrys-shoes.com; 2299 Broadway at 83rd St; 🕒10am-6:45pm Tue, Wed, Fri & Sat, to 7:45pm Mon & Thu, 11am-6pm Sun; [S]1 to 86th St)

Westsider Books BOOKS

38 🛍 Map p178, B5

A great little shop packed to the gills with rare and used books, including a good selection of fiction and illustrated tomes. There are first editions and a smattering of vintage vinyl. (www.westsiderbooks.com; 2246 Broadway btwn 80th & 81st Sts; 🕒10am-late; [S]1 to 79th St)

Westsider Records MUSIC

39 🛍 Map p178, B6

Featuring more than 30,000 LPs, this shop has got you covered when it comes to everything from funk to jazz to classical. A good place to lose all track of time. (☎212-874-1588; www.westsiderbooks.com/recordstore.html; 233 W 72nd St btwn Broadway & West End Ave; 🕒11am-7pm Mon-Thu, to 9pm Fri-Sat, noon-6pm Sun; [S]1/2/3 to 72nd St)

Local Life
Harlem

This is the neighborhood where Cab Calloway crooned. Where Ralph Ellison penned his epic novel on truth and intolerance, *Invisible Man*. Where acclaimed artist Romare Bearden pieced together his first collages. It's a place that is soaked in history – and then some. And it remains one of the country's most fabled centers of black American life.

Getting There

Harlem is 5 miles north of Midtown.

S Take the A/D one stop from Columbus Circle. The 2/3 takes 15 minutes to reach Harlem from Times Sq.

🚌 The M10 follows the west side of Central Park up into Harlem.

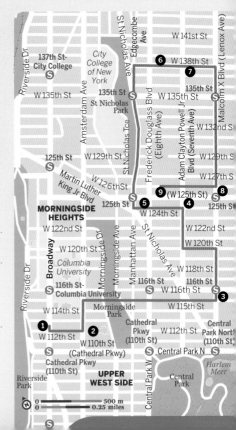

❶ College Campus Caffeine

Rev your engine with a cuppa joe alongside Columbia University students at **Community Food & Juice** (www.communityrestaurant.com; 2893 Broadway btwn 112th & 113th Sts; mains $14-29; ⏱8am-3:30pm & 5-9:30pm Mon-Fri, from 9am Sat & Sun; 🍴♿; 🚇1 to 110th St).

❷ Come to Jesus

The **Cathedral Church of St John the Divine** (📞tours 212-932-7347; www.stjohndivine.org; 1047 Amsterdam Ave at W 112th St; admission by donation, tours $6, vertical tours $15; ⏱7am-6pm Mon-Sat, to 7pm Sun; ♿; 🚇B, C, 1 to 110th St-Cathedral Pkwy) is the largest place of worship in the US.

❸ Rows of Cornrows

The semi-enclosed **Malcolm Shabazz Harlem Market** (52 W 116th btwn Malcolm X Blvd & Fifth Ave; ⏱10am-7pm; 🚇2/3 to 116th St) does a brisk trade in almost everything: textiles, essential oils, leather goods, weaves.

❹ Art & Community

The small **Studio Museum in Harlem** (www.studiomuseum.org; 144 W 125th St at Adam Clayton Powell Jr Blvd; suggested donation $7; ⏱noon-9pm Thu & Fri, 10am-6pm Sat, noon-6pm Sun; ♿; 🚇2/3 to 125th St) has been exhibiting the works of African American artists for more than 40 years. It's also an important point of connection for Harlem cultural figures.

❺ Books for Hue-Man-Ity

Hue-Man Bookstore (www.huemanbookstore.com; 2319 Frederick Douglass Blvd btwn 124th & 125th Sts; ⏱10am-8pm Mon-Sat, 11am-7pm Sun; 🚇A/C, B/D to 125th St), the largest independent African American bookstore in the country, offers a good selection of works from black literary heavyweights and pop writers alike.

❻ Strivers' Row

On the blocks of 138th and 139th Sts, **Strivers' Row** (138th & 139th Sts btwn Frederick Douglass & Adam Clayton Powell Jr Blvds; 🚇B, C to 135th St) is filled with 1890s townhouses. The area earned its nickname in the 1920s when aspiring African Americans first moved here.

❼ Come to Jesus

Sunday gospel services are best done at the **Abyssinian Baptist Church** (www.abyssinian.org; 132 W 138th St btwn Adam Clayton Powell Jr & Malcolm X Blvds; ♿; 🚇2/3 to 135th St) – there's even a designated 'tourist' section.

❽ Cock-A-Doodle-Do

Dine at **Red Rooster** (www.redroosterharlem.com; 310 Malcolm X Blvd btwn 125th & 126th Sts; mains $16-35; ⏱lunch & dinner daily, brunch Sat & Sun; 🚇2/3 to 125th St), where upscale comfort food is swirled with a world of flavors.

❾ Cheers & Jeers

End at the **Apollo Theater** (📞212-531-5305, tours 212-531-5337; www.apollotheater.org; 253 W 125th St at Frederick Douglass Blvd; admission weeknights/weekends $16/18; 🚇A/C, B/D to 125th St), Harlem's leading space for concerts and political rallies. The ever-popular Wednesday 'Amateur Night' draws notorious crowds.

Local Life
South Brooklyn

Getting There

South Brooklyn is about 6 miles south-east of Times Sq.

S The 2/3, 4/5, B and Q stop at Atlantic–Pacific. The 2/3 also stops at Grand Army Plaza.

To really know New York City is to explore its other boroughs, and no one will blame you for starting here. A city unto itself (it's three times larger than Manhattan), Brooklyn is a sprawling checkerboard of distinct neighborhoods where hipsters engage in their ironic pursuits. If you can, check out the following walk over the weekend to maximize your experience.

❶ The Other Central Park

Prospect Park (www.prospectpark.org; Grand Army Plaza; ⏱5am-1am; **S**2/3 to Grand Army Plaza, F to 15th St-Prospect Park), Brooklyn's version of Central Park, features many of the same landscape features but with far fewer crowds.

❷ Grand Army Plaza

At the park's northwest corner, **Grand Army Plaza** (Prospect Park West & Flatbush Ave; ⏱6am-midnight; **S**2/3 to Grand Army Plaza, B, Q to 7th Ave) is a giant traffic circle crowned by a massive arch. Don't miss the Saturday greenmarket.

❸ Unique Finds

Situated on the grounds of a school, the **Brooklyn Flea** (www.brooklynflea.com; 176 Lafayette Ave btwn Clermont & Vanderbilt Aves; ⏱10am-5pm Sat Apr-Dec; 🚻; **S**G to Clinton-Washington Aves) hosts over 200 vendors who congregate to sell their wares, ranging from antiques and vintage clothes to enticing to-go snacks.

❹ Winter Flea

During the winter months, the Brooklyn Flea is tucked safely inside the **Williamsburgh Savings Bank Tower** (1 Hanson Pl at Flatbush Ave; admission free; **S**2/3, 4/5 to Atlantic Ave, D, N/R to Atlantic Ave-Pacific St), which was at one time the tallest building in the borough.

❺ BAM!

The country's oldest performing arts center, **Brooklyn Academy of Music** (BAM; ☎718-636-4139; www.bam.org; 30 Lafayette Ave at Ashland Pl; **S**2/3, 4/5, B, Q to Atlantic Ave) supplies NYC with edgier works of modern dance, music and theater. Free performances are known to boil up on weekends.

❻ Rock Climbing

Get the blood rushing at **Brooklyn Boulders** (www.brooklynboulders.com; 575 Degraw St at Third Ave; day pass $22; ⏱noon-10pm Mon-Thu, to midnight Fri & Sat, to 8pm Sun; **S**R to Union St), NYC's biggest indoor climbing area – the perfect place to unleash your inner Spiderman.

❼ Dinner: Big Spender

Plan ahead and book a seat at the **Chef's Table** (☎718-243-0050; www.brooklynfare.com/chefs-table; 200 Schermerhorn St btwn Hoyt & Bond Sts; prix fixe from $135; ⏱7am-10pm Mon-Sat, 8am-9pm Sun; **S**A/C, G to Hoyt-Schermerhorn), a three-star Michelin phenomenon that has foodies frothing at the mouth with a seafood-centric tasting menu.

❽ Dinner: Small Wallet

Big on flavor, small in size, **Mile End** (www.mileendbrooklyn.com; 97A Hoyt St; sandwiches $8-12; ⏱breakfast, lunch & dinner daily, brunch Sat & Sun) offers the perfect smoked-meat sandwich – pair it with a gut-busting portion of *poutine*.

❾ Beer Garden

Finish the evening at **61 Local** (www.61local.com; 61 Bergen St btwn Smith St & Boerum Pl; ⏱11am-midnight Sun-Thu, to 1am Fri & Sat; **S**F, G to Bergen), a brick-and-wood hall with communal tables and a good selection of craft brews.

Local Life
Williamsburg

Williamsburg is essentially a college town without a college – it's New York's of-the-moment Bohemian magnet, drawing slouchy, baby-faced artists, musicians, writers and graphic designers. Once a bastion of Latino working-class life, it's become a prominent dining and nightlife center – and although it's not full of traditional attractions, the neighborhood nonetheless offers plenty to do.

Getting There

Williamburg is less than 5 miles from Times Sq.

S Hop on the L train – Williamsburg is one stop outside of Manhattan. Not bad, eh?

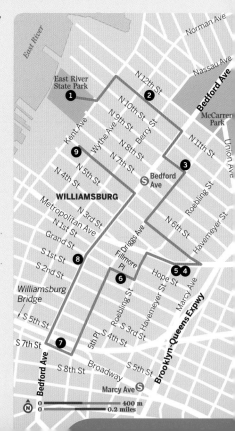

❶ Seeing Green

The seven-acre **East River State Park** (www.nysparks.com/parks/155; Kent Ave btwn 8th and 9th Sts; ⏱9am-dusk; 🚻; 🆂L to Bedford Ave) is the latest hot spot for outdoor parties and free summer concerts. During the summer, the Brooklyn Flea sets up shop here as well.

❷ Homegrown Hops

Hearkening back to when the area was NYC's beer-brewing center, **Brooklyn Brewery** (www.brooklynbrewery. com; 79 N 11th St btwn Berry St & Wythe Ave; ⏱free tours on the hour 1-4pm Sat & Sun; 🆂L to Bedford Ave) brews and serves tasty local suds. It also offers tours.

❸ Hipster Threads

The large **Buffalo Exchange** (504 Driggs Ave at 9th St; ⏱11am-7pm Mon-Sat, noon-8pm Sun; 🆂L to Bedford Ave) is the go-to spot for Brooklynites on a budget. Warning: you'll waste hours searching for vintage treasure.

❹ Bodega Ephemera

Housed in a former bodega, the curious **City Reliquary** (www.cityreliquary.org; 370 Metropolitan Ave near Havemeyer St; by donation; ⏱noon-6pm Sat & Sun, 7-10pm Thu; 🆂L to Lorimer Ave) is filled with sundry New Yorkiana, from shop signs and vintage postcards to subway tokens and a 'very old shovel.'

❺ Throw One Back at the Throw-Back

Pause for a mint julep at '70s-style **Commodore** (366 Metropolitan Ave cnr Havemeyer St; ⏱4pm-midnight Sun-Thu, to 1am Fri & Sat; 🆂L to Lorimer St) and go for the bar burger if you're feeling peckish.

❻ Made with Love

The adorable **Love Brigade Co-Op** (www.lovebrigade.com; 230 Grand St btwn Roebling St & Driggs Ave; ⏱noon-8pm Wed-Sun; 🆂L to Bedford Ave) features wearables by over two dozen independent designers from around the globe.

❼ Williamsburg's (Michelin) Star

Go for dinner at **Dressler** (📞718-384-6343; www.dresslernyc.com; 149 Broadway btwn Bedford & Driggs Aves; mains $26-35, bar menu $14-16; ⏱dinner Mon-Fri, lunch & dinner Sat & Sun; 🆂J/M/Z to Marcy Ave) and enjoy New American fare amid sleek surrounds. You can sit at the bar for a menu that's a bit easier on the wallet.

❽ More Brooklyn Booze

Crank that time machine back one more notch at **Maison Premiere** (www. maisonpremiere.com; 298 Bedford Ave btwn 1st & Grand Sts; ⏱4pm-4am Mon-Fri, noon-4am Sat & Sun; 🆂L to Bedford Ave), which features a laboratory's worth of punch and poison.

❾ Indie HQ

The perennially popular (and surprisingly intimate) **Music Hall of Williamsburg** (www.musichallofwilliamsburg. com; 66 N 6th St btwn Wythe & Kent Aves; 🆂L to Bedford Ave) is *the* place to see indie bands in Brooklyn.

The Best of
New York City

Central Park (p174)
JEAN-PIERRE LESCOURRET/LONELY PLANET IMAGES ©

Best Walks
Village Vibe

🏃 The Walk

Of all the neighborhoods in New York City, the West Village is easily the most walkable, its cobbled corners straying from the signature gridiron that unfurls across the rest of the island. An afternoon stroll is not to be missed; hidden landmarks and quaint cafes abound.

Start Commerce St; **S** 1 to Christopher St–Sheridan Sq, 1 to Houston

Finish Washington Sq Park; **S** A/C/E, B/D/F/M to W 4th St

Length 1 mile; one hour

🍴 Take a Break

There are perhaps more cafes per acreage in the West Village than anywhere else. Pause at any point during your stroll to slurp a latte street-side and enjoy the colorful crew of passing pedestrians: students, hipsters, moneyed professionals and celebrities hiding behind oversized sunglasses.

ROGER GAESS/LONELY PLANET IMAGES ©

Greenwich Village

❶ Cherry Lane Theater

Start your walkabout at the **Cherry Lane Theater** (p103). Established in 1924, the small theater is the city's longest continuously running off-Broadway establishment and was the center of the city's creative performance art moment during the 1940s.

❷ The Friends Apartment

Turn left and you'll see **90 Bedford St** on the corner of Grove St. You might recognize the apartment block as the fictitious home of the cast of *Friends* (sadly Central Perk was just a figment of the writers' imaginations).

❸ Carrie Bradshaw's Stoop

For another iconic TV landmark, wander up Bleecker and make a right stopping at **66 Perry St**, which was used as the apartment of the city's it girl, Carrie Bradshaw, in *Sex and the City* (though in the show, her address was on the Upper East Side).

❹ Christopher Park

Follow West 4th St until your reach **Christopher Park**, where two white, life-sized statues of same-sex couples (*Gay Liberation*, 1992) stand guard. On the north side of the green space is the legendary Stonewall Inn, where a clutch of fed-up drag queens rioted for their civil rights in 1969, signaling the start of what would become the gay revolution.

❺ Jefferson Market Library

Head toward Sixth Ave to find the **Jefferson Market Library** straddling a triangular plot of land at the intersection of several roads. The unmissable 'Ruskinian Gothic' spire was once a fire lookout tower. In the 1870s, it was used as a courthouse and today it houses a branch of the public library.

❻ Café Wha?

Take in the flurry of passers-by on Sixth Ave, then swing by **Café Wha?**, the notorious institution where many young musicians and comedians – like Bob Dylan and Richard Pryor – got their start.

❼ Washington Square Park

Further down MacDougal St is **Washington Square Park** (p90), the Village's unofficial town square, which plays host to loitering students, buskers and a regular crowd of protestors chanting about various injustices.

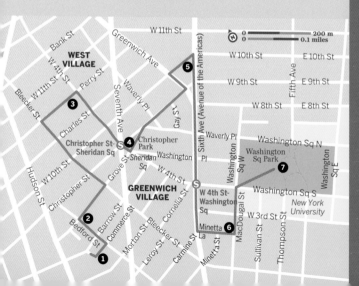

Best Walks
Iconic Architecture

🏃 The Walk

NYC has plenty of skyscrapers in every shape and size. Staring into the city's infinite abyss of twinkling lights from atop a skyscraper ranks high on everyone's to-do list, but we often prefer those quintessential New York moments on the street when the crown of a soaring spire winks hello amid honking taxis in the early evening.

Start St Patrick's Cathedral; **S** B/D/F/M to Rockerfeller Center

Finish Empire State Building; **S** N/Q/R to Herald Sq

Length 2 miles; two to three hours

🍴 Take a Break

Koreatown is Midtown's biggest surprise. If you're looking for the latest iteration of Korean fusion, make a beeline to 52nd St for a bite at Danji (p132), one of the brightest newcomers in the city's constellation of Michelin stars.

ATLANTIDE PHOTOTRAVEL/CORBIS ©

Grand Central Terminal

❶ St Patrick's Cathedral

The neo-Gothic **St Patrick's Cathedral** (p136) was built at a cost of nearly $2 million during the Civil War. Today is remains the largest Catholic cathedral in America, with seven open Masses a day from 7am to 5.30pm. All noontime Masses are accompanied by music and confession after the ceremony.

❷ Rockefeller Center

Rockefeller Center (p134) is a magnificent complex of art deco skyscrapers and sculptures. Enter between 49th and 50th Sts into the main plaza and its golden statue of Prometheus, then head up to the 70th floor of the GE Building just behind for an unforgettable view at Top of the Rock observation deck.

❸ Bank of America Tower

The **Bank of America Tower** is New York City's third-tallest building and – perhaps surprisingly – one of the most ecofriendly.

4 New York Public Library

At the corner of 42nd St and Fifth Ave stands the stately **New York Public Library** (p136), guarded by a pair of regal lions called Patience and Fortitude. Step inside to peek at the spectacular Rose Main Reading Room with its coifered ceiling. Cartography buffs will love thumbing through the collection of over 431,000 maps.

5 Grand Central Terminal

New York's beaux arts darling is **Grand Central Terminal** (p134). Star gaze at the Main Concourse ceiling, share sweet nothings at the Whispering Gallery and pick up a gourmet treat at the Grand Central Market.

6 Chrysler Building

Although William Van Alen's 1930 masterpiece, the **Chrysler Building** (p134), is best appreciated from afar, it's worth slipping into the Chrysler Building's sumptuous art deco lobby, lavished with exotic inlaid wood, marble and purportedly the world's largest ceiling mural.

7 Empire State Building

End your Midtown meander at the **Empire State Building** (p128), which provides a beautiful bird's-eye view of Manhattan and beyond. It's especially magical at sunset from the open-air observation deck on the 86th floor.

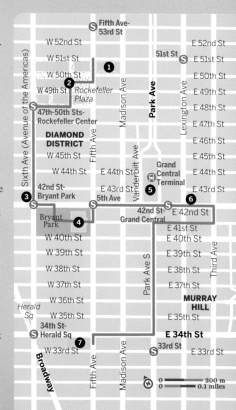

Best Walks
Memorable Manhattan Movies

🏃 The Walk

NYC has featured in more movies than any other city and the town is littered with cinematic landmarks. It was on these streets that a bumbling Woody Allen fell for Diane Keaton in *Annie Hall* and Meg Ryan faked her orgasm in *When Harry Met Sally*. Traversing the city can feel like one big déjà vu of memorable scenes, characters and one-liners.

Start Bloomingdale's; **S** N/Q/R to Lexington Ave or 4/5/6 to 59th St

Finish Metropolitan Museum of Art; **S** 4/5/6 to 86th St

Length 1.5 miles; two hours

✕ Take a Break

Stick around the Metropolitan Museum of Art and head up to the roof terrace. Enjoy a much-deserved cocktail at the Roof Garden Café & Martini Bar (p160) – the views of Central Park and its fortress of skyscrapers are worthy of any camera lens.

Wollman Skating Rink (p181) in Central Park

❶ Bloomingdale's

Start outside **Bloomingdale's** (p149), where Darryl Hannah and Tom Hanks shattered televisions in *Splash* (1984) and Dustin Hoffman hailed a cab in *Tootsie* (1982).

❷ Copacabana

West of here, 10 60th St is the site of the now defunct **Copacabana**, the night club (now a health food restaurant) that hosted Ray Liotta and Lorraine Bracco in *Goodfellas* (1990) and a coked-up lawyer played by Sean Penn in *Carlito's Way* (1993).

❸ Central Park

Continue west to **Central Park** (p174), which has appeared in *The Royal Tenenbaums* (2001), *Ghostbusters* (1983), *The Muppets Take Manhattan* (1983), *Barefoot in the Park* (1967) and the cult classic *The Warriors* (1979), among many others.

❹ 620 Park Ave

From here, head east to Park Ave. At 620 Park Ave at 65th St, you'll find the building that served as **John Malkovich's apartment** in Charlie Kaufman's *Being John Malkovich* (1999).

❺ 114 72nd St

To the north at 114 72nd St is the **high-rise** where Sylvia Miles lured John Voight in *Midnight Cowboy* (1969).

❻ 171 E 71st St

One block to the east and south is 171 E 71st St, a townhouse featured in one of the most famous movies to star New York: this was **Holly Golightly's apartment** in *Breakfast at Tiffany's* (1961).

❼ JG Melon

Continuing east to Third Ave, you'll find **JG Melon** (p165) at the corner of 74th St It's a good spot for beer and burger – plus the site of a meeting between Dustin Hoffman and Meryl Streep in *Kramer vs. Kramer* (1979).

❽ Carlyle

Heading west to Madison Ave, the **Carlyle** hotel at 35 76th St is where Woody Allen and Dianne Wiest had a date

from hell in *Hannah and Her Sisters* (1986).

❾ Metropolitan Museum of Art

From the Carlyle, it's a short jaunt west to the **Metropolitan Museum of Art** (p154) at 82nd St and Fifth Ave, where Angie Dickinson had a fatal encounter in *Dressed to Kill* (1980) and Billy Crystal chatted up Meg Ryan in *When Harry Met Sally* (1989).

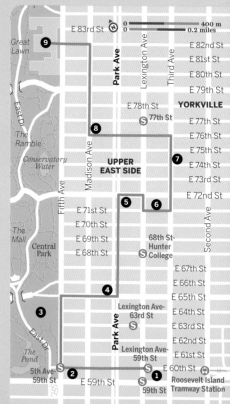

Best
Fine Dining

Tasting trends in New York City come and go, but there's one thing that will forever remain certain: fine dining never goes out of style. Sure, the culture of haute eats has changed over the years, but locals and visitors alike will never tire of dressing up to chow down. These days the scene revolves around 'New American' cuisine and high-end comfort food.

Reservations

Booking ahead is essential at any popular venue that takes reservations. Sometimes you'll need to call long before you've departed on your vacation. If tables are booked up, ask about bar service or whether you can sneak a seat at the end of the night (around 11pm). Lunch is another option – many restaurants have midday prix fixe service.

Celebrity Chefs

The era of reality TV shows continues the trend of celebrity chef-dom in NYC, a city where restaurateurs are just as famous as their fare. It's not just buzz though – these taste masters really know their trade. Big-ticket names abound: Mario Batali has painted the town red with his spaghetti sauces while David Chang's Momofuku empire continues to expand with heart-stoppingly delicious pork buns.

New American Eats

A gourmet spin on traditional comfort food – or peasant food – the 'New American' movement seeks to fuse repast standards with a lofty dedication to market-fresh produce and seasonal ingredients. Many of the city's most critically acclaimed chow houses offer souped-up versions of family recipes – a tribute to New York's citizenry of immigrants.

SETH WENIG/CORBIS ©

☑ Top Tips

▶ New Yorkers are famous for offering their opinion, so why not capitalize on their taste-bud experiences and click through scores of websites catering to the discerning diner. Some of our favorite blog-style rags include **Eater** (http://ny.eater.com), **New York Magazine** (www.nymag.com) and **Tasting Table NYC** (http://www.tastingtable.com/nyc/index.htm).

Best Celebrity-Chef Restaurants

Dutch Oysters on ice and fresh homemade pies bookend the dining experience – in the mid-

JAMES LEYNSE/CORBIS ©

Pasta for sale in Eataly

dle is comfort food, fresh from the farm. (p53)

Les Halles Anthony Bourdain's elegant brasserie – a carnivore's delight with evocative French fare. (p37)

Birreria Star of gourmet market Eataly. Feast on pork shoulder as you enjoy a variety of curated frosty ones. (p115)

Locanda Verde Contemporary Italian fare by Andrew Carmellini in the Greenwich Hotel. (p35)

Best Gourmet Groceries

Eataly Gorgeous (and massive!) gourmet grocery that pays tribute to the bustling markets of Italy. (p122)

Zabar's The Upper West Side's kosher contribu-

tion to upscale market eats. (p182)

Dean & DeLuca Luxury grocer boasting a seemingly infinite assortment of edibles from around the globe. (p56)

Best Buzzworthy Bites

RedFarm Sino fusion dishes with bold flavors. Doesn't take itself too seriously. (p93)

Danji Masterfully prepared and inventive 'Korean tapas' crafted by a young-gun pro. (p202)

Dovetail Simplicity is key – vegetarians unite on Mondays for a divine tasting menu. (p183)

Le Bernardin Triple Michelin-star earner and New York's holy grail of fine dining. (p137)

Worth a Trip

There are scores of Brooklyn restaurants that lure stalwart Manhattanites out for a foodie pilgrimage. Try **Vinegar Hill House** (www.vinegarhillhouse.com; 72 Hudson Ave btwn Water & Front Sts, Vinegar Hill; mains $15-30; ⏰ dinner daily, brunch Sat & Sun; 🚇; S F to York St) for dinner, then trek out to **Dough** (305 Franklin Ave cnr Lafayette Ave, Clinton Hill; doughnuts $2; ⏰ 7am-5pm; S G to Classon Ave) for a memorable dessert.

Best
Local Eats

From inspired iterations of world cuisine to quintessentially local nibbles, New York City's dining scene is infinite, all-consuming and a proud testament to the kaleidoscope of citizens that call the city home. So go ahead, take a bite out of the Big Apple – we promise you won't be sorry.

To Market, to Market

Don't let the concrete streets fool you – NYC has a thriving greens scene. At the top of your list should be the New Amsterdam Market (p36) – a seasonal Sunday food market near the South St Seaport. It's here that you'll find the best artisanal meats, cheeses, pasta and bread from the Northeast. Also worth a look is the Union Square Greenmarket (p122), open Monday, Wednesday, Friday and Saturday throughout the year (with reduced hours in winter). Brought to the public by **Grow NYC** (www.grownyc.org/ourmarkets), it could be considered the flagship venue of their market movement.

Food Trucks & Carts

The hot tin carts along the sides of busy intersections have long been a NYC staple as they dish out steaming halal snacks or plump bagels to overworked business folk or on-the-go tourists. But these days, there's a new crew in town that has classed up the meals-on-wheels culture with high-end treats and unique fusion fare. The trucks ply various routes, stopping in designated parking zones throughout the city – namely around Union Sq, Midtown and the Financial District. Our favourites are **Big Gay Ice Cream Truck** (www.twitter.com/biggayicecream), **Korilla BBQ** (www.twitter.com/korillabbq) and **Calexico Cart** (www.twitter.com/calexiconyc).

NY DAILY NEWS/GETTY IMAGES ©

☑ **Top Tips**

▶ Reserve a table at a number of restaurants around the city using **Open Table** (www.opentable.com).

Best for Old-School NYC

Katz's Delicatessen Classic pastrami on rye is the name of the game at this New York stalwart and tourist haven. (p71)

Zabar's New York Jewish charm fills the knish-tinged air on the Upper West Side. (p182)

William Greenberg Desserts Sweet treats à la New York yenta await: hamantaschen (you'll see) and the best black-and-white cookies around. (p166)

Katz's Delicatessen

Sarge's Deli Matzo ball soup for everyone's soul is served to diners sitting at brown vinyl booths. (p141)

Best Bakeries

ChiKaLicious This self-proclaimed 'dessert club' does all sorts of fusion desserts – the ice-cream-on-an-éclair is the clear winner. (p72)

City Bakery Don't miss the gooey cookies and the superlative hot chocolate topped by a homemade marshmallow. (p116)

Ess-a-Bagel New York bagels galore at this old-time-y joint near Stuyvesant Town. (p116)

Best Lunch Spots

Cafe Orlin A favorite East Village haunt with brag-worthy omelets and pillowy pitas atop Middle Eastern faves. (p69)

Cookshop Great on weekends for Bloody Marys, baked goods, hearty egg platters and unpretentious service. (p94)

Via Quadronno Expertly crafted Italian sandwiches go down smooth with a designer coffee. (p165)

Gray's Papaya New York's wieners are perfect to grab on the go for a fast lunch between sightseeing. (p185)

Worth a Trip

Serious gastronomes go to Queens. This multicultural borough spans all palates and kitchens, from the steaming Chinese noodle houses in Flushing – such as **Hunan Kitchen of Grand Sichuan** (www.thegrandsichuan.com; 42-47 Main St; mains $9-23; 🕒7am-2am; [S]7 to Flushing-Main St) – to the Greek eats of Astoria: try **Taverna Kyclades** (www.tavernakyclades.com; 33-07 Ditmars Ave at 33rd St; mains $12-26; [S]N/Q to Astoria-Ditmars Blvd).

Best
Drinking

Considering that 'Manhattan' is thought to be a derivation of the Munsee word *manahactanienk* ('place of general inebriation'), it shouldn't be surprising that New York truly lives up to its nickname 'the city that never sleeps.' In fact, some 20 years after the city was founded, over a quarter of New Amsterdam's buildings were taverns. Sometimes it feels like things have barely changed.

Prohibition-Chic

Here in the land where the term 'cocktail' was born, mixed drinks are still stirred with the utmost seriousness. And these days, researched cocktails are very much in – especially with a Prohibition or swinging '20s theme.

Craft Beer

Once upon a time, Brooklyn was a major beer export, and although that's no longer the case, there's been a recent rise in craft brews. In fact, beer-toting has become such a popular evening pastime that it's starting to rival wine-bar soirees.

Cafe Culture

In the land of limited apartment space, cafes often feel like an extension of one's home: a cosy place where you can gather with friends to catch up or finish that novel you've been working on in your free time. In recent years, however, cafe culture has been elevated – more often than not the corner cup of joe now comes with scrumptious home-made meals and snacks which have firmly planted the cafe deep within the foundation of the city's ever-changing dining scene.

MASCARUCCI/CORBIS ©

Best Cocktails

Little Branch Travel back to the Prohibition Era – barkeeps, dressed in slacks and suspenders, mix carefully blended cocktails in the basement. (p98)

Bathtub Gin This secret bar behind a trick wall does throw-back drinks that are easy to throw back. (p99)

Boom Boom Room Get your name on the guest list and you're in for a chilled-out lounge atmosphere with top-notch tipples. (p100)

Maison Premiere A chemistry-lab-style bar full of syrups and essences that costume-clad barkeeps mix up and shake around. (p197)

Terroir

Best Wine Selection

Vin Sur Vingt A varied assortments of one-time grapes served at reasonable prices in a quaint space. (p98)

Terroir A binder full of vino, opinionated waitstaff and a small menu of great nibbles. (p73)

Barcibo Enoteca Wine HQ a stone's throw from Lincoln Center. (p186)

Best for Beer

Vol de Nuit Belgian beer bar par excellence with themed food. (p99)

McSorley's Old Ale House One of the oldest bars in town serves two-for-ones. (p73)

Keg No 229 A who's who of boutique American brews. (p40)

Birreria Lengthy list of bottles and draughts. (p115)

Best for Spirits

Pravda House-made vodka infusions in a subterranean space. (p56)

Brandy Library A menu of encyclopedic proportions climbs all the way to triple digits. Knowledgeable waiters sweeten the deal. (p39)

Best Bar Bites

Commodore This corner bar is a faux '70s rec room with wood paneling and a few big booths to spread out in. (p197)

Tertulia Down that Spanish white with a delightful assortment of farm-fresh tapas treats. (p97)

Weather Up Come for the cocktails, stay for the excellent grub. (p40)

Best for Coffee

Abraço Expertly made espresso – a clear local fave – is brewed in this closet-sized cafe. (p70)

Via Quadronno This haven for 'ladies who lunch' touts brilliant sandwiches, but its coffee is worthy of much praise as well. (p165)

Stumptown Coffee Hipster-chic brewmasters wield perfectly brewed cups of steaming caffeine. (p143)

Kaffe 1668 Coffee-sippers of every ilk swing by for smooth house blends down in Tribeca. (p39)

Best
Entertainment

Hollywood may hold court when it comes to the motion picture, but it's NYC that reigns supreme over the pantheon of other arts. Actors, musicians, dancers and artists flock to the bright lights of the Big Apple like moths to a flame. It's like the old saying goes: if you can make it here, you can make it anywhere.

Comedy

A good laugh is easy to find in the Big Apple, where comedians sharpen their stand-up and improv chops hoping to get scouted by a producer or agent. The best spots for some chuckles are downtown – particularly around Chelsea and Greenwich Village.

Dance

Dance fans are spoiled for choice in this town, home to both the New York City Ballet (p188) and the American Ballet Theatre (p188), plus modern dance companies galore. There are two major dance seasons: first in spring (March to May), then in late fall (October to December).

Live Music

NYC is the country's capital of live music and just about every taste can be catered for here. For current listings, check out **New York Magazine** (www.nymag.com) and the **Village Voice** (www.villagevoice.com).

Theater

From the legendary hit factories of Broadway to the scruffy black-box theaters that dot countless downtown blocks, NYC boasts the full gamut of theater experiences. The term 'off-Broadway' is not geographical – it refers to theaters that are smaller in size and with less glitzy production budgets.

WALTER MCBRIDE/CORBIS ©

☑ **Top Tips**

▶ Cheaper, classical concerts can be scouted at various churches (oh the acoustics!) and smaller recital halls.

Best Broadway Shows

Book of Mormon A resounding triumph of talent both on stage and behind the scenes; from the creators of *South Park*. (p145)

Chicago Fosse hands swirl and the girls from the cell block make dirty deals, cabaret-style. (p145)

Wicked Beloved musical that drops a veritable house on the well-known tale of the *The Wizard of Oz*. (p146)

WALTER MCBRIDE/CORBIS ©

VILLAGE VANGUARD

Village Vanguard

Best for Theater (non-Broadway)

Playwrights Horizons The place to catch what could be the next big thing to hit the stages of New York. (p146)

Flea Theater One of New York's top off-off-Broadway companies performs a regular rotation of theater. (p41)

Lincoln Center The mother ship of the performing arts on the Upper West Side. (p180)

Brooklyn Academy of Music The country's oldest performing arts center and supplies New York City with its edgier works of modern dance, music and theater. (p195)

Best for Laughs

Upright Citizens' Brigade Theatre Improv at its finest by many who go on to star in *Saturday Night Live*. (p101)

Comedy Cellar Celebrity joke-tellers regularly plow through this basement club. (p102)

Best for Film

Angelika Film Center Foreign and independent films galore; comes with quirky charms (subway rumbles and occasionally bad sound). (p104)

92YTribeca Well placed on the festival circuit, this theater offers a bit of everything. (p41)

Film Society of Lincoln Center One of New York's cinematic gems, providing an invaluable platform for a wide gamut of moving pictures. (p187)

Best for Jazz

Village Vanguard Major jazz haven for over 50 years – the heart and soul of the Village scene. (p103)

Blue Note Famous world wide for its rotating cast of visiting musicians. (p103)

Best
LGBT

The future has arrived in NYC: men seek out other men using apps with geolocators, drag queens are so 'out' that they're practically 'in,' bouncers thumb through guest lists on their iPads and gay marriage is – at long last – legal. It's time to hop in your time machine and join the fray.

OCEAN/CORBIS ©

Mo Money, No Matter

Although New York City has a smattering of neighborhoods that are infamous for their gay hangouts, the city's LGBT scene is hardly segregated, let alone ghettoized. With one of the largest disposable incomes of any demographic, the gays seem to run the city, from the fashion runways and major music labels to Wall Street downtown. The new marriage laws of 2011 are a further acknowledgement that here in New York it's totally 'in' to be 'out'.

Weekdays are the New Weekend

Here in the Big Apple, any night of the week is fair game to paint the town rouge – especially for the gay community, who attack the weekday social scene with gusto. Wednesdays and Thursdays roar with a steady stream of parties and locals love raging on Sundays (especially in summer).

Promoters

One of the best ways to dial into the party hotline is to follow the various goings-on of your favorite promoter, such as **Josh Wood** (www.joshwoodproductions.com), **Susanne Bartsch** (www.susannebartsch.com), **Brian Rafferty** and **Shawn Paul Mazur** (www.raffertymazurevents.com), **Sean B** and **Will Automagic** (www.spankartmag.com) and **Erich Conrad** (www.twitter.com/ZIGZAGLeBain).

☑ Top Tips

► Figure out which scene you are a part of (Brooklyn hipster? Fashionista?) to find exactly the crowd you're after.

► Some of the best stuff happens at private parties, so make some friends then follow them.

► If it's hip and cool, odds are there will be plenty of gays in sight, so don't limit yourself to gay-specific places.

Best for Classic NYC Gay

Julius Bar The oldest operating gay establishment in the entire city. (p100)

Pier 45

Marie's Crisis The ultimate cramped piano bar where no one's afraid to be themselves. (p98)

Boxers NYC Sports bar where patrons tackle the tight ends on and off the field. (p120)

Best for Weeknights

Splash Bar A staple of the west-side gay scene continues to lure the crowds with DJed dance nights and drag shows. (p120)

Eastern Bloc Iron Curtain chic meets a sweaty sea of boys exchanging glances and ordering mixed drinks. (p74)

Industry Lounge chairs, dance beats and cute boys – the perfect gay ol' time. (p142)

Best Daytime Scene

Brunch on Eighth Ave Pick an outdoor eatery and hunker down for an afternoon of Bloody Marys while cruising Marys. (p95)

Pier 45 Spruced up with spruces, this concrete finger poking out into the water is a popular gay hangout spot, especially in good weather. (p92)

Worth a Trip

The Brooklyn gays go to **Metropolitan** (559 Lorimer St at Metropolitan Ave, Williamsburg; 🕒3pm-4am; [S] L to Lorimer St, G to Metropolitan Ave), which draws a steady stream of artsy types with its cool staff, cheap drinks, outdoor patio and groovy DJs. During the summer, it's known for its Sunday backyard cookouts, and on Wednesday nights, it's all about the girls.

Best
Shopping

You can blame the likes of Holly Golightly and Carrie Bradshaw for making it darned impossible not to associate New York City with diamonds for breakfast or designer labels for dinner – and the locals are all too happy to oblige. NYC isn't the world's fashion or technology capital, but private capital reigns supreme: there's no better place to shop to your heart's content.

BLOOMBERG/GETTY ©

An Homage to Luxury

At the top of NYC's shopping pyramid are those bastions of aspirational trends known worldwide as the department store. These high-end mega-boutiques offer all the big designer names.

Sample Sales

While clothing sales happen year-round – usually when the seasons change and the old stock must be moved out – sample sales are held frequently, mostly in the huge warehouses in the Meatpacking District or SoHo. While the original sample sale was a way for designers to get rid of one-of-a-kind prototypes that weren't quite up to snuff, most sample sales these days are for high-end labels to get rid of overstock at wonderfully deep discounts.

Flea Markets and Vintage Adventures

As much as New Yorkers gravitate toward all that's shiny and new, it can be infinitely fun to rifle through the closets of unwanted wares and threads. The most popular flea market is the Brooklyn Flea Market (p195), housed in all sorts of spaces throughout the year. The East Village is the city's de facto neighborhood for secondhand items – the uniform of the unwavering legion of hipsters.

Best Department Stores

Barneys Perfectly curated fashion labels lure serious New York fashionistas. (p149)

Bergdorf Goodman Exclusive labels and brilliant Christmas window installations. (p149)

Bloomingdale's A veritable museum to the world of shopping. (p149)

Best for Unique Souvenirs & Gifts

MoMA Design & Book Store Take home a piece of the Museum of Modern Art at its famous store, which is curated as beautifully as the museum itself. (p149)

ABC Carpet & Home A massive department store dedicated to everything you could

Patricia Field

ever want for your home. (p122)

Philip Williams Posters Over half a million original posters of all shapes and sizes await your perusal. (p42)

Kiosk A quirky collection of doodads from all over the globe. (p57)

Purl Soho Knit one, purl two at this craft shop, yarn vendor and dealer of memorable keepsakes. (p58)

Best Bookshops

McNally Jackson Everyone's favorite indie bookshop has a slew of tomes and hosts regular speaker series. (p57)

Printed Matter Limited-edition magazine and monographs – it's a

veritable art gallery unto itself. (p106)

Housing Works Book Store Funds go to charity and patrons all to happy to oblige in this cute cafe-cum-bookshop. (p57)

Strand Book Store Easily the most beloved bookstore in the city proudly boasts over 18 miles of books. (p106)

Three Lives & Company Receive expert advice on your latest finds – this definitely beats Amazon. (p106)

Best Apparel Boutiques

Opening Ceremony Indie labels galore cycle through this fashion gallery of global aspirations. (p58)

Patricia Field Famous fashionista of *Sex and the City* fame offers outrageous apparel in her large boutique. (p79)

Built by Wendy Snug boutique just beyond SoHo's reach with carefully cut designer wares. (p59)

Best
Architecture

New York's architectural history is a layer cake of ideas and styles. Colonial farmhouses and graceful Federal-style buildings are found alongside ornate beaux arts palaces from the early 1900s. There are the revivals (Greek, Gothic, Romanesque and Renaissance) and the unadorned forms of the International Style. For the architecture buff, it's a bonanza.

BRIAN LAWRENCE/GETTY ©

City of Skyscrapers

By the time New York settled into the 20th century, elevators and steel-frame engineering had allowed the city to grow up – literally. This period saw a building boom of skyscrapers, starting with Cass Gilbert's neo-Gothic 57-story Woolworth Building (1913). To this day it remains one of the 50 tallest buildings in the United States.

Others soon followed. In 1930, the Chrysler Building, the 77-story art deco masterpiece designed by William Van Alen, became the world's tallest structure. The following year, the record was broken by the Empire State Building, a clean-lined art deco monolith crafted from Indiana limestone. Its spire was meant to be used as a mooring mast for dirigibles – an idea that made for good publicity, but proved to be impractical and unfeasible.

A Starchitect's Canvas

New York City's heterogenous landscape lends itself well to the dabbling sketching pencils of some of the world's leading architectural personalities, or 'starchitects' as they've come to be known. You'll find Frank O Gehry's rippling structures, SANAA's white-box exteriors and Renzo Piano's signature facade flip-flopping tucked between the city's glass towers and low-rise bricked behemoths.

Best Skyscrapers

Empire State Building Like a martini, a good steak and jazz, this Depression-era skyscraper never ever gets old. (p128)

Chrysler Building Manhattan's most elegant skyscraper boasts steel ornamentation inspired by the automobile, including gargoyles that are shaped like retro hood ornaments. (p134)

Flatiron Building This is NYC's original skyscraper flavor with 20 triangularly shaped floors tucked behind ornate brick. (p113)

Flatiron Building

Best Places of Worship

St Patrick's Cathedral A neo-Gothic wonder and the largest Catholic cathedral in America. (p136)

Grace Church Rescued from disrepair, it's now one of the daintiest structures in the city, complete with spires and ornate carvings. (p92)

Trinity Church Stunning stained glass accents what was once the tallest structure in New York. Don't miss the on-site cemetery. (p34)

Temple Emanu-el This imposing Romanesque synagogue on the Upper East Side has ceilings that are painted in gold. (p163)

Best of the Rest

Whitney Museum of American Art Modernism doesn't get more brutal than this: Marcel Breuer's inverted staircase structure looks like the very well-designed lair of an action movie baddie. Bring it on. (p161)

Grand Central Terminal A classic beaux arts stunner, with an airy concourse capped by vaulted ceilings decorated with an astronomical pattern. (p134)

New Museum of Contemporary Art A stacked-cube structure by SANAA has a translucent aluminum exterior that is all kinds of sexy (even if the galleries have a detention-center vibe). (p66)

TETRA IMAGES/GETTY ©

Best
Museums

New York City is America's culture capital and sports dozens upon dozens of museums, showcasing an incredible spectrum of exhibits. You'll find everything from big-ticket attractions known throughout the world for their cache of treasures to tiny super-specialized showrooms exploring a single – and oftentimes offbeat – subject.

NELSON BARNARD/STRINGER/GETTY ©

Planning Your Visit

Most museums close at least one day a week, usually Monday, and sometimes Sunday and/or Tuesday. Many stay open late one or more nights a week – often a Thursday or Friday. You can save time at the most popular museums by purchasing tickets in advance online.

Galleries

Chelsea is home to the highest concentration of art galleries in the entire city – and the cluster continues to grow with each passing season. Most lie in the 20s, on the blocks between Tenth and Eleventh Aves. For a complete guide and map, pick up Art Info's *Gallery Guide*, available for free at most galleries, or visit www.westchelseaarts. com. Wine-and-cheese openings for new shows are typically held on Thursday evenings, while most art houses tend to shutter their doors on Sundays and Mondays.

For Free

Many museums offer free or reduced admission once a month – check the museum websites to find out when. Although most of the city's gallery openings occur on Thursday, you'll find gratis events throughout the week.

Best Art Museums

Museum of Modern Art NYC's darling museum space has brilliantly curated spaces boasting the best of the world's modern art. (p130)

Metropolitan Museum of Art The most incredible encyclopedic museum in the Americas comes stocked with its own Egyptian temple and the country's most famous canvas of George Washington. (p154)

Guggenheim Museum The exhibits can be uneven, but the architecture is the real star in this Frank Lloyd Wright–designed building. (p158)

Frick Collection A Gilded Age mansion has Vermeers, El Grecos and Goyas, and a stunning courtyard fountain. (p161)

Neue Galerie

Neue Galerie Fans of Klimt and Schiele should not miss this intimate space in a former Rockefeller mansion. (p162)

Best New York Museums

Lower East Side Tenement Museum Fantastic insight into life as an immigrant during the 19th and early 20th centuries. (p67)

Merchant's House Museum Step back in time to this perfectly preserved Federal home from well over a century ago. It's a great glimpse of old-school New York. (p50)

Museum of the City of New York Details of the city's colorful past abound in this refur-

bished Georgian mansion. (p163)

New York City Fire Museum Situated in an old firehouse, this museum recounts the story of New York's firemen and includes a haunting tribute to those who perished in 9/11. (p52)

New York City Police Museum Details the history of the city's police force. (p35)

Best Offbeat Museums

Museum of Comic & Cartoon Art A cult favorite for those seeking out graphic novels, old-school posters and everything in between. (p52)

Museum of Sex Need we say more? (p137)

Worth a Trip

On a hilltop overlooking the Hudson River, the **Cloisters Museum & Gardens** (www.metmuseum.org/cloisters; Fort Tryon Park; suggested donation adult/child $25/free; ⏱9:30am-4:45pm Tue-Sun Nov-Feb, to 5:15pm Mar-Oct; Ⓢ A to 190th St) is a mish-mash of European monasteries. Built in the 1930s to house the Metropolitan Museum of Art's medieval treasures, it also contains the beguiling 16th-century tapestry *The Hunt of the Unicorn*.

Best
Festivals & Events

CAMILO MORALES/CORBIS ©

It seems as though there's always some sort of celebration going on in NYC. National holidays, religious observances, arts festivals and just plain ol' weekends prompt parades, parties or street fairs.

Mercedes-Benz Fashion Week (www.mbfashion week.com/newyork) The infamous February fashion shows are not open to the public, but being in the city this week could provide a vicarious thrill.

St Patrick's Day Parade (www.nycstpatricksparade. org) A massive audience lines Fifth Ave on March 17 for this popular parade of bagpipe blowers, sparkly floats and clusters of Irish-lovin' politicians.

Tribeca Film Festival (www.tribecafilm.com) Robert De Niro's downtown film festival has quickly become a star in the indie movie circuit.

Gay Pride (www.nycpride. org) Gay Pride culminates in a major march down Fifth Ave on the last Sunday of June.

HBO Bryant Park Summer Film Festival (www. bryantpark.org) Beginning in June and ending in August, Bank of America sponsors weekly outdoor screenings of some of the most beloved films in Hollywood history.

Independence Day America's Independence Day – July 4 – is celebrated with fireworks

Shakespeare in the Park (www.shakespea reinthepark.org) Free performances in Central Park. You'll have to wait hours in line to score tickets or win them in the online lottery.

Open House New York (www.ohny.org) The country's largest architecture and design event is held in October, and features special, architect-led tours and other events.

Thanksgiving Day Parade (www.macys.com) Massive helium-filled cartoons soar overhead, high-school marching bands rattle their snares and millions of onlookers bundle up with scarves.

New York City Marathon (www.nycmarathon. org) Held in November, this run draws thousands of athletes from around the world and just as many excited spectators.

Rockefeller Center Christmas Tree Lighting (www.rockefellercenter. com) The flick of a switch ignites the massive Christmas tree in Rockefeller Center, bedecked with over 25,000 lights.

New Year's Eve (www. timessquarenyc.org/nye/) Times Sq is the ultimate place to ring in the New Year.

Best Sports & Activities

Although hailing cabs in New York City can feel like a blood sport and waiting on subway platforms in summer heat is steamier than a sauna, New Yorkers still love to stay active in their spare time. And considering how limited the green spaces are in New York, it's surprising for some visitors just how active the locals can be.

RICHARD LEVINE / ALAMY ©

Running & Bicycling

The 1.6-mile path surrounding the Jacqueline Kennedy Onassis Reservoir is for runners and walkers only. Also try the paths along the Hudson River or FDR Dr and the East River. NYC has added more than 200 miles of bike lanes in the last five years, but we recommend the uninitiated stick to the less hectic trails in the parks and along the waterways.

Indoor Sports & Activities

Yoga and Pilates studios dot the city. If you're looking to score some gym action, try your luck at scoring a complimentary pass from one of the franchised studios.

Best Spectator Sports

New York Yankees (www.yankees.com; Yankee Stadium, E 161st St at River Ave, the Bronx; **S** B, D, 4 to 161st St-Yankee Stadium) Even if you're not into baseball, it's worth trekking out to Queens to experience the rabid fandom.

New York Mets (www.mets.com; Citi Field, 123-01 Roosevelt Ave, Flushing; **S** 7 to Mets-Willets Pt) New York's other baseball team has its own legion of faithful fans.

New York Knicks (www.nyknicks.com; Madison Sq Garden, Seventh Ave btwn 31st & 33rd Sts, Midtown West; **S** A/C/E, 1/2/3 to 34th St-Penn Station) Pro-league basketball team that calls Madison Square Garden home.

☑ **Top Tips**

▶ Most teams sell tickets via **Ticketmaster** (☎800-448-7849; www.ticketmaster.com). The other major outlet is **StubHub** (☎866-788-2482; www.stubhub.com).

New Jersey Devils (www.newjerseydevils.com; Prudential Center, 165 Mulberry St, Newark, NJ; **R** NJ Transit, PATH to Newark Penn Station) Your best bet for a riveting hockey game.

New York Giants (www.giants.com; Meadowlands Stadium, East Rutherford, NJ; **R** NJ Transit from Penn Station to Meadowlands) One of the National Football League's oldest teams.

Best
Nightlife & Clubbing

JERRIT CLARK/WIREIMAGE/GETTY ©

Trendy all-night lounges tucked behind the walls of a crumby Chinese restaurant, taco shops that clandestinely host late-night tranny cabarets, stadium-size discotheques that clang to the thump of DJ-ed beats and after-after-after-parties on the roof as the sun rises. An alternate universe lurks between the cracks of everyday life and it welcomes savvy visitors just as much as the locals in the know.

Neighbourhoods

Choose where to go based on the kind of night you're after. The East Village is the proud home of the original flavor of dive bar while The Lower East Side's mix of nightclubs draws bands of youthful party-goers. The jet-set crowd flocks to the Meatpacking District, with wine bars, backdoor lounges and homo hangouts radiating out into the West Village and Chelsea. If you're after skyscraper views, historic cocktail salons or a time-warped dive bar with Hollywood credentials, you're bound to find your perfect drinking hole in Midtown's canyons. And

don't forget Brooklyn, which offers everything on the nightlife spectrum with Williamsburg as its drinking capital.

Best Clubs

Le Bain Theme parties roar throughout the week at this Meatpacking hotspot at the Standard Hotel. (p100)

Boom Boom Room If you got into Le Bain, try your luck next door at this more selective spot where you can actually make conversation with the *Vogue* photographers as you sway to DJed beats. (p100)

Heathers Induct yourself into East Village hipsterdom at this local haunt where the bar space is wee but it won't keep you

from busting a move – especially on weekends. (p75)

☑ **Top Tips**

▸ It never hurts to plan ahead: having your name on a guest list can relieve unnecessary frustration and disappointment.

▸ If you're fed the 'private party' line, try to bluff – chances are high that you've been bounced.

▸ Don't forget a wad of cash – many nightspots (even the swankiest ones) often refuse credit cards and in-house ATMs scam a fortune in fees.

Best
Parks

New York's parks, gardens and squares are the city's backyards. The larger parks are ideal for strolling or simply soaking up the sunshine, with plenty of seating as well as kiosks and nearby cafes. Smaller squares offer serendipitous moments of encounter, wonder and surprise.

Outdoor Activities

New Yorkers have perfected the art of turning their green spaces into places of recreation and encounter. During the summer months you'll find outdoor film screenings, Shakespeare performed in Central Park, concerts at Battery Park's Hudson River Park, not to mention Lincoln Center Dance Nights.

Beyond Manhattan

If you're looking for sprawling acres of green space beyond Central Park, it's best to head to Brooklyn. The borough's newest park is the 85-acre **Brooklyn Bridge Park** (www.brooklyn bridgeparknyc.org; East River Waterfront btwn Atlantic Ave & Adams St; ⏰6am-1am; 🚹; Ⓢ A/C to High St, 2/3

to Clark St, F to York St), which has revitalized a once-barren stretch of shoreline, turning a series of abandoned piers into public park land. Two of these are now open (Piers 1 and 6); others are scheduled to open in 2012 and 2013. Once completed, it will be the biggest new park in Brooklyn since Calvert Vaux and Frederick Law Olmsted designed the 585-acre Prospect Park.

Best Parks

Central Park The city's most famous park has more than 800 acres of rolling meadows and boulder-topped hillocks. (p174)

The High Line A thin stripe of green that unfurls up the western slice of downtown. (p84)

Gramercy Park New York exclusivity at its finest: it's cut off from the public by wrought-iron fences, but it's oh-so wonderful to peek in. (p114)

Madison Square Park A refurbished green space that showcases large-scale sculptures, wields popular burgers from its Shake Shack and has a state-of-the-art public restroom facility. (p114)

Riverside Park A 100-block park runs alongside the Hudson on Manhattan's west side – the ideal spot for a bike ride. (p182)

Bryant Park A welcome respite from the hecticness of Midtown, Bryant Park offers film screenings in summer and ice-skating in winter. (p137)

Best
Tours

While the streets of New York lend themselves well to unguided discovery, it's often worth joining a tour to gain greater insight into the city's history and treasures.

Strayboots (☎877-787-2929; www.strayboots.com; tours from $12) Self-guided hybrid tours that fuse interesting urban info and a scavenger hunt element to help New York neophytes find their way around the neighborhood of their choice. Go at your own pace as you text in your answers to central command to receive your next clue.

Municipal Art Society (☎212-935-3960; www.mas.org; 111 W 57th St; tours adult $15) With an expert focus on architecture, this non-profit society is dedicated to championing urban design. It takes groups on walking or bus tours of structural gems. Its most popular is a walk-through of the beaux arts Grand Central Terminal.

Gray Line (☎212-397-2620; www.newyorksightseeing.com; tours $50-75) The most ubiquitous guided tour in the city, Gray Line is responsible for bombarding New York streets with the red double-decker buses that locals love to hate. Really, though, for a comprehensive tour of the big sights, it's a great way to go.

Foods of New York (☎212-239-1124; www.foodsofny.com; tours $40-75) The official foodie tour of NYC & Company offers various three-hour tours that help you eat your way through the city. Prepare thyself for a moving feast of fresh Italian pasta, sushi, global cheeses and real New York pizza.

Bike the Big Apple (☎877-865-0078; www.bikethebigapple.com; tours incl bike & helmet $70-80) Recommended by NYC & Company, this operator offers a variety of tours including an Ethnic Apple Tour that covers Williamsburg, Roosevelt Island and the east side of Manhattan.

Big Apple Greeter Program (☎212-669-8159; www.bigapplegreeter.org; tours free) Set up an intimate stroll in the neighborhood of your choice, led by a local volunteer who just can't wait to show off his or her city to you.

RICHARD CUMMINS/LONELY PLANET IMAGES ©

Best
For Free

If the best things in life are free, then there are a ton of great things in New York. Besides wandering the endlessly fascinating streets and parks, there are a slew of world-class museums that offer free admission during different times of the month.

GAIL MOONEY/CORBIS ©

Staten Island Ferry Hop on the free ferry bound for Staten Island for postcard-perfect views of Manhattan's southern edge. (p32)

Chelsea Galleries Over 300 galleries are open to the public along Manhattan's West 20s. (p86)

Brooklyn Brewery Four-dollar draughts are easy on the wallet; free afternoon tours on weekends are even better. (p197)

New Museum of Contemporary Art Ethereal tooth-white boxes house a serious stash of contemporary art that's free for visitors on Thursday evenings after 7pm. (p66)

Central Park New York's giant backyard is yours for the taking, with acre after acre of tree-lined bliss. Go for a jog, relax on the lawn or throw bread crumbs at the ducks in the pond. (p174)

The High Line The city's proudest achievement in urban renewal in the last decade, this catwalk of parkland is great for a stroll and some skyline ogling. (p84)

New York Public Library The grand, beaux arts gem (aka the Stephen A Schwarzman Building) turned 100 in 2011 and is worth checking out for its sumptuous architecture in addition to the great collection of books. (p136)

Museum of Modern Art The glorious MoMA is free from 4pm to 8pm on Fridays – be prepared for massive crowds and long lines. (p130)

Neue Galerie The gracious Neue is gratis from 6pm to 8pm on the first Friday of the month. It's well worth visiting this somewhat under-the-radar treasure on the Upper East Side. (p162)

Studio Museum in Harlem Up in the heart of the city's African American roots, this museum is free to browse on Sundays. (p193)

American Museum of Natural History If you rock up to the museum an hour before closing, they'll let you in for free. (p180)

Best
For Kids

RAY LASKOWITZ/LONELY PLANET IMAGES ©

It may come as a surprise that the city known for never sleeping is actually quite kid-friendly. With enough museums to fill an entire week, you'll never want for additional exhibits that tickle the senses and expand the mind. Recently, imaginative new playgrounds have been built around the city's public spaces and child-focused attractions, like the Central Park Zoo, have received much-needed refurbishments.

Dining with Kids

Restaurants in the most touristy corners of the city are ready at a moment's notice to bust out the highchairs and kiddy menus. In general, however, dining venues are small – eating at popular joints sans reservation can often be more of a hassle with the little ones in tow. Early dinners can alleviate some of the stress, as most locals tend to take to their tables between 7:30pm and 9:30pm. In good weather, we recommend grabbing a blanket and food from one of the city's excellent grocers, and heading to Central Park or one of the many other green spaces for a picnic in the grass.

Best Museums

American Museum of Natural History Dinosaurs, planets and butterflies, oh my! (p180)

Metropolitan Museum of Art A fun trip back in time for the young ones – make sure to stop at the wondrous Egyptian Wing. (p154)

Best Shopping

FAO Schwarz Santa's workshop has crash-landed in the heart of Midtown. (p150)

Yoyamart Memorable gifts for kids, but a much more interesting shopping experience for their parents. (p105)

Forbidden Planet There's *Star Trek* and *Magic The Gathering* (and everything in between) at this nerd paradise. (p109)

Best Carousels

Bryant Park Steps from Times Sq and the New York Public Library, find Le Carrousel in Bryant Park, which revolves to the tune of French cabaret music. (p137)

Central Park At the level of 64th St in the heart of Central Park is a 1908 carousel with colorful painted horses. (p174)

Survival Guide

Survival Guide

Before You Go

When to Go

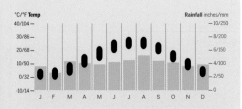

⇒ Winter (Dec–Feb)
Snowfalls and sub-zero temperature. The holiday season keep things light despite the shivers.

⇒ Spring (Mar–May)
Eager cafes drag their patio furniture out at the first hint of warm weather.

⇒ Summer (Jun–Aug)
Oppressively hot in height of summer. Locals flock to their Hamptons share on weekends.

⇒ Fall (Sep–Nov)
Brilliant bursts of red and gold illuminate the city's parks.

Book Your Stay

⇒ The average room rate is well over $300. But don't let that scare you, there are great deals to be had – almost all of which can be found through savvy online snooping.

⇒ Unlike many destinations, New York City doesn't have a 'high season.' Sure, there are busier times of the year when it comes to tourist traffic, but at over 51 million visitor per annum, the Big Apple never needs to worry when it comes to filling up beds. As such, room rates fluctuate based on availability; in fact, most hotels have a booking algorithm in place that spits out a price quote relative to the number of rooms already booked on the same night. The busier the evening, the higher the price.

⇒ If you're looking to find the best room rates, flexibility is key – weekdays are often cheaper and you'll generally find that accommodations in winter months have smaller price tags. If you are visiting over a weekend, try the business hotels in the Financial District, which tend to empty out when the work week ends.

➡ If you don't have your heart set on a particular property, check out discount juggernauts like **Expedia** (www.expedia. com), **Orbitz** (www.orbitz. com) and **Priceline** (www. priceline.com).

➡ If you do have an inkling of where you'd like to stay, it's best to start at your desired hotel's website as it'll often include deals and package rates.

➡ Also worth checking out are the slew of members-only websites, such as **Jetsetter** (www. jetsetter.com), that offer discounted rates and 'flash sales' for their devotees.

➡ These days, finding a place to sleep is hardly restricted to the traditional spectrum of lodging. Websites like **Airbnb** (www.airbnb.com) are providing a truly unique – and not to mention economical – alternative to the wallet-busting glitz and glam by offering locals the opportunity to rent out their apartments while they're out of town or lease a space (be it a bedroom or pull-out couch) in their home.

Useful Websites

Lonely Planet (www. lonelyplanet.com) Lots of accommodation reviews and online booking.

Playbill (www.playbill.com) It may seem counter intuitive to join the Playbill Club, but members get select rates on a variety of Manhattan hotels.

Kayak (www.kayak.com) Simple all-purpose search engine.

Best Budget

Cosmopolitan Hotel (www.cosmohotel.com) Cosmo is a hero if you'd rather save your bills for chic eateries and boutiques. It's clean and comfy but there's not too much to brag about.

Pod Hotel (www.thepod hotel.com) A dream come true for folks who would like to live inside their iPod – or at least curl up and sleep with it. This affordable hot spot has a range of room types, most barely big enough for the bed.

East Village Bed & Coffee (www.bedandcoffee.com) Owner Anne has turned her family home into an offbeat B&B with colorful, themed private rooms (one shared bathroom per floor) and great amenities

Sugar Hill Harlem (www. sugarhillharleminn.com) An airy townhouse restored to its turn-of-the-century splendor, with suites named after African American jazz greats.

Best Midrange

Ace Hotel New York City (www.acehotel.com/newyork) A hit with social-media types and cashed-up creatives, the standard and deluxe rooms are best described as upscale bachelor pads.

Nu Hotel (www.nuho telbrooklyn.com) The 93 rooms in this Brooklyn hotel are of the stripped-down variety, featuring lots of crisp whiteness (sheets, walls, duvets) and furnishings made from recycled teak.

Country Inn the City (www.countryinnthecity.com) Just like staying with your big-city friend – if, that is, your big-city friend happens to own a landmark 1891 limestone townhouse on a picturesque tree-lined block.

Hôtel Americano (www.hotel-americano.com) It's like sleeping in a bento box, but the food's been replaced by a carefully curated selection of minimalist furniture.

B&B On the Park (www.bbnyc.com) This beautiful Victorian B&B has five rooms splashed out in Persian-style rugs, potted plants and poster beds covered in pillows.

Gild Hall Wall Street (www.wallstreetdistrict.com) Gild Hall's entryway leads to a bi-level library and champagne bar oozing hunting lodge chic. Rooms fuse Euro elegance and American comfort.

Best Top End

Gramercy Park Hotel (www.gramercyparkhotel.com) The rooms – overlooking Gramercy Park – have customized oak furnishings, 400-count Italian linens, and big, feather-stuffed mattresses on sprawling beds.

Andaz Fifth Avenue (http://andaz.hyatt.com) Uber-chic yet youthful and relaxed, the Andaz ditches stuffy reception desks for mobile staff who check you in on tablets in lobby.

Surrey (www.thesurrey.com) This steely Upper East Side gem – literally, everything is decorated in silvery shades of grey – is all about luxury.

Greenwich Hotel (www.greenwichhotelny.com) From the plush drawing room to the lantern-lit pool inside a reconstructed Japanese farmhouse, nothing about Robert De Niro's hotel is generic.

Setai Fifth Avenue (www.capellahotels.com/newyork) Rooms at the luxurious, skyscraping Setai are more akin to suites. Understatedly chic, all feature neutral hues, handsome wood paneling, Duxiana mattresses and Nespresso machines.

Chatwal New York (www.thechatwalny.com) A restored art deco jewel in the Theater District, the Chatwal is as atmospheric as it is historic.

Arriving in New York City

☑ **Top Tip** For the best way to get to your accommodations, see p17.

John F Kennedy International Airport

John F Kennedy International Airport (JFK), 15 miles from Midtown in southeastern Queens, has eight terminals, serves 45 million passengers annually and hosts flights coming and going from all corners of the globe.

Taxi A yellow taxi from Manhattan to the airport will use the meter. Prices depend on traffic, often running about $55, and it can take 45 to 60 minutes. From JFK, taxis charge a flat rate of $45 to any destination in Manhattan (not including tolls or tip).

Car service Car services have set fares from $45.

Private vehicle If you're driving from the airport, either go around Brooklyn's south tip via the

Belt Parkway to US 278 (the Brooklyn-Queens Expressway or BQE), or via US678 (Van Wyck Expressway) to US 495 (Long Island Expressway or LIE), which heads into Manhattan via the Queens-Midtown Tunnel.

Express bus The New York Airport Service Express Bus costs $15.50.

AirTrain The overpriced AirTrain stops at every terminal at JFK. You pay the $5 fee with a Metro Card after exiting the train.

Subway The AirTrain links JFK to the subway. Take the AirTrain to Howard Beach–JFK Airport station for the A line through Brooklyn and into Manhattan, or opt for Sutphin Blvd–Archer Ave (Jamaica Station) for the E, J or Z line to Queens and Manhattan.

LaGuardia Airport

Used mainly for domestic flights, LaGuardia Airport (LGA) is smaller than JFK but only eight miles from midtown Manhattan; it sees about 26 million passengers per year. It's been open for commercial use since 1939, making it considerably older than JFK, too. US Airways and Delta have their own terminals.

Taxi A taxi to Manhattan will cost you about $40 for the approximately half-hour ride from LaGuardia. If your driver takes the Queens-Midtown tunnel, it's an additional $6.

Car service A car service from LaGuardia runs about $40 to $50.

Express bus The New York Airport Service Express Bus to Manhattan costs $12.

Private vehicle The most common driving route from the airport is along Grand Central Expressway to the BQE (US 278), then to the Queens-Midtown Tunnel via the LIE (US 495). Downtown-bound drivers can stay on the BQE and cross (free) via the Williamsburg Bridge.

Subway/bus It's somewhat less convenient to use public transportation to get from LaGuardia into the city. From LaGuardia, take the M60 bus bound for Manhattan, then switch to the 4/5/6 subway at the corner of 125th St and Lexington Ave.

Newark Liberty International Airport

Don't write off New Jersey when looking for air fares to New York. The same distance from Midtown as JFK (16 miles), Newark Liberty International Airport (EWR), brings many New Yorkers out for flights (around 36 million passengers annually). Actually it became the metropolis' first major airport in 1928.

Car service /taxi A car service runs about $55 for the 45-minute ride to Midtown – a taxi is roughly the same. You only have to pay the toll to go through the Lincoln Tunnel (at 42nd St) or Holland Tunnel (at Canal St) coming into Manhattan from Jersey ($8).

Subway/train Public transportation from Newark is convenient, but a bit of a rip-off. NJ Transit runs rail service (with an AirTrain connection) between Newark and New York's Penn Station for $12.50 each way. The trip uses a commuter train, takes 25 minutes and runs every 20 or 30 minutes from 4:20am to about 1:40am. When travelling to the airport,

Subway Cheat Sheet

Numbers, letters, colors Subway train lines have a color and a letter or number. Trains with the same color run on the same tracks, often following roughly the same path through Manhattan before branching out into the other boroughs.

Express & local lines Each color-coded line is shared by local trains and express trains; the latter make only select stops in Manhattan (indicated by a white circle on subway maps). If you're covering a greater distance, you're better off transferring to the express train (usually just across the platform) to save time.

Getting in the right station Some stations have separate entrances for downtown and uptown lines (read the sign carefully). If you swipe in at the wrong one, you'll either need to ride the subway to a station where you can transfer for free, or lose the $2.25 and re-enter the station (usually across the street). Also look for the green and red lamps above the stairs at each station entrance; green means that it's always open, while red means that particular entrance will be closed at certain hours, usually late at night.

Lost weekend All the rules switch on weekends, when some lines combine with others and some get suspended, some stations get passed and others get reached. Locals and tourists alike stand on platforms confused, sometimes irate. Check the www.mta.info website for weekend schedules. Sometimes posted signs aren't visible until after you reach the platform.

hold onto your ticket, which you must show upon exiting.

Train/bus A clumsier, 'stick-it-to-the-man' alternative is taking the 62 bus (every 10 or 20 minutes) for the 20-minute ride from the airport ($1.35) to Newark's Penn Station where you connect to the NJ Transit for New York's Penn Station ($4 one way).

Express bus The Newark Liberty Airport Express has a bus service between the airport and Port Authority Bus Terminal, Bryant Park and Grand Central Terminal in Midtown ($15 one way). The 45-minute ride goes every 15 minutes from 6:45am to 11:15pm (and every half hour from 4:45am to 6:45am and 11:15pm to 1:15am).

Getting Around

Subway

☑ **Best for...** making a beeline across town – up or down – regardless of the above-ground traffic situation.

➡ The New York subway's 660-mile system, run by the **Metropolitan Transportation Authority**

(MTA; 📞718-330-1234; www. mta.info), is iconic, cheap ($2.25 per ride), round-the-clock and easily the fastest and most reliable way to get around the city. It's also safer and (a bit) cleaner than it used to be (and now has overly cheerful automated announcements on some lines).

➡ New York's classic subway tokens now belong to the ages: today all buses and subways use the yellow-and-blue MetroCard, which you can purchase or add value to at one of several easy-to-use automated machines at any station. You can use cash or an ATM or credit card. Just select 'Get new card' and follow the prompts.

➡ It's a good idea to grab a free map, available from any attendant. When in doubt, ask someone who looks like they know what they're doing. They may not, but subway confusion (and consternation) is the great unifier in this diverse city. And if you're new to the underground, never wear headphones when you're riding, as you might miss an important announcement about track changes or skipped stops.

Taxi

☑ **Best for...** getting to and from the airports with luggage in tow, or zigzagging across Manhattan.

➡ The Taxi & Limousine Commission has set fares for taxi rides. It's $2.50 for the initial charge (first one-fifth of a mile), then 40¢ for each additional one-fifth mile as well as every 60 seconds of being stopped in traffic. There's also a $1 peak surcharge (weekdays 4pm to 8pm) and a 50¢ night surcharge (8pm to 6am), plus a New York State surcharge of 50¢ per ride.

➡ Tips are expected to be 10% to 15%, but give less if you feel in any way mistreated – and be sure to ask for a receipt and use it to note the driver's license number.

➡ The TLC keeps a Passenger's Bill of Rights, which gives you the right to tell the driver which route you'd like to take, or ask your driver to stop smoking or turn off an annoying radio station. Also, the driver does not have the right to refuse you a ride based on where you are going.

➡ To hail a cab, look for one with a lit (center) light on its roof. It's particularly difficult to score a taxi in the rain, at rush hour and around 4pm, when many drivers end their shifts.

Tickets & Passes

There are two types of **MetroCard** (📞718-330-1234; www.mta.info/metrocard). The 'pay-per-ride' is $2.25 per ride, though the Metropolitan Transportation Authority (MTA) tacks on an extra 15% value on MetroCards $8 and over. (If you buy a $20 card, you'll receive $23 worth of credit.) If you plan to use the subway quite a bit, you can also buy an 'unlimited ride' card (it's $8.25 for a one-day 'fun pass' or $27 for a seven-day pass). These cards are handy for travelers – particularly if you're jumping around town to a few different places in one day.

Note that the MetroCard works for buses as well as subways (and offers free transfers between them).

➜ Private car services are a common taxi alternative in the outer boroughs. Fares differ depending on the neighborhood and length of ride, and must be determined beforehand, as they have no meters.

Walking

☑ **Best for...** exploring quaint neighborhoods like the West Village, the East Village, Chinatown and SoHo.

➜ Screw the subway, cabs and buses, and go green. New York, down deep, can't be seen until you've taken the time to hit the sidewalks: the whole thing, like Nancy Sinatra's boots, is made for pedestrian transport.

➜ Broadway runs the length of Manhattan, about 13.5 miles. Crossing the East River on the pedestrian planks of the Brooklyn Bridge is a New York classic. Central Park trails can get you to wooded pockets where you can't even see or hear the city.

Bus

☑ **Best for...** taking in the city's atmosphere as you make your way across town.

➜ Buses are operated by the MTA, the same folks that run the subway. They share an identical ticketing system.

➜ Express buses run north–south along the city's eastern avenues – just make sure to purchase your ticket in advance.

➜ Crosstown buses are numbered according to the street they traverse.

Boat

☑ **Best for...** visiting the Statue of Liberty and snapping photos of the skyline.

➜ The zippy yellow boats that make up the fleet of **New York Water Taxi** (☎212-742-1969; www. nywatertaxi.com; hop-on-hop-off service 1 day $26) are an interesting alternative way of getting around. Boats run along several different routes, including a hop-on, hop-off weekend service around Manhattan and Brooklyn.

➜ New York Water Taxi also runs year-round commuter services connecting a variety of locations in Manhattan, Queens and Brooklyn.

➜ A good trip to consider is from E 34th St to

Fulton Ferry Landing in Brooklyn

➜ **New York Waterway** (☎800-533-3779; www.ny waterway.com) offers regular ferry service along the East and Hudson Rivers.

➜ Another bigger, brighter ferry (it's orange) is the commuter-oriented Staten Island Ferry (p32), which makes constant free journeys across the New York Harbor.

Essential Information

Business Hours

Nonstandard hours are listed in specific reviews through the neighborhood chapters in the Explore section of this guide. Standard business hours are as follows:

Banks 9am to 6pm Monday to Friday, some also 9am to noon on Saturday

Bars & clubs Around 5pm to 2am

Businesses 9am to 5pm Monday to Friday.

Entertainment Around 6pm to midnight

Restaurants Breakfast 6am to noon, lunch 11am to 3pm and dinner 5pm to 11pm. The popular Sunday brunch (often served on Saturdays too) lasts from 11am until 4pm.

Shops 10am to 7pm Monday to Friday, 11am to Saturdays. Sundays can be variable – some stores stay closed while others keep weekday hours. Stores tend to stay open later in the neighborhoods downtown.

Discount Cards

The following discount cards offer a variety of passes and perks to some of the city's must-sees. Check the websites for more details.

Downtown Culture Pass (www.downtownculturepass. org)

New York CityPASS (www. citypass.com)

Explorer Pass (www. nyexplorerpass.com)

The New York Pass (www. newyorkpass.com)

Electricity

The United States electric current is 110V to 115V, 60Hz AC. Outlets are made for flat two-prong plugs (which often have a third, rounded prong for grounding). If your appliance is made for another electrical system

120V/60Hz

120V/60Hz

(eg 220V), you'll need a step-down converter, which can be bought at hardware stores and drugstores for around $25 to $60. However, most electronic devices (laptops, camera-battery chargers etc) are built for dual-voltage use, and will only need a plug adapter.

The website www.kropla.com provides useful information on electricity and adapters.

Emergency

Police, Fire & Ambulance (☎ 911)
Poison control (☎ 800-222-1222)

Money

☑ **Top Tip** US dollars are the only accepted currency in NYC. While debit and credit cards are widely accepted, it's wise to have a combination of cash and cards on hand.

ATMs

➡ Automatic teller machines are on practically every corner. You can either use your card at banks – usually in a 24-hour-access lobby, filled with up to a dozen monitors at major branches – or you can opt for the lone wolves, which sit in delis, restaurants, bars and grocery stores, charging fierce service fees that go as high as $5.

➡ Most New York banks are linked by the New York Cash Exchange (NYCE) system and you can use local bankcards interchangeably at ATMs – for an extra fee if you're banking outside your system.

Credit Cards

➡ Major credit cards are accepted at most hotels, restaurants and shops throughout New York City. In fact, you'll find it difficult to perform certain transactions, such as purchasing tickets to performances and renting a car, without one.

➡ Stack your deck with a Visa, MasterCard or American Express, as these are the cards of choice. Places that accept Visa and MasterCard also accept debit cards, but first check with your bank to confirm that your debit card will be accepted in other states or countries.

➡ If your cards are lost or stolen, contact the company immediately.

Changing Money

Banks and moneychangers, found all over New York City (including all three major airports), will give you US currency based on the current exchange rate.

Public Holidays

This is a list of major New York City holidays and special events. These holidays may force the closure of many businesses or attract crowds, making dining and accommodations reservations difficult.

New Year's Day
January 1

Martin Luther King Day
Third Monday in January

Presidents' Day
Third Monday in February

Easter March/April

Memorial Day
Late May

Gay Pride
Last Sunday in June

Independence Day
July 4

Labor Day
Early September

Rosh Hashanah & Yom Kippur Mid-September to mid-October

Halloween October 31

Thanksgiving Fourth Thursday in November

Christmas Day
December 25

New Year's Eve
December 31

Safe Travel

Crime rates in NYC are still at their lowest in years. There are few neighborhoods remaining where you might feel apprehensive, no matter what time of night (and they're mainly in the outer boroughs). Subway stations are generally safe, too, though some in low-income neighborhoods, especially in the outer boroughs, can be dicey.

There's no reason to be paranoid, but it's better to be safe than sorry, so use common sense. Don't walk around alone at night in unfamiliar, sparsely populated areas, especially if you're a woman. Carry your daily walking-around money somewhere inside your clothing or in a front pocket rather than in a handbag or a back pocket, and be aware of pickpockets particularly in mobbed areas, like Times Sq or Penn Station at rush hour.

Telephone

Cell Phones

Most US cell phones besides the iPhone operate on CDMA, not the European standard GSM, so make sure you check compatibility with your phone service provider. North Americans should have no problem, but it is best to check with your service provider about roaming charges.

If you require a cell phone, you'll find many store fronts – Verizon, T-Mobile or AT&T – where you can buy a cheap phone and load it with prepaid minutes, avoiding a long-term contract.

Phone Codes

No matter where you're calling within New York City, even if it's just across the street in the same area code, you must always dial 1 + the area code first.

Manhattan ☎212, 646

Outer boroughs
☎347, 718, 929

All boroughs (usually cell phones) ☎917

International & Domestic Calls

Phone numbers within the US consist of a three-digit area code followed by a seven-digit local number. If you're calling long distance, dial ☎1 + the three-digit area code + the seven-digit number. To make an international call, call ☎011+ country code + area code + number. When calling Canada, you don't need to use the ☎011.

Useful Numbers

Local directory ☎411

Municipal offices and information ☎311

National directory information ☎1-212-555-1212

Operator ☎0

Toll-free number information ☎800-555-1212

Toilets

☑ **Top Tip** The NY Restroom website (www.nyrestroom.com) is a handy resource for scouting out a loo.

Considering the number of pedestrians, there's a noticeable lack of public restrooms around the city.

You'll find spots to relieve yourself in Grand Central Terminal, Penn Station and Port Authority Bus Terminal. There are also restrooms in parks, including Madison Sq Park, Battery Park, Tompkins Sq Park, Washington Sq Park and Columbus Park in Chinatown, plus several places scattered around Central Park. The best bet, though, is to pop into a Starbucks (there's one about every three blocks) and head straight to the bathroom in the back; just don't tell the baristas that we told you do so.

Money-Saving Tips

➡ Browse our list of free attractions (p227).

➡ Check museum websites to see when they offer free admission.

➡ Save on theater tickets by buying tickets at the TKTs booth at Times Square (p127) or in Lower Manhattan (p42).

➡ Stock up on picnic fodder at the many fun, gourmet markets.

Dos & Don'ts

➡ Hail a cab only if the roof light is on. Look carefully though: if the middle light is on, the cab is available, but if only the side lights are on the cab is off-duty.

➡ You needn't obey 'walk' signs – simply cross the street when there isn't oncoming traffic.

➡ When negotiating pedestrian traffic on the sidewalk, think of yourself as a vehicle – don't stop short, follow the speed of the crowd around you and pull off to the side if you need to take out your map or umbrella. Most New Yorkers are respectful of personal space, but they will bump into you – and not apologize – if you get in the way.

➡ When boarding the subway, wait until the passengers disembark, then be aggressive enough when you hop on so that the doors don't close in front of you.

➡ In New York you wait 'on line' instead of 'in line.'

➡ Oh, and it's How-sten Street, not Hew-sten.

Tourist Information

In this wonderful web-based world, you'll find infinite online sources to get up-to-the-minute information about New York City.

In person, try one of the five official bureaus (the Midtown office is the shining star) of **NYC & Company** (☎212-484-1200; www.nycgo.com).

Midtown (Map p132, D2; ☎212-484-1222; 810 Seventh Ave btwn 52nd & 53rd Sts; ⏰8:30am-6pm Mon-Fri, 9am-5pm Sat & Sun; Ⓢ B/D, E to 7th Ave)

Times Square (Map p132, D3; ☎212-484-1222; Seventh Ave btwn 46th & 47th Sts; ⏰9am-7pm; Ⓢ1/2/3, 7, N/Q/R to Times Sq)

Lower Manhattan (Map p30, C4; ☎212-484-1222; City Hall Park at Broadway; ⏰9am-6pm Mon-Fri, 10am-5pm Sat & Sun; Ⓢ R/W to to City Hall)

Harlem (☎212-222-1014; 163 W 125th at Adam Clayton Powell Jr Blvd; ⏰noon-6pm Mon-Fri, 10am-6pm Sat & Sun; Ⓢ1 to 125th St)

Chinatown (Map p48, D7; ☎212-484-1222; cnr Canal, Walker & Baxter Sts; ⏰10am-6pm; Ⓢ J/M/Z, N/Q/R/W, 6 to Canal St)

The **Brooklyn Tourism & Visitors Center** (☎718-802-3846; www.visitbrooklyn. org; 209 Joralemon St btwn Court St & Brooklyn Bridge Blvd; ⏰10am-6pm Mon-Fri; Ⓢ2/3, 4/5 to Borough Hall) in Downtown Brooklyn has information on the other favorite borough.

Travelers with Disabilities

Federal laws guarantee that all government offices and facilities are accessible to the disabled. For information on specific places, you can contact the mayor's **Office for People with Disabilities** (☎212-788-2830; ⏰9am-5pm Mon-Fri), which will send you a free copy of its *Access New York* guide if you call and request it.

Another excellent resource is the **Society for Accessible Travel & Hospitality** (SATH; ☎212-447-7284; www.sath.org; 347 Fifth Ave at 34th St; 🕐9am-5pm; [S]6 to 33rd St, 🚌M34 to 5th Ave, M1 to 34th St), which gives advice on how to travel with a wheelchair, kidney disease, sight impairment or deafness.

For detailed information on subway and bus wheelchair accessibility, call the **Accessible Line** (☎718-596-8585) or visit www.mta.info/mta/ada for a list of subway stations with elevators or escalators. Also visit www.nycgo.com and search for 'accessibility.'

Visas

The USA Visa Waiver Program (VWP) allows nationals from 36 countries to enter the US without a visa, provided they are carrying a machine-readable passport. For the updated list of countries included in the program and current requirements, see the **US Department of State** (http://travel.state.gov/visa) website.

Citizens of VWP countries need to register with the **US Department of Homeland Security** (http://esta.cbp.dhs.gov) three days before their visit. There is a $14 fee for registration application; when approved, the registration is valid for two years.

You must obtain a visa from a US embassy or consulate in your home country if you:

- do not currently hold a passport from a VWP country
- are from a VWP country, but don't have a machine-readable passport
- are from a VWP country, but currently hold a passport issued between October 26, 2005, and October 25, 2006, that does not have a digital photo on the information page or an integrated chip from the data page. (After October 25, 2006, the integrated chip is required on all machine-readable passports.)
- are planning to stay longer than 90 days
- are planning to work or study in the US.

Behind the Scenes

Send Us Your Feedback

We love to hear from travelers – your comments help make our books better. We read every word, and we guarantee that your feedback goes straight to the authors. Visit **lonelyplanet.com/contact** to submit your updates and suggestions.

Note: We may edit, reproduce and incorporate your comments in Lonely Planet products such as guidebooks, websites and digital products, so let us know if you don't want your comments reproduced or your name acknowledged. For a copy of our privacy policy visit lonelyplanet.com/privacy.

Brandon's Thanks

Thank you to Jennye for helming the triad of NYC projects and a special shout-out to Joanne for all of her love and support. Props to Cristian and Carolina for their brilliant writing and local savvy. Thanks also to New York know-it-alls Mollie, Allidah and Greg.

Acknowledgments

Cover photograph: Taxis at Times Sq, Manhattan, New York City; Rachel Lewis/Lonely Planet Images. Many of the images in this guide are available for licensing from Lonely Planet Images: www.lonelyplanetimages.com.

This Book

This 4th edition of Lonely Planet's *Pocket New York City* was researched and written by Brandon Presser with contributions by Cristian Bonetto and Carolina Miranda. This guidebook was commissioned in Lonely Planet's Oakland office, and produced by the following:

Commissioning Editor Jennye Garibaldi **Coordinating Editor** Elin Berglund **Coordinating Cartographer** Anthony Phelan **Coordinating Layout Designer** Mazzy Prinsep **Managing Editor** Anna Metcalfe **Managing Cartographers** Shahara Ahmed, Alison Lyall **Managing Layout Designer** Jane Hart **Assisting Editor** Kristin Odijk **Assisting Cartographer** Peter Shields **Cover Research** Naomi Parker **Internal Image Research** Nicholas Colicchia **Thanks to** Imogen Bannister, Tim Carpentier, Daniel Corbett, Laura Crawford, Janine Eberle, Ryan Evans, Larissa Frost, Chris Girdler, Liz Heynes, Laura Jane, Jouve India, David Kemp, Ross Macaw, Trent Paton, Adrian Persoglia, Piers Pickard, Martine Power, Sharron Reiher, Raphael Richards, Averil Robertson, Lachlan Ross, Michael Ruff, Julie Sheridan, Amanda Sierp, Laura Stansfeld, John Taufa, Angela Tinson, Gerard Walker, Clifton Wilkinson

Index

See also separate subindexes for:

🍴 **Eating p251**

🍸 **Drinking p252**

⭐ **Entertainment p253**

🔒 **Shopping p254**

Sights p000
Map Pages **p000**

Sights p000
Map Pages **p000**

⊗ Eating

Sights p000
Map Pages p000

✪ Entertainment

Our Writer

Brandon Presser

After earning an art history degree from Harvard University and working at the Musée du Louvre, Brandon swapped landscape canvases for the real deal and joined the glamorous ranks of eternal nomadism. Today, Brandon works as a full-time freelance writer and photographer. He's penned over 40 guidebooks to far-flung destinations across the globe, from Iceland to Thailand and many 'lands' in between. When he's not on the road, he calls New York City home – he lives a block from Union Sq.

Published by Lonely Planet Publications Pty Ltd
ABN 36 005 607 983
4th edition – Oct 2012
ISBN 978 1 74220 024 8
© Lonely Planet 2012   Photographs © as indicated 2012
10 9 8 7 6 5 4 3 2 1
Printed in China